The
Pygmalion
Project

The Pygmalion Project:

Love and Coercion Among the Types

Stephen Montgomery

 Prometheus Nemesis Book Company

Design and Composition: Regina Books

Printing and Bindery: San Dieguito Press

First Edition

10   9   8   7   6   5   4   3   2   1

ISBN: 0-9606954-9-4

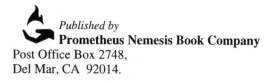
Published by
Prometheus Nemesis Book Company
Post Office Box 2748,
Del Mar, CA 92014.

Manufactured in the United States of America

Volume Three:

The Idealist

Acknowledgements

Thanks are due the following publishers for permission to reprint passages from the works cited:

Bantam Books: *The Brothers Karamazov*, by Fyodor Dostoevsky, trans. Andrew H. MacAndrew, copyright 1970.

New American Library: *Anna Karenina*, by Leo Tolstoy, trans. David Margarshack, copyright 1961; *The Death of Ivan Ilych, and Other Stories*, trans. J.D. Duff; *Jane Eyre*, by Charlotte Brontë; *Tess of the d'Urbervilles*, by Thomas Hardy.

Random House: *Howards End*, by E.M. Forster, copyright 1921 by E.M. Forster.

Charles Scribner's Sons: *The Age of Innocence*, by Edith Wharton, copyright 1920 by D. Appleton and Company.

Viking Penguin, Inc.: *Sons and Lovers*, by D.H. Lawrence, copyright 1913 by Thomas Seltzer, Inc.

Contents

Foreword by David Keirsey x

INTRODUCTION TO THE SERIES

The Mirror of Fiction 1

CHAPTER *1*

The Apollonian Ideal 11

CHAPTER *2*

The Monastic..39

Alyosha Karamazov, from
    Fyodor Dostoevsky's *The Brothers Karamazov* 43
Miriam Leivers, from
    D.H. Lawrence's *Sons and Lovers* 66

CHAPTER 3

The Advocate 93

Newland Archer, from
   Edith Wharton's *The Age of Innocence* 95
Marya Alexandrovna, from
   Leo Tolstoy's *Family Happiness* 123

CHAPTER 4

The Counselor...163

Konstantin Levin, from
   Leo Tostoy's *Anna Karenina* *165*
Jane Eyre, from
   Charlotte Brontë's *Jane Eyre* 201

CHAPTER 5

The Teacher...233

Angel Clare, from
   Thomas Hardy's *Tess of the d'Urbervilles* 234
Margaret Schlegel, from
   E.M. Forster's *Howards End* 253

Afterword...283

Appendix: The Keirsey Temperament Sorter.................287

Bibliography...299

Index...301

FOREWORD

Now here is a book to conjure with. I find nothing like it in communication studies or the other behavioral sciences. And I must say it surpasses its two predecessors, *The Pygmalion Project, Volume One* and *Volume Two*, on the Artisans and the Guardians, in its depth and clarity.

The study of persons, which I call "Personology," is a unique interdisciplinary science at the crossroads of Anthropology, Biology, Communication, Ethology, Psychology, and Sociology, and Montgomery's work is located at the center of those crossroads. As I commented in the Foreword to the volume on the Artisans, it is quite unusual for a writer specializing in literature to pay even cursory attention to system-field theory in communication science. Montgomery's attention has been much more than cursory: he has followed the invasion of communication field-theory into the behavioral sciences, especially as the theory has informed psychopathology and psychotherapy. And thus his studies of the Pygmalion projects of the various types of temperament and character rest upon a solid scientific foundation.

Let me remind you that character must follow temperament—temperament is predisposition, character post-disposition. In other words, character is acquired gradually as nature collides with nurture, and is built, trait by trait, on the foundation of temperament. So it is that personality comes with two faces: inborn temperament and learned character, what we are given by nature and what our life experience sculpts us into. Which brings me to George Bernard Shaw's play, *Pygmalion*, and Eliza Doolittle and her would-be sculptor, professor Henry Higgins.

In the film *My Fair Lady*, which is based on Shaw's play, Higgins wondered why the cockney flower girl Eliza couldn't be "more like me." Seeing himself as a splendid model of humanity, why then did she not emulate him? Montgomery's answer, of course, is that he and Eliza were of fundamentally different temperaments (he a Rational and she a Guardian)—that this difference attracted him in the first place, and that, for all Higgins' efforts to train Eliza's speech and behavior, he had not succeeded in making her over in his own image. However, in fairness, it must be said that Higgins *had* helped release Eliza from the cage of her "guttersnipe" existence. He had given her the means to live independently.

But *My Fair Lady* is not the only film with a Pygmalion theme that has captured the American audience. At the time of this writing E.M. Forster's *Howards End* is revisiting American theaters, having been nominated as best picture of 1992—and with the film's leading lady having been awarded the Oscar for her role as Margaret Schlegel, the Idealist wife of Henry Wilcox, a Guardian businessman. Remarkable! How can a quiet story like *Howards End*, about nothing more eventful than social transactions in Edwardian England, compete with the far more compelling scenes of violence and cultural strife in the other nominated movies? Montgomery's answer is intriguing—the story presents to the viewer something basic about the two temperaments depicted in the film, the Guardian and the Idealist. It appeals to the Guardian because the story is about possessions and property, and their *beneficent* ownership (Howards End in the name of a cottage in the English countryside). At the same time, it appeals to the Idealist because the story is about sensitive interpersonal relationships, both threatened and resolved by dint of Margaret's *benevolent* concern for her ethical conduct, and for Henry's.

By the way, almost all of the novels and plays Montgomery discusses in all three volumes have been made into films, some of them several times (*Jane Eyre*, for instance), and because of this *The Pygmalion Project* attracts a surprisingly wide audience. Yes, many of the novels he analyzes are said to be "classics," scarcely best-sellers in today's market. But gold is where you find it, and Montgomery allows himself to dig only in those books that best display the Pygmalion projects of the different temperaments. And in this volume about the Idealists, the vein is rich. Let's face it, Idealists are often drawn to writing "literature," and Idealist authors are far better prepared to unveil the soul-sculpting acts of their Idealist characters than any other kind of author. Indeed, I agree with Montgomery that (except for universal writers like Shakespeare, a Rational) an Idealist author is the *only* one who can do it, and more than that, only the most intuitive of them.

In reading this book one is reminded that most of us try, unwittingly and inadvertently to be sure (at least during the first several years of marriage) to change our spouse into our own image. Do not we Rationals pressure our spouse "to be more reasonable"; we Guardians "to come up to our expectations"; we Artisans "to lighten up"? So it is with the Rationals, Guardians, and Artisans. But what of the Idealists? Surely they would not seek to change their spouse. Surely they would let us be.

Unfortunately, as Montgomery shows us, Idealists appear to engage in Pygmalion projects just as much as the other temperaments, perhaps even more often than others—and more blamelessly. After all, who among the character types is more bent on finding and releasing the hidden potential in each of us than the Idealists? And if the Idealists (I now call them the "Intuitive Ethicists") divine in us the potential to be as spiritual as they, and then try to help us caterpillars emerge from our cocoons as butterflies, how can we criticize them for so benevolent an error? And though they inevitably fail in their project to turn us into Idealists like themselves, still are we injured by their efforts? That, I suppose, is for each of us to decide.

Having written so well of the Artisans and Guardians in their Pygmalion projects, Stephen Montgomery now turns his attention to the always enthusiastic and often metaphorical messages of the Idealists. An Idealist himself, Montgomery is able to describe such Pygmalion game tactics with an insider's perspective, and so bring a special expertise to his discussion. Thus Montgomery's essay on the Idealist is, as the saying goes, "from the horse's mouth"—though this is clearly a horse of a different kind, namely the kind with a horn-like antenna protruding from its forebrain: behold the Unicorn.

David Keirsey
June, 1993

Introduction
to the Series

The Mirror
of Fiction

> It is not our purpose to become each other; it is to
> recognize each other, to learn to see the other and
> honor him for what he is.
>
> ——Hermann Hesse[1]

In Greek legend, a brash young sculptor named Pygmalion
found the women of Cyprus so impossibly flawed that he
resolved to carve a statue of his ideal woman, embodying
every feminine grace and virtue. For months he labored
with all his prodigious skill (and also with a strange
compulsion), rounding here, smoothing there, until he had
fashioned the most exquisite figure ever conceived by art.
So exquisite indeed was his creation that Pygmalion fell
passionately in love with the statue, and could be seen in his
studio kissing its marble lips, fingering its marble hands,
dressing and grooming the figure as if caring for a doll. But
soon, and in spite of the work's incomparable loveliness,
Pygmalion was desperately unhappy, for the lifeless statue
could not respond to his desires, the cold stone could not

---

1 Hermann Hesse, *Narcissus and Goldmund*, trans. Ursule Molinaro
 (New York: Farrar, Straus and Giroux, 1968), p. 43.

return the warmth of his love. He had set out to shape his perfect woman, but had succeeded only in creating his own frustration and despair.[2]

The premise of this book is that, in our closest relationships, we all behave like Pygmalion to some extent. Many of us seem attracted at first to creatures quite different from ourselves, and seem to take pleasure in the contrast. But as we become more involved and start to vie for control of our relationships, we begin to see these differences as flaws. No longer satisfied with our loved ones as they are, we set about to change them, to transform them into our conception of what they should be. No longer able to appreciate our loved ones' distinctive ways of living, we try to shape them according to our own values or agendas. Like Pygmalion, in short, we take up the project of sculpting them little by little to suit ourselves. We snipe and criticize, brow-beat and bully, we sculpt with guilt and with praise, with logic and with tears—whatever methods are most natural to us. Not that we do this ceaselessly, nor always maliciously, but all too often, almost without thinking, we fall into this pattern of coercive behavior.

And like Pygmalion, we are inevitably frustrated, since our well-intentioned efforts to make over our mates bring us little more than disappointment and conflict. Our loved ones do not—cannot—comply meekly with our interference in their lives, and even if they were to surrender to our pressure, they would have to destroy in themselves what attracted us in the first place, their individuality, their distinct breath of life. Our Pygmalion projects must fail:

---

[2]Summarized from Edith Hamilton's *Mythology* (Mentor edition.), pp. 108-111.

either our loved ones fight back, and our relationships become battlegrounds; or they give in to us, and become as lifeless as Pygmalion's statue. In this paradoxical game, we lose even if we win.

In the legend, as it turns out, Venus took pity on Pygmalion and brought his statue to life, and he and "Galatea," as he named her, blushed, embraced, and married with the goddess's blessing. The rest of us, however, cannot rely on such miraculous intervention. Living in the real world, we are responsible ourselves for the success our relationships, and this means we must find a way to abandon our Pygmalion projects, by learning, if we can, to honor our fundamental differences in personality. For only by respecting the right of our loved ones to be different from ourselves—to be perfect in their own ways—can we begin to bring the beauty of our own relationships alive.

The argument of my books is not entirely new. I take my main title, in fact, from David Keirsey and Marilyn Bates's *Please Understand Me: Character and Temperament Types*, and throughout these pages I am indebted to their wonderfully perceptive analysis of human behavior and relationship styles. However, the nature of my evidence—literary characters—*is* unusual, and needs perhaps a few words of explanation.

I make at the outset one I hope not too obvious assumption: that the skillful novelist or playwright and the skillful temperament psychologist are both, of necessity, skillful people-watchers. The cornerstone of realistic fiction has always been the story-teller's astute observation of human behavior, and thus we marvel at how "lifelike" are his characters or how "true-to-life" are their experiences. The so-called "Romantic" and "Symbolist" writers might have loftier visions, but they base their characters nonetheless on real human types before they transcend to their ideal worlds or retreat into their private fantasies. Even such clearly unrealistic forms of fiction as myth and caricature build upon a thorough knowledge of human characteristics. The Greek epic heroes, as well as the gods, are plagued with all our human foibles, and Charles Dickens's most grotesque characters exaggerate our most familiar human traits. As one literary critic has put it:

> Literature portrays almost every conceivable human action, thought, attitude, emotion, situation, or problem. In one way or another people are basic to the literary imagination, even in its most fanciful flights.[3]

Certainly fictional characters are not real people, and to insist on their reality might close us off from an author's unique imagination. And yet, in most cases, even in the eccentric world of a writer like Franz Kafka, a story lives for us and catches us up in its artifice because we see ourselves and our predicaments in its characters. In other words, when a story catches, as Henry James put it, "the very note and trick, the strange irregular rhythm" of human behavior, we know that we are "touching [the] truth" of life and breathing the "air of reality."[4] And such a personal recognition can delight us—or disturb us profoundly—with its accuracy. Suspecting this, Hamlet instructed a troupe of actors to touch his uncle's conscience with a scene from a play, and in his famous speech he defined the power of fiction to make us perceive ourselves more clearly:

> the purpose of playing...was and is, to hold, as 'twere, the mirror up to nature. [5]

---

[3]B. Bernard Cohen, *Writing About Literature* (Glenview, Illinois: Scott, Foresman and Co., 1973), p. 37.

[4]Henry James, "The Art of Fiction" in *Partial Portraits* (Ann Arbor, The University of Michigan Press, 1970), pp. 398, 390.

[5]William Shakespeare, *Hamlet*, III,ii,19-20.

In much the same way, the writing of the more perceptive temperament psychologists also unnerves us with this rush of recognition. To read David Keirsey's sixteen character portraits in *Please Understand Me* is indeed to look in a mirror. When I began to edit *Please Understand Me*, I remember browsing ahead in the manuscript and being quite shaken by the air of truth in my own portrait, the "INFJ" Author, as Keirsey called it then. I felt quite found out at the time, almost as if some novelist or playwright had sketched me in his working notebook. (More than a decade of reports from *Please Understand Me* readers of all types suggests such unmasking is frequently the case.) I found the other portraits nearly as fascinating (though no one is quite as fascinating as oneself), and as I worked on the manuscript I realized that Keirsey's word portraits of Isabel Myers's four-letter designations (the Inspector for Myers's "ISTJ," the Performer for the "ESFP," and so on) were offering me an extraordinary instrument—a flexible and surprisingly accurate vocabulary for discussing the vast array of human personality.

As with all experience of a new vocabulary, I began to see the world around me with new clarity and in new detail, and very soon my family, my students, my colleagues, friends and foes alike, found their way into the categories of personality I was internalizing. Not that they were reduced from complex individuals, but the broader lines of their attitudes and imperatives came into focus. And in my profession—reading and teaching literature—I made a two-fold discovery. Not only could I analyze characters and relationships with more insight, but I began to see that throughout history the great novelists and playwrights had been bringing to life the same gallery of real-life characters that Keirsey was describing in *Please Understand Me*, and in his more recent book, *Portraits of Temperament*. The impulsive Artisans ("SPs") and the spiritual Idealists ("NFs"), the logical Rationals ("NTs") and the dutiful Guardians ("SJs")—all kinds and combinations of these characters lived in the pages of Chaucer, Shakespeare, Jane Austen, Dickens, D.H. Lawrence, Hemingway, and many, many more.

It should not have surprised me, really, that characters in literature fit so naturally into Keirsey's categories. After all, as the esteemed critic Robert Scholes has argued, novelists and playwrights create their characters from two impulses: "the impulse to individualize and the impulse to typify."[6] One might even say that much of the interest (and the charm) of fiction lies in its power to be discriminating and representative at the same time. Writers (particularly Idealist ["NF"] writers) cherish the mystery of the authentic soul and bristle at the idea of putting unique human beings into "boxes"; but the best of them also admit that their characters typify larger categories of humanity. Thus Henry James cautions us that "Humanity is immense, and reality has a myriad forms,"[7] but he also understands that "Art is essentially selection…whose main care is to be typical."[8] Literary criticism has long endeavored to unravel characters' individual peculiarities with the help of so-called "depth" psychology; temperament theory can now provide us with a finer language (a finer "vocabulary" as I have called it) for describing the more fundamental, shared

---

[6]Robert Scholes, *Elements of Literature* (New York: Oxford University Press, 1978), p. 109.

[7]Henry James, "The Art of Fiction" in *Partial Portraits*, pp. 387-8.

[8]Henry James, "The Art of Fiction" in *Partial Portraits*, p. 398.

patterns of human behavior, first in the literary characters and then in ourselves.

My hope in these books, then, is to marry these two characterologies into an informative and I hope entertaining look at the different ways people go about their love relationships. Perhaps by seeing literary characters as portraits of human character styles (Jay Gatsby as a Promoter Artisan, say, or Jane Eyre as a Counselor Idealist), we can learn something about our own interpersonal styles with our loved ones. Perhaps by regarding the lives of literary characters as virtual case studies of the Keirseyan Types, we can, in the mirror of these fictions, better recognize ourselves and our own Pygmalion projects. Which returns me to the topic of my books, surely the most coercive relationship of all: Love.

Approaching temperament styles through literature in one way broadens the field of observation—all of those stories, all of those characters—but it also narrows the focus to those subjects about which literature is most discerning. And, without a doubt, love is the subject upon which literature lavishes most attention, and offers most insight. Love, courtship, passion, marriage, this "constant sensitiveness of characters for each other," as E.M. Forster described it, "this constant awareness, this endless readjustment, this ceaseless hunger"[9]—love in all its forms and complications dominates the literary imagination, and provides a wealth of detail for the reader with an eye for character types. To be sure, the games and the rituals, the dreams and the strategies of love so tirelessly pursued in novels and plays amply illustrate Keirsey's portraits of the Artisan, Guardian, Idealist, and Rational mating styles, as

---

[9]E.M. Forster, *Aspects of the Novel* (Harvest edition, 1954), pp. 54-5.

well as largely support his theory of the Pygmalion project. For better or for worse, we do seem irresistibly attracted to human types far different from ourselves, and we do attempt—and almost invariably with unfortunate consequences—to reshape our loved ones in our own image. This is the abundant evidence of literature.

Temperament theory and literature thus combined offer us more than either abstract psychological categories or esoteric "literary" characters. Broadly and systematically defined by the temperament psychologist, and then richly detailed by the novelist or playwright, these are *our* relationships, depicting our attractions and regrets, our fantasies and disillusionments, our coercions and compromises. If we will look into the mirror of fiction through the powerful lens of temperament theory, we might come to understand ourselves more clearly, and perhaps see the Pygmalion in us all.

But first, to those of you unfamiliar with temperament theory, or who have forgotten exactly what all the capital letters ("SP," "NT," etc.) and all the talk about "temperaments" and "types" is about, I want to offer the following diagnostic summary, printed with David Keirsey's permission. Remember that the following table is a short-hand classifier; for a more complete personality survey, take Keirsey's Temperament Sorter questionnaire in *Please Understand Me* (and reproduced in the Appendix at the end of this book). Remember also that all of us have *all* of these characteristics, and surely many more, and that our temperament is merely a dominance in our behavior of one style over the others.

To complete this questionnaire pick *one* word in each row that *best* fits you, and circle the letter in front of it. Please use a dictionary for unusual words and skip any lines in which you cannot choose one word over the others. Upon completion read the scoring instructions on the next page.

I prefer to be:	E seemly	Q efficient	Y pleasing	B effective
I prefer feeling:	X inspired	A excited	D concerned	P calm
I take pride in being:	A a winner	D accountable	P competent	X authentic
I'd like being a:	E magnate	Q wizard	Y sage	B prodigal
I'd rather be:	P pragmatic	X ethical	A practical	D traditional
There's virtue in:	Z goodwill	C boldness	F ownership	R independence
I'm confident when:	C dashing	F included	R self-willed	Z in rapport
I most often look for:	X my identity	A adventures	D security	P proof
I'm proud of being:	Y genuine	B ahead	E dependable	Q capable
I'm best at:	C expediting	F monitoring	R organizing	Z mentoring
I often crave:	A spontaneity	D ceremony	P achievement	X love
I put my trust in:	D authority	P reason	X intuition	A luck
I am a good:	B crafter	E inspector	Y counselor	Q sequencer
I can be:	B impetuous	E dispirited	Q preoccupied	Y alienated
I'd rather be:	P ingenius	X prophetic	A a prodigy	D dignified
I'm better at:	D logistics	P strategy	X diplomacy	A tactics
I count more on:	B chance	E certification	Q logic	Y instinct
I like being seen as:	R progressive	Z altruistic	C urbane	F forbearing
I'm better acting as:	Z an envoy	C a player	F a broker	R a planner
I tend to be rather:	X credulous	A optimistic	D pessimistic	P skeptical
I'm often:	A cynical	D fatalistic	P solipsistic	X mystical
I often speak in:	B street talk	E polite terms	Q shop talk	Y metaphors
I like myself more if:	D prosperous	P autonomous	X benevolent	A nervy
I often search for:	Q evidence	Y Self	B risks	E safety
I like being seen as:	R generative	Z unworldly	C worldly	F dedicated
I have more faith in:	Z feelings	C the breaks	F licensure	R grounds
I often yearn for:	R attainment	Z affection	C whims	F rites
I'm better at:	Q devising	Y championing	B adapting	E supplying
I often want more:	A pleasures	D services	P problems	X romance
I'm more capable in:	Z personalizing	C thematizing	F standardizing	R systemizing
My words are often:	D conventional	P technical	X allegorical	A lingo
Trouble is often:	Y paradoxical	B farcical	E predestined	Q meaningless
I tend to seek:	F immunity	R corroboration	Z uniqueness	C gambles
I'm rather often:	Q a doubter	Y a believer	B buoyant	E leery
I often speak:	Z figuratively	C slang	F establishment	R jargon
I'm self-confident if:	P self-directed	X empathic	A impactful	D belonging
I often feel:	Q tranquil	Y enthused	B elated	E serious
I have a hunger for:	Y caring	B impulses	E rituals	Q accomplishment
I often speak of:	P entailment	X cues	A facets	D amounts
Sometimes I get:	Z estranged	C reckless	F downcast	R distracted
I'm better at:	B composing	E insuring	Q configuring	Y conciliating
Bad times are often:	R random	Z inexplicable	C a mockery	F inevitable
Maybe I'll become:	C top dog	F an official	R a mastermind	Z a seer
My best ability is:	D stabilizing	P patterning	X humanizing	A fashioning
I'd be good as:	P a marshaller	X a teacher	A an expediter	D a supervisor
I can do well in:	X advocating	A improvising	D providing	P contriving
I'd like to be:	C a virtuoso	F a magistrate	R a genius	Z an oracle
I prefer to feel:	F solemn	R serene	Z fervent	C thrilled
There's virtue in:	B daring	E affluence	Q independence	Y kindliness
I emphasize:	C description	F evaluation	R definition	Z interpretation
I'm better at:	F providing	R inventing	Z revealing	C performing
I like being seen as:	Y warm	B sophisticated	E staunch	Q productive
I'm confident if I'm:	E a member	Q strong-willed	Y sympathetic	B impressive
I like myself if I'm:	R skilled	Z sincere	C competitive	F responsible
Under stress I can get:	D depressed	P preoccupied	X confused	A impulsive

Determine your score by adding together the number of A, B, and C choices, then the D, E, and F choices, then the P, Q, and R, and finally the X, Y, and Z choices. The largest of these sums indicates which of the four temperaments you are probably most like.

A ☐ +B ☐ +C ☐ = ☐ **The Artisan Temperament**

D ☐ +E ☐ +F ☐ = ☐ **The Guardian Temperament**

P ☐ +Q ☐ +R ☐ = ☐ **The Rational Temperament**

X ☐ +Y ☐ +Z ☐ = ☐ **The Idealist Temperament**

THE ARTISAN TEMPERAMENT: Abilities. The thirty five to fourty percent among us of Artisan temperament have an instinct for thematic variation, learn operational techniques avidly and easily, can become tactical leaders, and tend to speak descriptively and colorfully of the concrete world about them. **Interests.** Artisan types search for new adventures, hunger for functioning, want to have pleasure every day, trust their impulses implicitly, aspire to virtuosity, but are too optimistic in expectation, and too cynical in retrospection. **Self-Image.** They personify themselves as sophisticated, are proud of their competitiveness, respect themselves in the degree they are daring, and feel confident of themselves in the degree they can impress others. **Social Relationships.** In their family interactions the Artisans are egalitarian, providing entertainment for their mates, free play for their children, and a variety of indulgences for themselves. **Four Kinds of Artisans.** The *operator* kinds are natural *promoters* and *crafters*, while the *player* kinds are natural *performers* and *composers*.

THE GUARDIAN TEMPERAMENT: Abilities. The forty to forty five percent among us of Guardian temperament have an instinct for maintaining standards, learn manners and morals of their membership groups quickly and dutifully, can become logistical leaders, and tend to speak quantitatively and exactingly of the concrete world about them. **Interests.** Guardian types search for increasing security, hunger for rite and ceremony, wish for some services each day, trust authority implicitly, aspire to honor and dignity, but are too pessimistic in expectation and too fatalistic in retrospection. **Self-Image.** They personify themselves as prosperous and self-supporting, are proud of their accountabiltiy, respect themselves in the degree they are staunch and steadfast, and are confident of themselves in the degree they are members in good standing. **Social Relationships.** In their family interactions they are hierarchical, wanting respectability in their mates, conformity in their children, and self-sacrifice in themselves. **Four Kinds of Guardians.** The *monitor* kinds are natural *supervisors* and *inspectors*, while the *conservator* kinds are natural *providers* and *protectors*.

THE RATIONAL TEMPERAMENT: Abilities. The six or seven percent among us of Rational temperament have an instinct for systemic analysis, learn technology with ever increasing zeal, sometimes become strategic leaders, and often speak categorically and definitively of the abstract world of their imagination. **Interests.** Rational types search for evidence for their theories, hunger for achievement, wish to grapple with puzzles and enigmas, trust logic and reason implicitly, aspire to ingenuity, but are too skeptical in expectation and too solipsistic in retrospection. **Self-Image.** They personify themselves as productive, are proud of their competencies, respect themselves in the degree they are autonomous, and feel confident of themselves in the degree they are strongwilled. **Social Relationships.** In their family interactions they are libertarian, providing enlightenment for their mates, learning options for their children, and for themselves continuous self-improvement. **Four Kinds of Rationals.** The *organizer* kinds are natural *fieldmarshals* and *planners*, while the *engineer* kinds are natural *prototypers* and *architects*.

THE IDEALIST TEMPERAMENT: Abilities. The eight or nine percent among us of Idealist temperament have an instinct for interpersonal integration, learn ethics with ever increasing zeal, sometimes become diplomatic leaders, and often speak interpretively and metaphorically of the abstract world of their imagination. **Interests.** Idealist types search for their unique identity, hunger for deep and meaningful relationships, wish for a little romance each day, trust their intuitive feelings implicitly, aspire to profundity, but are too credulous in expectation and too mystical in retrospection. **Self-Image.** They tend to personify themselves as altruistic, are proud of their authenticity, respect themselves in the degree they are benevolent, and feel confident of themselves in the degree they are empathic. **Social Relationships.** In their family interactions they strive for mutuality, provide spiritual intimacy for their mates, opportunity for fantasy for their children, and for themselves continuous self-renewal. **Four Kinds of Idealists.** The *mentor* kinds are natural *teachers* and *counselors*, while the *advocate* kinds are natural *revealers* and *conciliators*.

Chapter 1

The Apollonian Ideal

O the sun of the world will ascend, dazzling, and take his
height—and you too, O my Ideal will surely ascend!

——Walt Whitman[1]

Although nearly all of the Greek gods revealed both a
physical and a metaphysical dimension in their
personalities, two, Dionysus and Demeter, seemed
primarily involved with the cycles of concrete, earthly
existence—birth and death, spring and fall, sowing and
reaping—while two others, Prometheus and Apollo, had
more to do with the abstractions of mind and spirit, of logic
and intuition. Needless to say, Dionysus and Demeter had
their own characteristic mental lives, but they seemed to
turn their hands naturally to the material world of *things*,
either making things (Dionysus was the fertility god), or
managing things (Demeter was the goddess of the harvest).
In the same way, Prometheus and Apollo certainly had

---

[1] Walt Whitman, "O Sun of Real Peace," ll. 3-4.

some interests and talents in the physical world, but they seemed to turn their minds naturally to the ideas *behind* things, or the symbols that stand *for* things, either offering man technological control over nature (Prometheus stole the knowledge of fire from the gods), or holding out the promise of spiritual enlightenment (Apollo was the god of light and truth).

In David Keirsey's theory of temperament styles, and in my volumes of *The Pygmalion Project*, these four Olympians serve as totem gods for the four fundamental ways of life first observed by the Greeks, and then validated again and again in western culture over the past twenty-three hundred years: Dionysus for the **Artisans** ("SPs") in *Volume One*, Demeter for the **Guardians** ("SJs") in *Volume Two*, Prometheus for the **Rationals** ("NTs") in *Volume Four*, and Apollo for the subject of this third volume, the deeply intuitive and interpersonally sensitive temperament Keirsey calls the **Idealists** ("NFs").

Phoebus Apollo is often spoken of as the sun-god, but the Greeks did not clearly associate him with the earthly cycle of day and night. Helios in fact was the sun-god, while Apollo (whose first name "Phoebus" meant "brilliant" or "shining") was, as I have said, the god of light, particularly in the symbolical sense of the word, and thus he was the god of truth or insight, in whom was no falsehood or darkness. Apollo was also the voice of truth, the seer and the revealer, whose trance-like oracle at Delphi was renowned throughout the ancient world for its enigmatic yet inescapable prophecies. And Apollo was the god of music, master of the golden lyre, although his playing was famous not so much for its virtuosity as for its power of inspiration.[2] In his music, Apollo was the spiritual healer

---

[2]In *The Birth of Tragedy out of the Spirit of Music* (1872), Nietzsche makes a similar distinction between virtuosity and inspiration when he

and peacemaker—the god of harmony—purifying his listeners, making them whole, and lifting them to the realm of the gods. Occasionally, Apollo would stoop to fight for causes he believed in, but even in battle he was above the fray: no hand-to-hand warrior, he was lord of the silver bow, the archer-god aiming his radiant shafts from afar. At rare times Apollo could be brutal and lustful, lowering himself to take a bloody revenge, or (overcome with love) forcing himself on a terrified maiden. And yet, while some fascination with the primitive and the profane seemed to lurk just beneath his shining surface, Apollo was by far the purest and most benevolent of the gods, embodying almost perfectly the Greek ideals of wisdom and virtue.[3]

Apollo symbolizes the Idealists so well because these apollonian ideals—truth, purity, peace, spirit—shine through the Idealists' most basic attitudes toward life and inspire their most characteristic behavior. First of all, Idealists are the most visionary or utopian of the four temperaments, forever imagining a more perfect state of being, both in themselves and in the world around them. The Idealist is Goethe's young Werther, a wistful, introspective young man who describes his life as awash in poetical fantasies:

> I examine my own life and there find a world, but a world rather of imagination and dim desires, than of distinctness and living power. Everything swims before my senses, and I smile and dream my way through the world.[4]

---

describes the two gods of Greek art, the ecstatic Dionysus and the contemplative Apollo.

[3]Summarized from Edith Hamilton's *Mythology* (Mentor edition, 1942), pp. 30-31.

[4]Johann Wofgang Von Goethe, *The Sorrows of Young Werther* (Rinehart edition, 1965), p. 8.

Idealists are often in this state of self-examination, outside of themselves watching their thoughts and feelings, trying to make their lives conform to their dreams—it is their gift and at times their curse. The Idealist is James Joyce's Stephen Dedalus, a young Irish intellectual who yearns to rise above the dirt and futility of Dublin and embrace his ideal imaginings:

> He was different from others....He wanted to meet in the real world the unsubstantial image which his soul so constantly beheld. He did not know where to seek it or how: but a premonition which led him on told him that this image would, without any overt act of his, encounter him.[5]

Armed with their romantic image of perfection, Idealists often devote themselves to what they consider true and honorable causes, seeking the holy grail in one form or another, "slaying the dragons" of corruption, or "making the world a better place to live in." Cervantes' Don Quixote de la Mancha is perhaps the archetypal Idealist in this sense, a gentle, elderly nobleman who dedicates himself to a medieval, almost mythical concept of honor:

> He had filled his imagination with everything that he had read, with enchantments, knightly encounters...with tales of love and its torments, and all sorts of impossible things, and as a result had come to believe that all these fictitious happenings were true; they were more real to him than anything else in the world. He would...become a knight-errant and roam the world on horseback, in a suit of armor; he would go in quest of adventures, by way of putting into practice all that he had read in his books; he would right every manner of wrong.[6]

Don Quixote's quest is uniquely Idealistic. He is not seeking adventure for the excitement of it, like an Artisan;

---

[5]James Joyce, *A Portrait of the Artist as a Young Man* (Viking Compass edition, 1969), p. 65.

[6]Miguel de Cervantes, *Don Quixote de la Mancha* (Modern Library, 1949), p. 27.

he is not simply upholding social traditions, like a Guardian; nor is he searching nature for theoretical problems to solve, like a Rational. Idealists can be, at times, just as bold as Artisans, just as vigilant as Guardians, and just as curious as Rationals; but their first desire is to live an ardently ethical life, as the true and valiant champions of some burning cause or some transcendent concept of good. In this way the Idealist is John Steinbeck's Tom Joad, the Dustbowl farm boy who slowly perceives a much larger injustice in his family's struggle with poverty, and who imagines uniting the Okies to fight back:

> I been thinkin' a hell of a lot, thinkin' about our people livin' like pigs, an' the good rich lan' layin' fallow, or maybe one fella with a million acres, while a hunderd thousan' good farmers is starvin.' An' I been wonderin' if all our folks got together an' yelled....[7]

Idealists often discover that their noble intentions do not survive for very long in the real world, but the dream of truth and justice is always the basis for their action, no matter how painful their eventual disillusionment. Tom Joad knows he will likely be killed for his agitating, but he has divined a greater spiritual basis for defying the big California landowners—"Well, maybe like Casy says, a fella ain't got a soul of his own, but on'y a piece of a big one"—and he believes his spirit of rebellion will survive even his death:

> I'll be aroun' in the dark. I'll be ever'where—wherever you look. Whenever they's a fight so hungry people can eat, I'll be there. Wherever they's a cop beatin' up a guy, I'll be there.[8]

---

[7]John Steinbeck, *The Grapes of Wrath* (Viking Compass edition, 1975), p. 571.
[8]John Steinbeck, *The Grapes of Wrath* (Viking Compass edition, 1975), p. 572.

And Don Quixote, despite the world's cruel treatment of him, picks himself up time and again on his adventures, straightens his makeshift helmet, and continues his crusade against evil, believing fervently in the ultimate triumph of the apollonian ideal of virtue:

> But in spite of all this [misfortune], virtue is omnipotent and ...will emerge triumphant from every peril and bestow light on the world as does the sun in the heavens.[9]

As much as Idealists involve themselves in meaningful social causes, they care even more deeply for what E.M. Forster calls the "sanctity of personal relationships." Idealists are the most instinctively interpersonal of all the temperaments, finding perhaps their greatest joy in creating and deepening the significant relationships in their lives. Idealists tolerate superficial relationships well enough— they try to be nice to everyone—but their real desire is always to nourish more intimate levels of understanding with their friends and loved ones, sharing insight, offering counsel, and communicating about meanings and feelings and personal growth. The Idealist is Bernard Shaw's Eugene Marchbanks, an impassioned young poet who tries to reveal his heart's truth to a young Guardian woman, only to run up against her outraged conventionality:

> MARCHBANKS [*secretly*]...We all go about longing for love: it is the first need of our natures, the first prayer of our hearts; but we dare not utter our longing: we are too shy. [*Very earnestly*] Oh, Miss Garnett, what would you not give to be without fear, without shame—
>
> PROSERPINE [*scandalized*] Well, upon my word!
>
> MARCHBANKS [*with petulant impatience*] Ah, don't say those...things to me: they don't deceive me: what use are they? Why are you afraid to be your real self with me?[10]

---

[9]Miguel de Cervantes, *Don Quixote de la Mancha* (Modern Library, 1949), p. 420.

[10]George Bernard Shaw, *Candida* (Penguin Books, 1977), p. 35.

Idealists typically search the world for ideal love, longing to find the one perfect "soul mate" with whom they can share their inner lives—what they often refer to as their "real self." This yearning for soul-communion makes the Idealists wonderfully close and imaginative lovers, but it can also create problems. At times, Idealists will commune so closely with their loved ones, identifying with the "other" so completely (Keirsey calls this "introjection"), that they put at risk their own sense of self. The Idealist is Shakespeare's Romeo, who seems happiest when lost in the agonizing paradoxes of love:

> O heavy lightness! serious vanity!...
> Feather of lead, bright smoke, cold fire, sick health!...
> I have lost myself; I am not here:
> This is not Romeo, he's some other where.[11]

In some cases, however, this intoxicating disconnection can disturb, and even terrify, the Idealist. D.H. Lawrence's Connie Chatterley is deeply troubled by her longing to surrender her conscious self to the dark, animal sensuality of Mellors the gamekeeper, for she knows that embracing such darkness means

> the loss of herself to herself....She knew she had always feared it, for it left her helpless; she feared it still, lest...she would lose herself, become effaced, and she did not want to be effaced.[12]

On the other hand, Idealists also run the risk of expecting so much perfection from their loved ones that normal human relationship never fully satisfy them. This is the other side of intuition, what Keirsey calls "attribution" or "projection," and Idealists find themselves again and again investing their own romantic ideals into loved ones who

---

[11]William Shakespeare, *Romeo and Juliet* (I,i,181-204).
[12]D.H. Lawrence, *Lady Chatterley's Lover* (Signet edition), pp. 126-127.

never quite measure up. The Idealist is Henry James's John Marcher who wastes his life, and the quiet love of a devoted woman, by insisting that his fate must be something "rare and strange, possibly prodigious." At the end of his life, and when it is too late, Marcher has a devastating vision of the genuine love he has missed by expecting love to overwhelm him:

> No passion had ever touched him....He had been *outside* his life, not learned it from within....The escape would have been to love her, *then* he would have lived. *She* had lived—who could say now with what passion?—since she had loved him for himself; whereas he had never thought of her (ah, how it hugely glared at him!) but in the chill of his own egotism. [13]

I want to explain this concept of "projection" more thoroughly, since it is so important in understanding the Idealists' way of dealing with other people. Plato first argued that the *idea* of a thing is more real than the concrete thing itself, and that whatever we perceive in this material world is merely an imperfect reflection of its ideal form. Immanuel Kant went a crucial step further, proposing that the very *perception* of reality is not objective, not independent of the observer, but is at least in part a projection of the individual's mind onto the material world. Then, Edmund Husserl and the phenomenologists concluded that reality was so mired in subjective perceptions that methods were needed to strip away the mind's presuppositions and rediscover the "thing itself" (the *"ding an sich"*).

All along, playwrights, poets, and novelists (particularly if they are Idealists or Rationals) have described the curious ways in which their characters project their own consciousness into the world around them, attributing to

---

[13]Henry James, "The Beast in the Jungle" in *The Turn of the Screw and Other Short Novels* (Signet edition), pp. 449-450.

others (and to nature—even to the simplest things) their own private thoughts and feelings and values. Shakespeare's Hamlet, for instance, said that "there is nothing either good or bad but thinking makes it so,"[14] while the Romantic movement (influenced by Kant) took as one of its great themes the creative relationship between the poet's imagination and the external reality of the senses. Thus William Wordsworth thrilled to the beauty of nature:

> Therefore am I still
> A lover of...this green earth; of all the mighty world
> Of eye and ear—

but he also felt that his own imaginative faculty was intimately involved in the formation of that beauty:

> Of eye and ear—both what they *half create*,
> And what *perceive*.[15]

Early in the twentieth century Marcel Proust offered perhaps the most famous, and certainly the most extended, description of projection in all of literature. Here, from *The Remembrance of Things Past*, is a moment of reverie on the imaginative realities held in a cup of tea:

> I put down my cup and examine my own mind. It is for it to discover the truth. But how? What an abyss of uncertainty whenever the mind feels that...it, the seeker, is at once the dark region through which it must go seeking....Seek? More than that: *create*. It is face to face with something which does not

---

[14]William Shakespeare, *Hamlet*, II,ii, 256-257.

[15]William Wordsworth, *Lines Composed a Few Miles Above Tintern Abbey*, ll.105-107 (italics are mine). Critics of Wordsworth, and of the emotional excesses of the Romantics in general, cautioned against such intrusion of the writer's personality: Keats (a Romantic himself) thought Wordsworth showed an undisciplined "egotistical sublime" in his verse, while Ruskin (a Victorian) coined the phrase "pathetic fallacy" to describe what he regarded as the Romantics' overzealous anthropomorphism.

so far exist, to which it alone can give reality and substance, which it alone can bring into the light of day.[16]

And Wallace Stevens, the most Husserlian of modern poets, describes a young woman singing by the seashore as

> . . .the single artificer of the world
> In which she sang. And when she sang, the sea,
> Whatever self it had, became the self
> That was her song, for she was the maker. Then we,
> As we beheld her striding there alone,
> Knew that there never was a world for her
> Except the one she sang and singing, made.[17]

My purpose here is not to join the debate in philosophy between Idealism and its opposites, Realism or Positivism, but only to suggest that, of the four temperaments, Idealists have the most attributive imaginations, and that they naturally—and endlessly—project their personal vision of life into the people around them, particularly their loved ones. As Virginia Woolf puts it for all her fellow Idealists, "Such is the manner of our seeing. Such the conditions of our love."[18] Let me add, however, that despite their irrepressible subjectivity, Idealists are keenly aware of human feelings, both their own feelings and the feelings of others, and in most cases they are quite skillful at

---

[16]Marcel Proust, *Swann's Way*, trans. C.K. Scott Moncrieff (Modern Library, 1956), p. 63 (italics are mine). For a more contemporary Idealist statement of this phenomenon, see John Lilly's meditation on "The Search for Reality" in his book *The Deep Self* (Warner Books): How can the mind render itself sufficiently objective to study itself? In other words, how are we able to use the mind to ponder on the mind?" (p. 67).

[17]Wallace Stevens, "The Idea of Order at Key West," ll. 36-42.

[18]Virginia Woolf, *Jacob's Room* (Harvest Books, 1950), p. 72.

reconciling their inner and outer worlds, establishing smooth, caring relations with their loved ones.[19]

This gift for rapport characterizes not only the Idealists' own personal relationships, but even their involvement in others' relationships. Keirsey calls the Idealists "the most benevolent of all the types,"[20] the natural diplomats and peacemakers among us, uncomfortable with almost any expression of conflict or argument, and gently determined to settle all disputes with kindness. The Idealist is Chaucer's Parson, a purely good man, and one of the few pilgrims in *The Canterbury Tales* who is spared Chaucer's magnificent irony:

> Holy and virtuous he was, but then
> Never contemptuous of sinful men,
> Never disdainful, never too proud or fine,
> But was discreet in teaching and benign.[21]

The Idealist is also E.M. Forster's Mrs. Moore, an elderly Englishwoman who simply cannot accept the undercurrents of animosity between the people of India and their English rulers. She fervently believes the British should base their colonial administration on the principle of "good will and more good will and more good will," and she insists to her son (a self-important government bureaucrat) that

> The English *are* out here to be pleasant....India is part of the earth. And God has put us on the earth to be pleasant to each other...to love our neighbors and to show it.[22]

---

[19]David Shapiro, in his book *Neurotic Styles* (Basic Books, 1965), argues that while subjective cognition necessarily occasions "empathic errors," it also characterizes "some people" (i.e. Keirsey's Idealists) as "imaginative and interpretive, and, most particularly,...empathic in their understanding of the world" (p. 69).

[20]David Keirsey, *Portraits of Temperament*, pp. 91, 103.

[21]Geoffrey Chaucer, *The Canterbury Tales*, trans. Nevill Coghill (Penguin Books, 1977), p. 35.

[22]E.M. Forster, *A Passage to India* (Harvest Books, 1952), pp. 51-52.

Mrs. Moore's attitude nicely summarizes the Idealist's dual commitments in the social world: championing utopian causes, and creating loving, altruistic relationships. But Idealists also take up one other mission in their inner lives, a search for perfection so unique to Idealists, and so hopelessly abstract, that the other temperaments find it almost impossible to understand: the search for the Self.

Idealists regard their sense of self, their personal identity, as an object of serious inquiry and conscious cultivation. "To be, or not to be: that is the question," ponders Hamlet, in perhaps the most famous Idealist speech in all of literature. And though Hamlet is weighing the value of life and death in this soliloquy, his question also suggests for a great many Idealists (and even for Hamlet himself) a more abstract process of internal discovery. This issue of exactly how "to be" themselves—and "not to be" one or more other selves—dominates Idealist thinking and distinguishes them clearly from the other three temperaments. Artisans, Guardians, and Rationals are much more interested in developing (respectively) what they can do, how they ought to behave, or what they might think, than in discovering who they *are*. The other temperaments master skills, or accumulate credentials, or acquire knowledge, but their "self" (when they think about their self at all) is simply the sort of person they happen to be, a "person-ality" more or less fixed at birth, and certainly not something they feel able to interfere with. Idealists, on the other hand, think of the self as protean, open-ended, a matter of "self-actualizing,"[23] or "becoming a person,"[24] or evolving their "human potential." The Idealist is Gabriel García

---

[23]See Abraham Maslow's *Motivation and Personality*, 1954.
[24]See Carl Rogers' *On Becoming a Person*, 1961.

Márquez's Uncle Leo Daza XII, a "genial lunatic" whose conviction is that

> human beings are not born once and for all on the day their mothers give birth to them, but that life obliges them over and over again to give birth to themselves.[25]

The metaphor of birthing is apt, for Idealists see the self not only as having the unlimited potential of a newborn child, but also (on the darker side) as an especially vulnerable identity that can be lost, or stolen, or somehow invaded and taken over by malevolent forces.[26] Indeed, self-conception is such a compelling issue for Idealists because they are, as a temperament, unsure of their identities, showing evidence of what R.D. Laing refers to as a "Divided Self,"[27] and what Andras Angyal terms a "Pattern of Vicarious Living."[28] Dostoevsky also understood this innately split (or schizoid) way-of-being, as when he has his innocent Prince Myshkin explain how he feels almost helplessly of two minds:

> "it's simply both things came at once. The two thoughts came together; that often happens. It's constantly so with me. I think it's not a good thing, though; and, do you know," Myshkin went on very earnestly, genuinely, profoundly interested, "...it is awfully difficult to struggle against the *double* thoughts; I've tried. God knows how they arise and come into one's mind."[29]

---

[25]Gabriel García Márquez, *Love in the Time of Cholera* (Penguin Books, 1989), p. 165.

[26]Shapiro, like Keirsey, sees the Idealists as essentially "paranoid" in their defensive behavior (*Neurotic Styles*, p. 69).

[27]R.D. Laing, *The Divided Self* (Tavistock, 1959).

[28]Andras Angyal, *Neurosis and Treatment: A Holistic Theory* (John Wiley & Sons, 1965).

[29]Fyodor Dostoevsky, *The Idiot* (Dell Laurel edition, 1966), p. 347.

Naturally, we all fall prey to emotional confusion at one time or another in our lives, but this kind of self-absorbed awareness of a "double self" characterizes, to one degree or another, the Idealists' common experience of life.

If aggravated and deepened by abusive parenting, such fundamental insecurity in the Idealist's self-concept can develop into various forms of hysterical behavior, and though few need resort to such extreme defensive tactics, even relatively well-adjusted Idealists live their lives with some vague feelings of uncertainty, some secret doubt about their wholeness, and recognize in themselves, if only slightly, the unsettling potential for some of the milder forms of emotional dissociation. Hamlet might wax "desperate with imagination" and put on an "antic disposition," but even ordinary Idealists can feel torn or estranged from themselves, can feel chronically irritable and self-conscious, can notice themselves imitating others unconsciously, trying too hard to please others, or feeling uncomfortable with their own darker impulses. In any event, given this intrinsic lack of a well-founded, unified sense of themselves, it is little wonder that Idealists speak meaningfully about searching for their "real self" or their "true self," about becoming "authentic" or "centered," about finding out "who they are" or getting "in touch with themselves." The Idealist is Hermann Hesse's Emil Sinclair, a shy student who, after a fierce internal conflict, finally comes to believe that

> Each man's life represents a road toward himself, an attempt at such a road, the intimation of a path. No man has ever been entirely and completely himself. Yet each one strives to become that—one in an awkward, the other in a more intelligent way, each as best he can.[30]

---

[30]Hermann Hesse, *Demian* (Perennial Library, 1989), p. 2.

This quintessential Idealist assumption that we are all on a "search for ourselves" is an attribution of spiritual hunger that often irritates the other temperaments: many Artisans react with sarcasm and ridicule; many Guardians seem impatient—or even angry—with such foolishness; and many Rationals fall upon the Idealist with the most skeptical interrogation. Further, and even more incomprehensibly to the other temperaments, when Idealists believe they have in fact "found" themselves, they often generalize their sense of harmony and project their inner-wholeness onto the world outside, imagining themselves to be one with all the universe. Thus, as soon as Hesse's most famous Idealist, Siddhartha, feels that "his Self had merged into unity," he comes to understand his place in a universal oneness:

> There shone in his face the serenity of knowledge, of one who is no longer confronted with conflict of desires, who has found salvation, who is in harmony with the stream of events, with the stream of life, full of sympathy and compassion... belonging to the unity of all things.[31]

Unfortunately, there is a troubling paradox coiled at the very center of the Idealist's search for self. As Keirsey argues in *Please Understand Me*,[32] the search for self is fundamentally incompatible with the experience of finding the self. For many Idealists (particularly young Idealists) the search for self becomes a romantic longing for identity—what Keirsey calls the "Identity-Seeking" way of life[33]—in which Idealists feel most authentically themselves only when they are seeking themselves. In their very enthusiasm for self-discovery, Idealists can become

---

[31]Hermann Hesse, *Siddhartha* (Bantam Books, 1972), p. 136.
[32]David Keirsey, *Please Understand Me*, pp. 58-59.
[33]David Keirsey, *Portraits of Temperament*, pp. 90, 101.

trapped in self-contradiction: they *are* themselves only if they are searching for themselves, and they would cease being themselves if they ever found themselves.

Late in his life Siddhartha tries to explain this contradiction between seeking and finding to his friend Govinda, an old Buddhist monk who has spent his life searching for himself. "Perhaps," Siddhartha offers,

> "you seek too much, that as a result of your seeking you cannot find."
>
> "How is that?" asked Govinda.
>
> "When someone is seeking," said Siddhartha, "it happens quite easily...that he is unable to find anything, unable to absorb anything, because he is only thinking of the thing he is seeking, because he has a goal, because he is obsessed with his goal. Seeking means: to have a goal; but finding means: to be free, to be receptive, to have no goal."[34]

The search impedes the finding; the striving for wisdom is its own obstacle. Some Idealists undoubtedly reach Siddhartha's perspective and find their "true" selves, which means that they finally give up struggling to become some perfected idea of themselves, and simply accept themselves as they are. But for many Idealists, the search for simplicity and personal unity only winds them more deeply in the complexities of inner division and self-contradiction: the more they seek themselves, the more intensely frustrated they are in their search.

This obscure feeling of living trapped in paradox is one of the causes, I believe, of the Idealists' peculiar interest in philosophies that offer release into metaphorical systems of reality. As Gregory Bateson and his colleagues observed in

---

[34]Hermann Hesse, *Siddhartha* (Bantam Books, 1972), p. 140.

their work on double-bind communication,[35] the only way to escape a paradox is to step mentally outside of its self-contradictory system, and thus Idealists seem particularly fascinated by theories that point the way to some alternative form of reality, either inside, outside, next to, or above ordinary reality: "deep self" psychology, "para"psychology, "meta"psychology and "meta"physics, "trans"cendental consciousness, "extra"sensory perception, the "super" natural, and so on. A curious note: although they are forever projecting their imaginations onto reality, Idealists will not often agree with the Rational's characteristic view that *all* of reality (including "the self") is a purely imaginary concept, a fiction made up each moment by each of us, and thus something to be dealt with pragmatically. On the contrary, so powerful is their need to find firm footing in reality, and so strong is their ability to conceptualize, that Idealists regard the imagination as the road to a higher reality, some Platonic realm of absolute authenticity, where the spirit or essence of things is more "real" than any manifestation in the material world.

Whatever the truth of the matter, Idealists believe they are ascending to an apollonian ideal in all the significant phases of their lives, undertaking what Plato called "the upward journey of the soul" from the dark prison of the material world to the true "lord of light."[36] And whether one thinks of their spiritual destination as a benign delusion or, indeed, as a more perfect reality, the Idealists' incessant striving for

---

[35]See Bateson's articles on the relationship between double-bind communication and hysterical symptoms, including hallucination, collected in *Steps to an Ecology of Mind* (Ballantine Books, 1972). See also Paul Watzlawick, Janet Beavin, and Don Jackson' *Pragmatics of Human Communication* (W.W. Norton & Company, 1967).
[36]Plato, *The Republic* (Oxford University Press, 1965), p. 231.

enlightenment seems the natural extension of their most characteristic traits: their love of myth and fantasy; their natural facility with symbols and metaphors; their uncanny sense of intuition and premonition; their deep caring about social ethics; their extraordinary empathy; and their sincere longing for personal unity and serenity.

Although Idealists comprise no more than ten percent of the general population,[37] they fill the pages of western literature, appearing again and again in novels and plays as the "pure" character aspiring to this paradoxical notion of a "spiritual reality." Idealists are often religious figures in literature, not the strict voices of church dogma (the role typically reserved for Guardians), but gentle, soul-searching characters devoted to spiritual growth, characters such as Dinah Morris in George Eliot's *Adam Bede*, or the prison chaplain in Camus's *The Stranger*—though they can also be conscience-wracked clergy, such as the Reverend Arthur Dimmesdale in Nathaniel Hawthorne's masterpiece of suppressed passion, *The Scarlet Letter*. Idealists are also secular figures with religious names that add mythological significance to their destinies, Bernard Shaw's Saint Joan, for example, but also Joseph Conrad's Lord Jim, little Simon in William Golding's *Lord of the Flies*, and "Ishmael" in Herman Melville's *Moby Dick*. At the very least, Idealists are pure-of-heart characters (quite often women) who hold the promise of spiritual salvation in their stories: the saintly Isabella in Shakespeare's *Measure for Measure*, or Sonia Marmeladov in Dostoevsky's *Crime and Punishment*.

Idealists are also frequently those memorable individuals who follow a calling rather than a profession. They are

---

[37]David Keirsey, *Portraits of Temperament*, pp. 96, 108.

charismatic teachers, often loved by their students, though at times troublesome in their unconventionality: Jean Brodie in Muriel Spark's *The Prime of Miss Jean Brodie*, for instance, or Mr. Keating in Peter Weir's film *Dead Poets Society*. By the way, Idealists are also highly imaginative and troubled students, like Quentin Compson in William Faulkner's *The Sound and the Fury*, or Sandy Stranger, Jean Brodie's aptly named protégée who eventually takes the veil as "Sister Helena of the Transfiguration." Idealists can be socially conscious journalists, such as Rambert in Camus's *The Plague*, or Nathaniel West's Miss Lonelyhearts. They can be artists waiting for inspiration, Jude Fawley in Hardy's *Jude the Obscure*, for instance, or Lily Briscoe in Virginia Woolf's *To the Lighthouse*. Idealists can be poets, such as Miles Coverdale in Hawthorne's *The Blithedale Romance*, or Boris Pasternak's Yuri Zhivago. Or they can be counselors, like old Doc Appleton, the sage family doctor (and Apollo figure) in John Updike's *The Centaur*, or the doomed psychotherapist Dick Diver in F. Scott Fitzgerald's *Tender is the Night*.

Literature often places the Idealist on the brink of life, searching for meaning and goodness and a sense of identity: Pierre Bezúhov in Tolstoy's *War and Peace*, for example, or the aptly named Adella "Quested" in E.M. Forster's *A Passage to India*. And in their quest for justice and peace, Idealists often become the romantic heroes of our most popular stories, from Malory's King Arthur, with his shining vision of Camelot, to the aspiring Jedi Knight Luke Skywalker (another superb apollonian name) in George Lucas's *StarWars* trilogy. As I have suggested, however, Idealists are only rarely the clear-eyed, fearless heroes in literature; they are more likely torn and tormented figures, filled with doubt and anxiety—the so-called "modern heroes" fighting themselves as much as their enemies, characters such as Don Quixote, Hamlet, Nora in *A Doll House*, or Lady Chatterley.

Not surprisingly, literature tends to portray its storytellers as Idealists, sometimes the novelist's own thinly disguised persona, such as "Marcel" in Proust's *The Remembrance of Things Past*, or "Chris" in Isherwood's *Berlin Stories*. And if not the authors themselves, Idealists are time and again the characters who narrate stories, self-revealing personalities like Conrad's Marlow who sits in "the pose of Buddha" as he pieces together the horrifying *Heart of Darkness*—as well as a host of other first person narrators, from Dickens's David Copperfield to Fitzgerald's Nick Carraway in *The Great Gatsby*. And though these narrators are often innocent characters (Stingo in William Styron's *Sophie's Choice* is a good example), they can also be oddly disturbed individuals, such as the haunted governess in Henry James's classic ghost story *The Turn of the Screw*, or Humbert Humbert, the sadly bewitched pedophile in Vladimir Nabokov's *Lolita*.

One intriguing discovery in my research: the Idealist's sensitivity and vulnerability are often represented in literature by a physical handicap, particularly lameness—think of the club-footed Philip Carey in Somerset Maugham's *Of Human Bondage*, the limping Rickie Elliot in E.M. Forster's *The Longest Journey*, and the crippled Laura Wingfield in Tennessee Williams's *The Glass Menagerie* (who is symbolized in the play by a fragile, shining unicorn, the mythical creature that embodies so much of the Idealist personality). In addition, Idealists are also the victims of a host of unnamed disorders, such as Milly Theale's mysterious illness in James's *The Wings of the Dove*, Elizabeth Barrett Browning's confining infirmity in Rudolf Besier's *The Barretts of Wimpole Street*, and Osvald's congenital brain disease in Ibsen's *Ghosts*.

And if Idealists in literature seem to be easily broken in body, they suffer as well from various psychosomatic afflictions: Prince Myshkin's epilepsy in Dostoevsky's *The Idiot*, for example, Billy's stammer in Melville's *Billy Budd, Sailor*, and Archibald Craven and his son Colin's spinal weakness in Frances Hodgson Burnett's magnificent children's novel, *The Secret Garden*. And finally, Idealists are subject to a wide range of clearly hysterical disorders, from Sarah Woodruff's *melancholia obscura* in John Fowles's *The French Lieutenant's Woman* to the lurid fantasies of Blanche DuBois in Williams's *A Street Car Named Desire*, from the illusion of divine conception in John Pielmeier's *Agnes of God* to the paranoid delusions of Septimus Warren Smith in Virginia Woolf's *Mrs. Dalloway*, from the knightly hallucinations of Don Quixote to the unspeakably savage visions of Mr. Kurtz in *Heart of Darkness*.

As many of the names in these last two paragraphs might suggest, Idealists are the pivotal characters in dozens of so-called "psychological" novels and plays, and certainly a good number of these characters (Hamlet most notably) have been made the subject of exhaustive psychological analysis, primarily from the point-of-view of Freudian instinct theory, but also using the Jungian theory of archetypes, and many other intra-personal approaches. My intention in *The Pygmalion Project*, however, is to observe the patterns of *inter*-personal behavior in these characters, particularly their interactions in love and marriage, and to describe not only their shared traits of character (their temperament), but also their innate style of manipulating their loved ones. And from this Gestalt perspective, Idealists can only be seen as masterful Pygmalions, bringing all the power of their projective imaginations to bear on reshaping the significant people in their lives.

As an example of the Idealist's Pygmalion disposition—and my use of literary evidence—I want to describe an ironic little scene from Walker Percy's comic novel, *Love in the Ruins* (1971). In the story, Doris More is tired of her husband Tom's insensitivity. Doris is a Louisiana housewife whose Idealism has recently flowered into what Tom calls a "yearning for esoteric doctrine: she has taken up with an English guru (a devout "disciple of Ramakrishna"), she has begun reading books like *"Siddhartha, Atlas Shrugged,* and *ESP and the New Spirituality,"* and she has developed the urgent need to go "in search of myself....To the lake isle of Innesfree." Tom is a psychologist (not clearly drawn, but either a pragmatic Artisan or Rational), and though he is accustomed to his clients' interpersonal gambits, he confesses that his wife has him one-down: "It was the one tactic against which I was defenseless, the portentous gravity of her new beliefs."

Tom might make fun of Doris's new-age credo ("she hoped to recover herself, learn quiet breathing in a simple place, etcetera etcetera"), but he loves his wife sincerely and even offers to accompany her on her search for inner-knowledge—but Doris has set her heart against him, and only sighs bleakly,

> we don't relate....There are no overtones in our relationship, no nuances, no upper mansions....Spiritual growth is the law of

life. Our obligation is to be true to ourselves and to relate to
this law of life.[38]

Tom looks confused, and hopes to lift his wife's spirits the
best way he knows how, with a little friendly sexual
interplay: "I'd like to relate now," he offers, his eyes
smiling. Idealists, however, often try to control their
relationships with an air of saintly superiority, and so Doris
turns even more somberly into the "priestess of high
places": "I know, I know," she shakes her head, "That's
how you see it....As physical." Tom shifts his ground,
trying not to look so shallow and lascivious (so much like
"a high school boy with impure thoughts"), and he promises
her, "But I don't want just your body." At which point
Doris, not to be won over, resorts to a familiar Idealist
rebuttal: she asks her husband, meaningfully, "What *do* you
want?" Feeling his way, Tom answers rather uncertainly,
"You...," but Doris only shakes her head again and wraps
herself in the mystery of a private identity, insisting "But
not the real me."[39] This step into a personal myth stymies
Tom and, knowing he cannot hope to prevail against an
Idealist in this battle of phantom ideas, he relents and
mutters, "Jesus."

---

[38]Walker Percy, *Love in the Ruins* (Noonday Books, 1971), p. 66. All
quotations from *Love in the Ruins* are from this edition.

[39]In *The Divided Self*, R.D. Laing describes how "the person whom we
call 'schizoid'" conceals himself in the message, "All that you can see
is not me" (p. 37); indeed, Laing observes that "the schizoid
individual...must *never* be what can be said of him. He must remain
always ungraspable, elusive, transcendent" (p. 88). And Andras Angyal
points out the same tactic in the "vicariously living person," or what he
also calls the "hysteric" personality (both apt descriptions of the
Idealists): "Since the 'I' of the vicariously living person is not his real I,
he says in effect, 'It was not I who did it'" (p. 191).

Doris next goes on the offensive. In the midst of their heart-to-heart talk, she asks Tom reproachfully, "Who was it who said the physical is the lowest common denominator of love?" This question is rhetorical, intended not to elicit an answer, but to show Tom how crude, and possibly how uneducated, he is. Tom feels trapped, and indeed when he tries to joke his way out by mumbling ("I don't know. Probably a Hindoo"), his weak attempt at sarcasm only proves his wife's point. Doris then presses her advantage with more sophisticated double-bind questions (much like the classic, "Have you stopped beating your wife?"), trying to attribute some sort of "problem" to her husband:

> "You know the trouble with you, Tom?"
> "What?"
> "You don't understand a purely spiritual relationship."[40]

Although Tom flatly admits, "that's true," he does understand that his wife is seriously unhappy, and he again offers to help settle their differences, asking "but why don't we work at it together?" Doris, however, wants a more self-incriminating concession from her husband, for as an Idealist she fully believes that she can make Tom a more sensitive man *by making him aware of his insensitivity*— and thus she resumes her manipulative questioning:

> "What are you, Tom?"
> "I don't know.".…
> "Who was it who said: if I were offered the choice between having the truth and searching for it, I'd take the search?"
> "I don't know. Probably Hermann Hesse.".…
> "You know the trouble with you, Tom?" She was always telling me the trouble with me. "You're not a seeker after truth."[41]

---

[40]Walker Percy, *Love in the Ruins*, p. 71.

[41]Walker Percy, *Love in the Ruins*, pp. 69-70.

Eventually (and though it might seem contradictory), Doris gives in to Tom's amorous overtures in the scene—Idealists, for all their protests of purity, are passionate creatures. And yet, even though Doris relaxes for the moment with Tom, her style of arguing illustrates three essential features of Idealist Pygmalion projects. It identifies Idealists as tactical in their communications (perhaps unconsciously so); it shows how the Idealists' enigmatical statements about "the self" leave the other temperaments almost helpless to respond; and most importantly, it reveals the underlying assumption of all Idealist Pygmalion projects, that there is something wrong with a person who is not, as Doris puts it, "a searcher like me, a pilgrim."

Not all Idealists are like Doris More, of course, nor do they all have exactly the same intentions in their Pygmalion projects. Doris is close to being a caricature of what David Keirsey calls the **Disciple** Idealists ("NFPs"), that branch of the temperament devoted to the spiritual journey, and who generally take a reporting or responding role in their relationships, what Keirsey refers to as a "role-informing" style. Disciples are the true Don Quixote's of the world, championing romantic causes with passionate intensity, searching for integrity in themselves and in their societies, and often preferring to be a fervent supporter than to assume a role of leadership. The seclusive Disciples, Keirsey's **Monastics** ("INFPs"), are the most seriously self-conscious and self-examining of all the Idealists, almost hypersensitive to their own good and evil impulses, often expecting of themselves, but also of their loved ones, an uncompromising sense of purity. The gregarious Disciples, the **Advocates** ("ENFPs"), are high-spirited, highly imaginative seekers after new and intense experiences; they are open to all of life's dramatic possibilities, and are often ardently committed to reforming their societies, as well as their loved ones.

The other half of the temperament is made up of the **Mentor** Idealists (Myers's "NFJs"), who search more for personal identity than for spiritual wholeness, and who are more the initiators or "role-directors" in their relationships. Although they resent being accused of direct manipulation, Mentors spend much of their lives urging others to deepen themselves and to develop their personal potential. The private Mentors, the **Counselors** ("INFJs"), are especially sensitive to conflict and thus are more subtle and complex in their directives, preferring to work behind the scenes, or with individuals, exerting a deeply-felt, almost psychic influence on their clients, their students, or their loved ones. The gregarious Mentors, which Keirsey names the **Teachers** (the "ENFJs"), are the most confident and charismatic of all the Idealists, and they broadcast their message of personal enlightenment with irresistible enthusiasm.

For clarity, let me summarize these type-categories and sub-categories, as well as the characters I examine in later chapters:

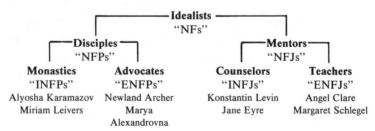

	Idealists "NFs"		
Disciples "NFPs"		**Mentors** "NFJs"	
Monastics "INFPs"	**Advocates** "ENFPs"	**Counselors** "INFJs"	**Teachers** "ENFJs"
Alyosha Karamazov	Newland Archer	Konstantin Levin	Angel Clare
Miriam Leivers	Marya Alexandrovna	Jane Eyre	Margaret Schlegel

Regardless of their particular style, however (and I suspect this is true of all four temperaments), Idealists do not think of themselves as interpersonally coercive. On the contrary, Idealists have little question that their plans for their loved ones are entirely unselfish efforts to help them evolve as human beings—after all, the Idealist assumes, everyone wants "deep down" to grow as a person, to unfold spiritually and become a better individual. Thus, Idealists think of themselves not as maneuvering their mates, trying to change them into their own Idealist image, but rather as assisting or guiding their loved ones to become more enlightened or virtuous in their lives—surely a benevolent undertaking. Despite the Idealists' protests of innocence, however, their manipulative pressure is very much in evidence, and because it seems to derive from the most benign instincts, it can be difficult to deal with.

First, Idealists have an all-encompassing need to help the people in their lives grow to their highest mental and spiritual potential. Idealists, whatever their walk of life, are born with a pedagogical imperative, encouraging others to learn about themselves or to deepen themselves, and revealing to others the sources of healthful and meaningful living. This innate desire to nurture personal growth makes Idealists, as I have said, inspiring figures in the classroom, the counseling session, the confessional, or in any other guidance relationship. But with their own mates, the Idealists' appeal for an "upward journey of the soul"—and their assumption that this journey is right for everyone—can turn into the most unwelcome Pygmalion maneuvering.

Moreover, the Idealists' desire for *self*-enlightenment actually increases their Pygmalion behavior with their loved ones. With their prodigious ability to enter imaginatively "into" other people (their intuitive ability), Idealists often see their mates as intimately involved with their own sense of themselves. Again, spouses are more than life-partners to the Idealist, they are soul-partners, joined with them (so the Idealist believes) in some profoundly spiritual identification. In *Wuthering Heights*, for example, Catherine Earnshaw cries that Heathcliff is "more myself than I am. Whatever our souls are made of, his and mine are the same."[42] And though we see in the novel that she has tragically misjudged Heathcliff's Artisan nature, few Idealists would deny that such a romantic union of souls is the very ideal of love. This passionate over-identification with their mates makes Idealists wonderfully loving and empathic spouses, but it can also set the stage for Pygmalion projects. Almost unconsciously Idealists can step from shaping their own sense of self to sculpting their loved ones in their own image.

In essence, Idealists see their personal lives as works of art, and they often expect their loved ones to be a perfect match for them, and their mating to fulfill some deeply-felt romantic dream. Sadly, human beings can rarely live up to such poetic ideals, and most Idealists are thus faced with serious disillusionment in their relationships. Although Idealists usually learn to accept their disenchantment philosophically, the ideal of the "match made in heaven" is always with them on some level—and while it inspires Idealists to be extraordinarily devoted to their loved ones when things are going well, it can also lead to Pygmalion manipulation when the spouse begins to fail the ideal, and the relationship comes under stress.

---

[42]Emily Brontë, *Wuthering Heights* (Norton Critical Edition, 1972), p. 72.

Keep in mind, however, that for all their Pygmalion talents, Idealists have perhaps the greatest gifts of all the temperaments for successful, even joyous, interpersonal relationships. Their spirit of cooperation, their passion for their mates, their desire for deep bonding, their personal warmth and enthusiasm—all these Idealist traits more than compensate for their coerciveness. If it can be assumed that Pygmalion projects are an inevitable part of any relationship, that at best such manipulation can be kept loving and sympathetic, then Idealists offer their Artisan, Guardian, and particularly their Rational mates the possibility of exceptional happiness.

Chapter 2

The
Monastic

When would the days begin of that active wifely
devotion which was to strengthen her husband's life
and exalt her own?

—George Eliot[1]

Shyest and most contemplative of all the Idealists, the
Monastics (Myers's "INFPs") might seem too gentle-
spirited to become involved in Pygmalion projects with
their loved ones. In *Please Understand Me* David Keirsey
describes this type's desire for harmony, both in their own
lives and in their closest relationships, while in *Portraits of
Temperament* he stresses their inherent need for
interpersonal cooperation and conciliation.[2] Similarly, the
evidence of literature clearly indicates that the Monastics

---

[1] George Eliot, *Middlemarch*, (Riverside edition, 1968). p. 202.

[2] David Keirsey, *Please Understand Me*, pp. 176-177; *Portraits of
Temperament*, pp. 99-100. Note that Keirsey called this type the
"Questor" in *Please Understand Me* and the "Hygienic" in *Portraits of
Temperament*.

try by all means to avoid contention with their loved ones, seeking their happiness instead in shared sympathy and mutual devotion, in what Henry James called "The peace of having loved...[and] having *been* loved."[3]

Like all the Idealists, one of the Monastics' first concerns in life is internal human development, and they devote much of their energy to their own spiritual enlightenment. But Monastics will also take it upon themselves to help strengthen their loved ones' spirituality—if anything, Monastics feel more religiously devoted to this duty than any other type, and more exalted in the effort. And, unfortunately, when they endeavor to bring this message of reverent living to their loved ones, the coercive effect is unmistakable.

Since they belong to the family of Disciple Idealists ("NFPs"), the typical Monastic relationship with others is "role-informing"—in other words, they try to nurture their loved ones' spiritual growth by sharing information with them, and not (or only reluctantly) by giving them orders. Thus, instead of commanding their loved ones to cleanse or to deepen their lives, Monastics will first discipline themselves, as if wanting to demonstrate in their own lives that harmony and personal morality are the keys to happiness. When they must interact more assertively, Monastics naturally assume the role of confidant, encouraging their mates to "talk it out," and hoping to inspire them with some life-altering insight. And in these intimate conversations Monastics will occasionally resort to what might be called interpersonal "front-loading," that is, praising their loved ones for virtues they do not have,

---

[3]Henry James, *The Wings of the Dove* (New York Edition, 1937), Vol. II, p. 332.

hoping to shape their behavior by investing them with the Monastic's own values.

On occasion, when stung by emotional indifference or when disappointed by their loved ones' shallowness or materialism, Monastics will break down and *tell* their mates to change their lives, but they become directive only in times of unnatural stress, and they are clearly strained and self-conscious in the role. In most cases, as I have suggested, Monastics attempt a more subtle Pygmalion appeal in their relationships. Either they model their own Monastic way as the only deeply satisfying manner of living, or they try to implant their own soulful Idealist traits in their loved ones, hoping their ideals will take root and grow.

Alyosha Karamazov

Fyodor Dostoevsky's *The Brothers Karamazov* (1879-80) is a vast novel, not only in its length, but also in the scope of its aspirations. Dostoevsky saw his novel as the culmination of both his story-telling art and his thinking on a wide range of subjects, from psychopathology to criminal justice, from erotic possession to religious transcendence, from the primordial tragedy of fathers and sons (anticipating Freud) to the emergence of the isolated god-man (anticipating Nietzsche). However, despite its enormous size and complexity, *The Brothers Karamazov* was intended only as an introductory novel; Dostoevsky planned a second novel, what he called "the main novel," that would follow "the life of my hero" up the present time.[4] And though Dostoevsky died before he could write this final masterwork, he

---

[4]Fyodor Dostoevsky, *The Brothers Karamazov*, "Author's Preface," (Bantam Classic edition, Andrew H. MacAndrew, trans., 1981), p. 2.

presented in *The Brothers Karamazov* more than enough detail about young Alyosha Karamazov—the brother he singled out as his "hero"—to frame a very nearly definitive portrait of the male Monastic Idealist.

Alyosha is the third son of the infamous Fyodor Karamazov, a provincial Russian landowner of considerable means, but an obscenely carnal man, bloated with lust and drunkenness—and certainly one of the most cruelly observed Promoter Artisans ("ESTPs") I know of in literature. Alyosha's mother is old Karamazov's second wife, Sofia, a strikingly beautiful sixteen-year-old orphaned girl from a neighboring province, a delicate Monastic herself who has been scolded and punished by her Monitor Guardian ("STJ") stepmother into terrible fits of shrieking, and whose sanity finally breaks under the added weight of Karamazov's sexual demands. Sofia dies in the throes of religious hysteria when Alyosha is just three years old, and "as in a dream" he remembers his mother sobbing and holding him up in supplication to an icon of the Virgin Mary. Alyosha is sent to live with another family after Sofia's haunting death, but Dostoevsky tells us that all his life the young man feels a mysterious connection with his mother (as well as with the Virgin Mary), a deep sense of identity with her and a yearning to find her grave.

Alyosha does indeed resemble his mother in his acute sensitivity—"You're just like her, just like the Crazy Woman," his father swears to him—but happily his nature shows few signs of Sofia's terrible frenzy and torment. Raised in a loving Conservator Guardian ("SFJ") family, Alyosha grows up a "bright, good-tempered boy," trustful and friendly, "an angel on the earth" as his older brother Dmitry calls him. He is genuinely liked by everyone he meets, blessed with the gift of "making people love him," and seemingly incapable of animosity, even against his father. Never once does Alyosha reproach his father for the "shocking debauchery" he carries on night and day in his house. "There was something in him," Dostoevsky points out,

> that made people realize that he refused to sit in judgment on others, that he felt he had no right to, and that, whatever happened, he would never condemn anything.[5]

Few Monastics ever achieve the depth of forbearance in their relationships that Alyosha Karamazov seems born with, and yet, no matter how rare, nor how difficult to maintain, Alyosha's sense of infinite tolerance remains a Monastic ideal, one of their most sacred aspirations.

Alyosha has his peculiarities, of course (Dostoevsky admits that he was "strange from the cradle"), but what might seem eccentric to the other types is simply normal Monastic behavior. For example, Alyosha seems a distant boy, "rather reserved," Dostoevsky says, "one might even say uncommunicative." In school, he is "seldom playful, or...even merry," not actually frightened of life, but serious-minded, and painfully shy about standing out and "showing off to the other boys." Monastics have an innate humility about them, a deep-rooted reserve that can get the better of them and actually keep them from accomplishing all they are capable of in life. And Dostoevsky seems well aware of the cost of his young hero's modesty. He makes a special point that Alyosha (like many bright Monastics) "was always among the top students" in his school, although never bold enough to be "first in his class."

---

[5]Fyodor Dostoevsky, *The Brothers Karamazov* (Bantam Classic edition, Andrew H. MacAndrew trans., 1981), p. 21. All quotations are from this edition.

Alyosha also shows the innate Monastic indifference to money, a trait that is indeed strange in a novel so filled with money—with loans and inheritances, bills of debt and payoffs, with all the greed and scheming and revenge over money the characters display. In singular contrast, Dostoevsky admits that Alyosha "did not seem to know the value of money," calling him (with some pride, it seems)

> one of those child-like, saintly creatures, who, if he were suddenly to come into a large fortune, would think nothing of giving it all away to some good cause.[6]

Even more oddly to the people around him, Alyosha is known to "plunge into his private thoughts," to become "absorbed in his thoughts and, as it were, withdraw from the world," often choosing to "go off into a quiet corner and read a book" rather than to socialize. This is not to say that he is sullen or frightened of people; on the contrary, Dostoevsky emphasizes that Alyosha has an enduring love of mankind, and that "throughout his life he seemed to believe in people and trust them." But the intensity of his inner life—his engrossment in his own interior world— simply supersedes at times his relationships with the people around him, as Dostoevsky explains:

> His apparently distant behavior was due to a constant inner preoccupation with something strictly personal, something which had nothing to do with other people, but which was so supremely important to him that it made him forget the rest of the world.[7]

Let me reiterate this point: Alyosha's inner-absorption is not born of fear or indifference, but derives from the Monastic's intrinsic self-awareness and penchant for internal contemplation, what Keirsey calls their need "to

---

[6]Fyodor Dostoevsky, *The Brothers Karamazov*, p. 23.

[7]Fyodor Dostoevsky, *The Brothers Karamazov*, p. 21.

retreat periodically to private places...to examine their virtues and vices."[8] Monastics are often thought to be timid or aloof when they are merely turned inward, assessing quite passionately the state of their souls.

Alyosha does shrink from one part of life, however. Perhaps in reaction to his father's depravity, but also in keeping with his Monastic's sensitivity, he cannot bear "to hear dirty words or a certain type of talk" about sexual matters. At school, surrounded by what Dostoevsky calls the astonishing "outward cynicism" of the little Artisan boys, Alyosha blushes and tries to "stop up his ears as soon as they started talking about 'those things.'" His schoolmates admire Alyosha for many of his virtues, but they see in his "frantic modesty and chastity" a perfect opportunity to bring him down to their level; and so they corner him and tease him, calling him "little girl" and mocking him with obscenities. Alyosha covers his ears with his hands and struggles to break free, but he must finally submit, "bearing it all in silence," until the other boys back away and leave him in peace.

Finally, and most importantly, Alyosha is different from others in his Monastic attitude toward religion and religious discipline. Alyosha's formal Christian name is "Alexei," which alludes to Russia's Saint Alexei (known as "the man of God"), and Alyosha seems determined to follow in the footsteps of his famous namesake. Throughout the first half of *The Brothers Karamazov*, Alyosha is a novice in the local monastery, and Dostoevsky assures us that the nineteen-year-old has every intention of spending "the rest of his life within its walls." Like all Idealists, Alyosha decides very early in life to search out some ethical basis

---

[8]David Keirsey, *Portraits of Temperament*, p. 109.

for his existence, and to pledge his loyalty to an apollonian sense of goodness and right—to find "the ideal way to escape from the darkness of a wicked world, a way that would lead him toward light and love." And thus, when he becomes convinced of the truth of God and immortality (having "given it serious thought"), he throws himself into his religious conversion with typical Monastic enthusiasm. The idea of becoming a monk "caught his imagination," Dostoevsky tells us, and

> he yearned to serve it and give it his whole strength...to sacrifice everything, his life itself, in an act of supreme devotion.[9]

I don't want to suggest that all Monastics choose the Christian deity as their object of worship, or that they are all inclined to cloistral discipline. This same selfless devotion can be inspired in them by almost any compelling social issue, by secular volunteer work of many kinds, by a personal commitment to physical or psychological health, or by a private conception of divinity. (Indeed, Dostoevsky confesses that had Alyosha decided against the existence of God, "he would immediately have joined the ranks of the atheists and socialists.") What Monastics seek in life is a higher calling, some ethical ideal to which they can dedicate their lives, and they are fully capable, as Keirsey notes, of "unusual sacrifices" for what they believe in.[10]

In Alyosha's case, and this is also typically Monastic, the source of inspiration is not merely an abstract principle or teaching, but is embodied in a *person*. Idealists are easily the most "personal" of all the temperaments, concerned about people even more than ideas—or, rather, they

---

[9]Fyodor Dostoevsky, *The Brothers Karamazov*, p. 30.

[10]David Keirsey, *Please Understand Me*, p. 176.

understand ideas most easily in the context of personal relations. (In contrast, Artisans grasp ideas through their senses, Guardians through protocol, Rationals through logic.) Here, Dostoevsky tells us that Alyosha was drawn into the monastery not because of Christian theology, but

> only because he had happened to meet a man who made an overwhelming impression on him—the famous Zosima, the elder of our monastery, to whom he had become attached with all the ardor of the first love kindled in his insatiable heart.[11]

Dostoevsky insists that "Alyosha was in no sense a fanatic" like his mother, and yet his "youthful imagination" is deeply stirred by Zosima's quiet spirituality, and his veneration of his mentor seems at times so compelling as to border on monomania:

> the elder had been his unquestionable ideal for so long that all his aspirations and youthful energies could not help but follow that ideal to the exclusion of all others, even to the point of forgetting everything and everyone else at certain moments.[12]

Monastics devote themselves to religious movements and metaphysical schools with great enthusiasm, often becoming the disciples[13] of admired leaders, whom they invest with transcendent qualities, hoping to find in the saint or the sage—and thus to experience vicariously—the spiritual perfection they long for in themselves.[14] Dostoevsky tells us that in Father Zosima's saintly presence

---

[11]Fyodor Dostoevsky, *The Brothers Karamazov*, p. 20.

[12]Fyodor Dostoevsky, *The Brothers Karamazov*, p. 409.

[13]In *Portraits of Temperament*, Keirsey actually uses the name "Disciples" to identify all the "NFPs."

[14]Andras Angyal makes the same point, explaining that "the vicariously living person...sets out to change or 'create' himself—through imitation, by living up to some borrowed standards, or by allying himself with a valued person" (*Neurosis and Treatment*, p. 190).

Alyosha hears an unspoken command: "If thou wouldst be perfect, go and give up all that thou hast and come and follow me." This is an appeal few Monastics can resist.

Father Zosima, however, gives Alyosha two more explicit directives in the novel, one that defines Alyosha's mission within the monastery, and the other that prescribes his eventual departure. In the first place, as a novice under Zosima's guidance, Alyosha must abide by his master's one uncompromising law: "you renounce your own will, you yield it...in total submission and self-renunciation." The purpose of what Dostoevsky calls Zosima's "terrible apprenticeship" is not so much to accustom Alyosha to the procedures of the Holy Order (an objective insisted upon by some Guardian monks in the monastery), as it is to prepare him for that most sacred, and most paradoxical, of Idealist journeys, the search for self.

Father Zosima is an archetypal Counselor Idealist ("INFJ"), imbued with mysterious healing power and the gift of prophecy, and as Dostoevsky struggles to summarize the elder's vision of Alyosha's future, he expresses the baffling contradiction that lies at the heart of all ascetic philosophies: that obedience is freedom, and that self-denial somehow leads to self-discovery. If Alyosha will submit to Zosima's austere regimen, he will

> finally attain, through a whole life of obedience, complete freedom (that is, freedom from himself) and thus avoid the fate of those who reach the end of their lives without ever having found themselves within themselves.[15]

It is difficult, even for many Idealists, to understand such an impenetrable statement; but, then, sages like Father Zosima often speak in mesmerizing riddles and paradoxes that

---

[15]Fyodor Dostoevsky, *The Brothers Karamazov*, pp. 31-32.

effectively disarm their listeners, causing them to suspend their critical judgment and open themselves to spiritual truth.

Father Zosima's second directive sends Alyosha on another journey, on "a long, long road" into the world of human relationships, and inevitably into the interpersonal intricacies of Pygmalion projects. Zosima is an ancient man, wizened and frail, with a serene knowledge that his long life is ending, and he tells Alyosha that after his death the young man must leave the monastery. "I am sending you out into the world," he confides to Alyosha, "and you will be of great service there." Zosima instructs Alyosha, "you will leave these walls, but in the world outside you will still be like a monk...you will bless your life and make other men bless their lives." And Zosima concludes (like Apollo's oracle) with the unsettling prophecy that his "chaste and pure" young novice will also take a wife.

This command to enter the outside world seems straightforward enough, but it too places Alyosha in a troubling dilemma. On the one hand, Alyosha's every instinct as a Monastic tells him that "the elder sent me out to reconcile and unite people," and taking Zosima's words to heart he is ready to start on his journey of peacemaking. On the other hand, the idea of leaving the monastery, and particularly of marrying, worries Alyosha dreadfully: "here in the hermitage there was peace and holiness," he broods (with a "quivering" heart), while "outside all was confusion and darkness, in which," Dostoevsky adds, "he was afraid to lose his way."

All his life, Alyosha's closest personal relationships have tended to overwhelm him with a sense of conflict, leaving him mentally and emotionally fragmented. After one typically explosive family quarrel, for example, Alyosha's

> thoughts were splintered and scattered and he...was afraid to bring all the fragments together to get a total picture of all the painful and conflicting feelings he had experienced.[16]

Alyosha's quandary is a common one for Monastics, their life-long mission to bring peace to others often existing uneasily side by side with their own sensitivity to conflict. It might even be fair to say that Monastics seek unity in the relationships around them because they feel the *lack* such unity in themselves. At the very least, a vague sense of uncertainty and inadequacy seems to plague the Monastics' relations with others, an almost unconscious feeling of discord that underlies their longing for harmony in the outside world.

Let me also point out that Alyosha's fear of facing his dark and painful feelings, as well as his fear of becoming lost in wickedness, are just two examples of a pervasive Monastic fear of entering into the corrupted world of flesh and blood. Monastics prefer to live in an ideal world of one sort or another, in ivory tower seclusion, or in some dream of their own innocence—behind monastery walls either physical or psychological. And in times of stress they will go to extraordinary lengths, even into a number of self-destructive avoidance behaviors, to keep from acknowledging their baser human impulses.[17]

---

[16]Fyodor Dostoevsky, *The Brothers Karamazov*, p. 171.

[17]In *Neurosis and Treatment*, Andras Angyal argues that "the hysteric, who represses all tabooed impulses so as to remain good and blameless, insists, in effect, that he must be perfect" (p. 191). And Angyal adds that the hysteric deals with threatening impulses "in one of two ways: they are either *transformed* so as to be more consistent with the reigning system principle or kept from becoming effective by *segregation*" (p.

Not that Alyosha is as horrified by indecency as he was in his school days, but Dostoevsky suggests several times in *The Brothers Karamazov* that, even as an adult, Alyosha has deep-seated anxiety about the life of his body, particularly about his sexual desires. For instance, Alyosha is undeniably stirred by the "dark, sparkling eyes" of Katerina, his brother Dmitry's fiancée, though he buries his feelings and then seems confused by "the indefinable origin of his anxiety." Also, when the ravishing Grushenka (Dmitry's mistress) teases and flirts with him, Alyosha is utterly fascinated by her beauty and is "shaken by tiny, imperceptible shivers" as she devours him with her gaze; but he is terrified of his attraction as well, and he feels "somehow tense and nervous" in her presence, finally turning "away from her, nervously clasping and unclasping his hands." Keirsey might very well have been describing Alyosha Karamazov when he observed that the Monastics often live in a profound moral ambivalence, ever-striving for innocence and purity in their lives, but also feeling stalked by perversion, and fascinated "with the profane."[18]

Despite his inner divisions and fears, however, Alyosha faithfully follows Father Zosima's dying wish and leaves the monastery, believing fervently in his mission to "reconcile and unite" his fellow men. Though still intimidated by the conflicting passions in relationships, and anxious lest he become "completely lost in all these complications," Alyosha knows he cannot escape his life's calling. Dostoevsky's insight into the young Monastic's

---

130). Keirsey believes that both of these defensive behaviors, transformation and segregation (i.e. dissociation), are characteristic of the Idealists.

[18]David Keirsey, *Please Understand Me*, p. 176.

nature is uncanny; he tells us that Alyosha cannot help but
minister to his loved ones,

> because his love was an active one. He was unable to love
> passively: as soon as he came to love someone, he had to help
> that person. And in order to help he had to set himself a goal.
> He had to be sure what was good for each person, what it was
> he needed, and then when he was sure of what was best for
> everyone, he got to work.[19]

As I have argued, Idealist Pygmalion projects are often
difficult to defend against because they come concealed in
lofty intentions, and Dostoevsky makes this case
eloquently. As Alyosha enters into the world of men and
women, his motives appear purely altruistic: he is quite sure
he wants "what was good for each person," and his only
goal is "to help that person" find "what it was he needed."
Such loving devotion to others certainly seems blameless,
and yet Dostoevsky shows us that it is a small step from
wanting what is good for each person to believing you
know, as Alyosha puts it, "what was best for everyone," an
attitude that is by no means peculiar to the Idealists, indeed,
that forms the basis of Pygmalion projects for all the
temperaments.

But what an Idealist believes is best for others is naturally
quite different from what an Artisan or a Guardian or a
Rational believes, and yet so instinctive is our desire to cast
the world in our own image that we ignore these
ineradicable differences among us. Innocently, and often
righteously, we take up our Pygmalion projects, and in this
case Alyosha spends much of the rest of his time in *The
Brothers Karamazov* trying to bring his ideal of soulful
salvation to the other characters. Alyosha's efforts in each
relationship meet with different degrees of success and

---

[19]Fyodor Dostoevsky, *The Brothers Karamazov* , p. 224.

failure, depending in large part on the temperament of the character involved, but his intention to spiritualize his loved ones is evident. Father Zosima had told Alyosha that a monk must try to help his fellow-men become "what [they] ought to strive to become," and the young Monastic loyally sets about this holy work.

Though it might seem odd, the three earthy Artisans in the novel are most immediately susceptible to Alyosha's saintly offices. Although Artisans care very little about spiritual rebirth, they can be surprisingly sentimental about receiving heavenly forgiveness, and Alyosha's compassion comes as blessed comfort to each of them. For example, when Alyosha offers to pray for his father's sins, the old man softens instantly, calling Alyosha his "clean angel," and weeping, "I know you're the only person on earth who hasn't condemned me." Alyosha also touches the souls of Dmitry and Grushenka, two more of Dostoevsky's "Sensualists," by listening with a loving heart to their lurid confessions. "You'll hear me out, you'll understand, and you'll forgive," Dmitry tells Alyosha, "and that is just what I need—for someone who is better than me to forgive me." And Grushenka calls Alyosha her "prince charming": "I knew he'd come one day and forgive me. I believed he'd love me, unclean as I am."

Compassion is not coercion, of course, unless it attempts to reshape its recipients; and clearly Alyosha crosses this fine line with a kind of behavior that Keirsey calls "front-loading." Very simply, Alyosha tries to encourage these three Artisans to become more spiritual by loading—or projecting—an expectation of spirituality into them. Thus he tries to convince his father that, for all his sins, he has a place in heaven awaiting him: "You're not wicked," he comforts him, and insists, "your heart is better than your head." He also promises Dmitry that without fail, "you'll find in yourself [a] new man" of conscience and faith. And he assures Grushenka that, no matter how wantonly she tempts him, she will always be his "true sister, a treasure, a loving soul."

Monastics put forward such benevolent attribution unconsciously and involuntarily in their Pygmalion projects. It is a Monastic's deep conviction that even the most sinful human beings have a seed of godliness in them—a latent soul waiting to be brought to life. Moreover, Monastics believe in the power of their words to inspire even the worst among us; if they say someone is a "loving soul" often enough, or with enough conviction, then they fully expect that person to become a loving soul. And their influence is undeniable.[20] Without knowing it, without even wanting to comply, their loved ones try to fulfill the Monastics' glowing expectations: old Karamazov confides to Alyosha that "with you alone I feel like a decent person," Dmitry admits that Alyosha is "like my conscience," and Grushenka cries, "he called me his sister and I'll never, never forget it."

However, Dostoevsky is careful to point out in *The Brothers Karamazov* that the Monastics' well-intentioned attribution of virtue can also result in vehement—and quite appropriate—irritation and resentment. Front-loading can make loved ones feel manipulated into virtue: "Aren't you going a bit far now?" Dmitry suddenly warns his brother. Front-loading tries to press loved ones onto the Monastic's

---

[20]Robert Rosenthal and Lenore Jacobson describe the amazing effectiveness of what they call the "self-fulfilling prophecy" in their seminal book, *Pygmalion in the Classroom; teacher expectation and pupils' intellectual development* (Holt, Rinehart and Winston, 1968).

own moral path, an imposition of holiness which old Karamazov finds very nearly insufferable:

> As for reaching your paradise, Alexei, my son, I don't even want to reach it—I want you to understand that....Now if you wish to have prayers said for my soul, you're welcome to, and if you don't wish to, you can go to hell yourself for all I care.[21]

And this sort of unwarranted praise can even have an unintentionally shaming effect, robbing loved ones of their self-respect and making them feel guilty for being who they are—as Grushenka pleads with Alyosha to understand:

> and you mustn't say kind things about me and insist that I'm good....If you praise me, you only make me ashamed of myself.[22]

As you might expect, Rationals are more perceptive than Artisans about this sort of coercive communication—at one point, in fact, Alyosha's Rational friend Rakitin very nearly names the technique: "They've loaded you with that elder of yours," he tells Alyosha, "and now you're firing your elder at me." And Rationals are more coldly indignant. Rationals anchor their self-respect in their personal autonomy (particularly their intellectual autonomy), and they are acutely aware of the slightest moral instruction, even though most often they keep their annoyance to themselves. In an early scene, for instance, Alyosha's Rational brother Ivan merely cautions Alyosha about his spiritual attributions. Ivan has been trying to describe his tenacious love for life (he likens it in his Rational's scientific way to the "centripetal force left in our planet"), when Alyosha over-interprets his words and flies into his Monastic enthusiasm for higher meaning:

---

[21]Fyodor Dostoevsky, *The Brothers Karamazov*, p. 207.

[22]Fyodor Dostoevsky, *The Brothers Karamazov*, p. 427.

Yes, that's right...love should come before logic....Only then will man come to understand the meaning of life. You know what I think, Ivan—half your work is already done; you love life. Now you must concentrate on the second half and you'll be saved.[23]

Ivan, however, has said nothing about higher "love" or some metaphysical "meaning of life," and divine salvation does not tempt him in the least. And with a slightly strained patience he stops Alyosha before he puts any more words in his mouth: "So you're saving me already!"

But later in the novel Alyosha tries manipulating him again, and this time Ivan is not so good-natured. Alyosha is praising his brother warmly for his goodness and innocence before God ("God has entrusted me to tell you this"), when Ivan turns on him "with an icy smile":

"You know, Alexei...there are two things I cannot stand— prophets and epileptics, especially messengers from God."[24]

When Ivan condemns epileptics in this passage, he is referring primarily to the twisted Smerdyakov, old Karamazov's bastard son, but he might very well have Alyosha also in mind. Earlier, and in front of Ivan and his father, Alyosha has what appears to be an epileptic seizure:

Alyosha suddenly leapt up from his seat, just as his mother had, threw up his hands, covered his face with them, then collapsed back into his chair as though his legs had been pulled out from under him, and suddenly started shaking in a succession of hysterical, violent, soundless sobs.[25]

---

[23]Fyodor Dostoevsky, *The Brothers Karamazov*, p. 277.

[24]Fyodor Dostoevsky, *The Brothers Karamazov*, p. 724.

[25]Fyodor Dostoevsky, *The Brothers Karamazov*, p. 164.

Dostoevsky knew about epilepsy first hand. He suffered from the malady himself,[26] and he made Prince Myshkin, the epileptic hero of his novel, *The Idiot*, endure the most graphically portrayed seizures I have ever seen depicted in fiction.[27] And while it cannot be said that Alyosha is an epileptic on that scale in the novel, Ivan knows how easily shaken Alyosha's nerves are, and he knows how far he can push his little brother in an argument: "It seems I'm hurting you, my boy. You don't look very well." Rationals do not usually go all out against a weaker opponent, but in this case, pushed by Alyosha's piety beyond his breaking point, Ivan shows us just how vicious a Rational can be.

Clearly, in his conviction that he knows "what is best for everyone" Alyosha repeatedly oversteps himself, and again with Katerina (an "ESTJ" Supervisor Guardian) his attempt at salvation results in bitter animosity. Katerina implores Alyosha to advise her on her tortuous relationship with Dmitry, whom she has vowed to save with her love, devoting her life to this Pygmalion project as to a "grim, painful, and...unrelenting duty." Dmitry and Katerina illustrate a classic Artisan-Guardian dysfunctional relationship in *The Brothers Karamazov*, similar to several of the relationships I detail in *The Pygmalion Project, Vols. One* and *Two*. However, Dostoevsky's statement of Katerina's position (in which devotion becomes a means of punishment) is particularly revealing:

---

[26]Dostoevsky began his epilepsy as a young man in prison, just after the severe trauma of standing before a firing squad, awaiting his execution—which was commuted at the last moment.

[27]In his theory of absurd family games, David Keirsey describes epileptic convulsions as one of the characteristic defensive behaviors of the Idealists. And Dostoevsky seems to make the same association, for next to Alyosha, the Christ-like Prince Myshkin is one of the purest Idealists I know of in literature.

> And let [Dmitry] see, as long as he lives, that I stay true to him
> and to the promise I have given him once and for all, even
> though he himself has been untrue and has betrayed me....I
> will become just a means to his happiness...and that until the
> end of my life. And I want him to see it and be aware of it as
> long as he lives.[28]

At first, Alyosha is reluctant to involve himself in the twists
and turns of such grimly coercive love, but under the
pressure of Katerina's plea for guidance he finally responds
with what can only be described as a holy epiphany: "It's as
if I had suddenly seen something," he whispers in a
"trembling, faltering voice." Alyosha believes he has
divined Katerina's true feelings for Dmitry—that she has
never really loved him—and this insight comes to Alyosha
with the power of a sacred revelation:

> I really don't know how I dare tell you all this, but somebody
> ought to tell you the truth...because no one here wants to tell
> the truth.[29]

Again, Idealists have a remarkable intuition about people
and relationships, but they can also take their powers too
seriously, coming to believe that they can effectively
change others with their insights. Idealists (especially
Monastics) believe implicitly that "The truth will set you
free," and Alyosha fully expects his penetrating words to
save Katerina from her twisted dependence on Dmitry. But
like front-loading, such truth-telling can also threaten the
other's privacy, actually creating resistance to change,[30]
and certainly in this case Katerina rejects Alyosha's insight,

---

[28]Fyodor Dostoevsky, *The Brothers Karamazov*, p. 226)

[29]Fyodor Dostoevsky, *The Brothers Karamazov*, p. 229.

[30]For a full discussion of the ambiguous role of truth or insight in
psychotherapy, see Paul Watzlawick, John Weakland, and Richard
Fisch's book *Change: Principles of Problem Formation and Problem
Resolution* (W.W. Norton & Co., 1974).

along with his implied Pygmalion message that she must begin living in the light of truth. Exploding with rage, she shrieks at him, "You're a holy little fool! That's all you are," and then storms from the room.

This same general pattern—first loving appreciation, and then violent rejection—appears in almost all of Alyosha's relationships, but it plays itself out most dramatically, and most tragically, in Alyosha's heartbreaking betrothal to a young girl named Lise Khokhlakov.

Lise is a rather badly disturbed Teacher Idealist ("ENFJ"), plagued by some of the same shrieking fits as Alyosha's mother, and also bound to a wheelchair by what appears to be a hysterical paralysis.[31] Although only fourteen, she has loved Alyosha for several years, from the time of his long visit to Moscow when he would sit with her and tell her of his thoughts and impressions, or share with her memories of his childhood—Dostoevsky tells us that "sometimes the two of them would dream up whole stories together." Like almost all the other characters in *The Brothers Karamazov*, Lise regards Alyosha as her confessor and savior, and so when she meets him again at the monastery (she has come from Moscow to be healed by Father Zosima) she risks her heart's secret and smuggles him a letter confessing her feelings. Lise is terrified that Alyosha will despise her for her boldness, but he is in fact overjoyed at the news; and though he admonishes himself that such human happiness "might be sinful," he rushes to her side to reassure her of his own wish to marry.

The scene of Lise and Alyosha's engagement, however, illustrates not only their typical Idealist innocence about

---

[31]Keirsey notes that Mentor Idealist in particular are "seizure hysterics, either paralytic, convulsive, or both" (*Portraits of Temperament*, p. 96).

love, but also introduces an unavoidable conflict of Pygmalion styles. At first, Lise and Alyosha are both nervous and embarrassed—though in their own characteristic ways—about acknowledging their feelings. As they talk over their plans Alyosha shyly tries to avoid physical contact, until Lise orders him, "Give me your hand, Alyosha! Why do you keep trying to pull it away?" Then, after he rather awkwardly embraces her, Lise advises him, "Well, Alyosha, we'd better postpone kissing for a while, because neither of us is very good at these things yet." Let me point out that, as a Teacher, Lise is a role-directing Idealist, quite willing to take command of this unfamiliar relationship; and indeed, as she relaxes with the idea of being married, her thoughts turn explicitly to matters of interpersonal control:

> Alyosha, you'll have to do what I tell you, do you agree to that? That must be settled in advance.[32]

Alyosha's Monastic role-informing style is less straightforward, but it operates just as actively in this scene. Alyosha quickly counteracts Lise's directiveness with his own saintly tolerance: when Lise tells him what suit he must wear when he leaves the monastery, Alyosha humors her, and acquiesces, "I'll wear whatever you want me to." Lise cannot help but admire such generosity—"You're an amazingly nice person, Alexei"—though his niceness also irritates her with its gentle righteousness: "but there are times," she adds, "when you sound rather smug."

When Lise blushes at her forwardness and asks Alyosha how he can love someone so young and "silly"—and so hopelessly crippled—Alyosha tries to lift her with the

---

[32]Fyodor Dostoevsky, *The Brothers Karamazov*, p. 263.

power of his words, heaping her with praise to convince her of her worthiness:

> you have many talents that I lack completely. You're a much gayer person than I am, and you're also much more innocent than I.[33]

And Alyosha also tries to help Lise believe in herself with a heartfelt Monastic suggestion of deeper truth: "while you laugh like a little girl," he promises her meaningfully, "you think like a martyr."

Sadly, and with startling consequences, this attribution of martyrdom is the most affecting part of Alyosha's Pygmalion project with Lise. She immediately begs him to explain this view of her—"Me, a martyr? What do you mean by that?"—and he tells Lise that her severe physical and spiritual suffering has surely awakened in her a true divinity of soul. "Take, for instance, the question you asked me earlier," he begins,

> Well that's something a martyr would ask...a person to whom such questions occur is himself capable of suffering. While sitting in your wheel-chair all this time, I'm sure you've given much thought to these things.[34]

Lise listens nervously to Alyosha's confidence-inspiring words, and clearly wants to live up to his expectation of loving self-sacrifice: "I'll yield to you joyfully," she promises him, "I'll be happy to." And as they part Lise seems radiant with hope: "We shall be happy, Alyosha, don't you think?"

But within a few days a radical—and truly puzzling—change has taken place in the hysterical young girl. Lise calls Alyosha to her and cruelly breaks off their

---

[33]Fyodor Dostoevsky, *The Brothers Karamazov*, p. 262.

[34]Fyodor Dostoevsky, *The Brothers Karamazov*, p. 262.

engagement, claiming that she is insatiably promiscuous, flaunting before him her desire for evil, and insulting him not only for his humility, but also for his unbearable Monastic purity. "You wouldn't be much of a husband," she mocks him:

> I'm terribly fond of you, but I have no respect for you at all....I want someone to marry me, tear me to pieces, betray me, and then desert me. I don't want to be happy.[35]

Dostoevsky gives no preparation or justification for this bizarre twist in Lise's behavior, and her actions might be considered incredible, except that they are quite in keeping with the schizoid characteristics of the disturbed Idealist. In the first place, Idealists are extremely vulnerable to feeling invaded and overwhelmed by another person, and they will resort to what R.D. Laing calls "the most strenuous, desperate" maneuvers—even inspiring hatred in the other— to maintain their precarious identity.[36] In this case, Alyosha's Pygmalion project has threatened to engulf Lise, and she suddenly feels she must repudiate Alyosha's belief in her goodness, what she calls his "unbearable" presumption of her saintliness. With the convoluted defensive logic of the schizoid personality, Lise feels she must destroy Alyosha's faith in her—she will even destroy herself—in order to keep control of her own life.[37]

Furthermore, Keirsey speaks of the Idealist's deeply hidden longing to experience "the ugly, the corrupt, and the

---

[35]Fyodor Dostoevsky, *The Brothers Karamazov*, pp. 697-698.

[36]R.D. Laing, *The Divided Self* (Pelican edition, 1965), p. 44.

[37]In *The Divided Self*, Laing describes the case of one young man, Peter, who "so deeply resented what he felt were everybody's efforts to make him into a saint" (p. 123) that his "schizoid defense...became an *intentional project of self-annihilation*" (p. 129).

fleshly"[38] parts of life, and so in this scene, when Lise sets out to free herself from the pressure of Alyosha's praise, she inevitably embraces the Idealist's darkest desires for wanton sexuality and violent destruction. "I want to do evil," she insists, "many, many horrible things": she threatens "to set fire to this house" and to bring all around her to ruin, "so that there is nothing left anywhere."[39] Alyosha listens patiently, and Lise tries to goad him into some sort of angry response:

> I know you're furious with me because I won't talk to you about holy things. But I have no wish to be holy. What will they do, in the next world, to someone who has committed the greatest sin? I'm sure you know what the penalty is.[40]

Alyosha is heartsick at Lise's unbelievable outburst, and yet he still tries to comfort her with gentle (and role-informing) words of hope and insight. Alyosha learned from Father Zosima that we "should always treat people as if they were children and sometimes...as if they were patients in a hospital," and so he promises Lise "this is just a momentary crisis, perhaps the result of your former illness." But Alyosha's imperturbable priestly understanding only enrages Lise all the more: "Oh you have the right ideas about things," she raves at him sarcastically, "you of all people, you, the monk!" Once again, and even more desperately in this case, Alyosha's best-intended efforts to

---

[38]David Keirsey, *Please Understand Me*, p. 66.

[39]Lise's desperate yearnings echo with a terrible clarity Laing's description of schizoid fantasies. He finds that "The image of fire recurs repeatedly" in the schizoid, as if symbolizing "the uncertain flickering of the individual's own inner aliveness" (*The Divided Self*, p. 45). And he observes further that the schizoid individual "is unable to believe that he can fill his own emptiness without reducing what is there to nothing" (p. 93).

[40]Fyodor Dostoevsky, *The Brothers Karamazov*, p. 699.

ennoble his loved ones result in resistance and resentment. Once again his Monastic front-loading backfires.

Since Dostoevsky did not live to write the "main novel" about Alyosha's adult life, we can never know if Lise was able to overcome her hysterical self-destructiveness, or if Alyosha ever learned to give up his saintly Pygmalion projects and allow his loved ones to live their own lives. From the evidence we have in *The Brothers Karamazov* we can only say that Dostoevsky had penetrated deeply into the shy, mysterious Monastic character, and that he had discerned with remarkable clarity the selflessness—and the paradoxical coerciveness—of their interpersonal aspirations.

Miriam Leivers

Although Dostoevsky is often spoken of as one of the first "psychological" novelists, he thought of himself more as a religious or metaphysical writer. In his notebooks Dostoevsky corrected those who praised his insights into the minds of his characters: "I am called a psychologist," he said, but "it's not true....I depict all the depths of the human soul." On the face of it, D.H. Lawrence would seem to have little in common with Dostoevsky. Lawrence is popularly known not for the depths of his characters' spirituality, but for the explicit sexuality—some have said pornography—in their relationships. And yet Lawrence has much to say about the human soul in his novels, and he also saw himself as "a profoundly religious man," though it is true he rejected the abstract *mental* spirituality of modern Christianity for the earthy "dark gods" and the phallic mystery of ancient pagan worship. "My great religion," he wrote, is a belief in the blood, the flesh, as being wiser than the intellect. We can go wrong in our minds. But what our blood feels and believes and says, is always true.[41]

Given what can only be called Lawrence's contempt for disembodied spirituality, it is little wonder that he treats Monastics quite critically in his novels. But so keen was Lawrence's eye for human behavior, and so intimately knowledgeable was he about the Disciple Idealists (he was most likely an "ENFP" Advocate himself), that he offers us one of literature's most remarkable portraits of the female Monastic: Miriam Leivers from his great early novel, *Sons and Lovers* (1913).

Miriam Leivers is a "shy...sensitive" girl of nearly sixteen when we first meet her in *Sons and Lovers*. Her family has lately taken over Willey Farm in the wild meadows surrounding the coal fields of Nottinghamshire, but Miriam holds herself above the rude farming life. "The girl was romantic in her soul," Lawrence tells us, "something of a princess turned into a swine-girl in her own imagination." Although she is a healthy, ripening girl, with deep brown eyes and a "beautiful warm colouring," there seems something distant, almost ghostly about her: "Miriam seemed as in some dreamy tale," Lawrence continues, "a maiden in bondage, her spirit dreaming in a land far away and magical." The Idealist's imagination is naturally given to transforming ordinary reality, and Miriam has clearly turned her crude, demeaning life into a private fairy-tale, what Lawrence calls "her inside dream." She moves about the farmhouse, doing her menial kitchen chores in a "strange, almost rhapsodic way," and her eyes dilate suddenly, "like an ecstasy," when she stares past her

---

[41]Quoted from Lawrence's letter to Ernest Collings, 17 Jan., 1913.

drudgery to the higher romantic world where she is sure she belongs.

Miriam also imagines herself above the farming folk—"the common fry," she calls them—preferring to read Walter Scott novels and fancying herself in the company of Scott's splendid heroes and heroines, the "Ediths, and Lucys, and Rowenas, Brian de Bois Guilberts, Rob Roys, and Guy Mannerings." Indeed, Lawrence tells us that "She could very rarely get into human relations with anyone," and that in particular she "scorned the male sex," refusing to mix with the neighboring farm boys, and shunning her Artisan brothers for their brutal, loutish ways. "She niver durst do anything," her brother Geoffrey taunts her, "except recite poitry." Even her amiable Artisan father earns her disfavor, because "he did not carry any mystical ideas cherished in his heart, but only wanted to have as easy a time as he could, and his meals when he was ready for them."

Not that her fantasies and her poetry bring Miriam much joy in her life. Her incessant need is to have "things kindling in her imagination or in her soul," and this makes her almost always too intense to find pleasure in simple human living. Miriam's face "scarcely ever altered from its look of brooding," Lawrence observes, and he confesses that

> she was cut off from ordinary life by her religious intensity which made the world for her either a nunnery garden or a paradise, where sin and knowledge were not, or else an ugly cruel thing.[42]

This propensity to see the world polarized into fervent moral extremes—as either heaven or hell, with no middle

---

[42]D.H. Lawrence, *Sons and Lovers* (Penguin Books, 1981), p. 148. All quotations are from this edition.

ground for normal human frailty—is quite typical of the Idealists, giving them an uncompromising desire for purity in their lives, but also leaving them very little room for "natural" or spontaneous living. In an extraordinary passage Lawrence describes Miriam's tendency—quintessentially Idealist—to make life so clenched with consequence that even the simplest tasks become difficult:

> Her body was not flexible and living....She was not clumsy, and yet none of her movements seemed quite *the* movement. Often, when wiping the dishes, she would stand in bewilderment and chagrin because she had pulled in two halves a cup or a tumbler....There was no looseness or abandon about her. Everything was gripped stiff with intensity, and her effort, overcharged, closed in on itself.[43]

Miriam's only soul companion is her mother, another rather shadowy Monastic who has tried to tame her unruly sons with "over-gentleness" and an "apologetic tone," and who has infused the house with an almost oppressive atmosphere of spirituality. Mrs. Leivers has the Idealist's incurably symbolical view of the world, the unconscious need, as Keirsey puts it, to give even "small transactions profound significance,"[44] or in Lawrence's words to "exalt everything—even a bit of housework—to the plane of a religious trust." And Lawrence points out that Miriam is cut from the same cloth as her mother, describing the two Monastics as "mystical" souls, "such women as treasure religion inside them, breathe it in their nostrils, and see the whole of life in a mist thereof."

To be sure, Miriam is religious as only a Monastic can be religious, with a mystical imagination and an ardent personal devotion. Much like her namesake "Miriam the

[43]D.H. Lawrence, *Sons and Lovers*, pp. 153-154.

[44]David Keirsey, *Please Understand Me*, p. 92.

prophetess" in the Old Testament, Miriam is a "worshipper," Lawrence tells us, one who believes we "should be religious in everything, have God—whatever God might be—present in everything."[45] She pays little attention to the forms or fellowship of organized religion, and little more to Christian theology. But the soaring spires of a Gothic church or the virginal scent of white Easter lilies make her "soul come into a glow," and she worships the Christ in all men—indeed, to Miriam, "Christ and God made one great figure, which she loved tremblingly and passionately." And yet, again, her religious passion brings her little human happiness. Eternally bowed and solemn, "she might have been one of the women who went with Mary when Jesus was dead," Lawrence describes her, adding that Miriam seems to enter effortlessly into "a rapture of self-sacrifice," eagerly "identifying herself with a God who was sacrificed."

Alyosha Karamazov had this same fascination with self-sacrifice—"I want to suffer too," he told his brother Ivan, like Jesus "our great idealist"—and, as we have seen, when Monastics attempt to impart their martyr's rapture to their loved ones, the stage is set for Pygmalion projects. For example, Miriam tries to act the saint with her surly brothers, submitting meekly to their callous jibes and demands, which is in truth a quiet attempt on her part to shame the boys into behaving more soulfully toward her. And Lawrence describes the results of such indirect manipulation with his usual clarity: "the boys resented...this eternal appeal to their deeper feelings," he says; they felt "themselves cut away underneath" as males, and they

---

[45]Miriam is the sister of Moses in the Bible, and her "song" (Exodus 15:21) gives us a good idea of Miriam Leivers' attitude toward holy worship: "Sing ye to the Lord, for he hath triumphed gloriously."

answer with even more brutal insults. At times Miriam loses her temper and reproaches her brothers for their scornful cruelty—and then the boys know they have won, and they mock her anger and reduce her to tears. But when Miriam maintains her saintly air, what Lawrence terms her "proud humility," she takes a subtle, paradoxical control over her brothers. Though "they hated her" for her righteousness, Lawrence admits "it had its effect on them," and they burn in the unwanted consciousness of their spiritual inferiority.

One autumn, amid this "jangle and discord" in the family, a new young man, Paul Morel, begins to spend time at Willey Farm. Paul is the sixteen-year-old son of a Nottingham coal-miner and his wife,[46] friends of Miriam's parents, but he is not at all like the coarse farming and mining boys of Miriam's acquaintance. On the contrary, Paul is a "quick, light, graceful" Teacher Idealist ("ENFJ"), a pale, poetic figure to Miriam "who could be gentle and who could be sad, and who was clever, and who knew a lot, and who had a death in the family." Indeed, Paul's older brother has just died, and while his Inspector Guardian ("ISTJ") mother grieves almost inconsolably, Paul visits the farm whenever possible to escape the gloom and to nurse his own fragile health.

After some initial hostility, the Leivers boys soon become fast friends with Paul, but Miriam stands off as usual, afraid Paul "might consider her simply as the swine-girl, unable to perceive the princess beneath." And yet she feels drawn to this slender, somewhat sickly young man whose "face was

---

[46]For a full discussion of Walter and Gertrude Morel's embattled marriage, including his Performer Artisan ("ESFP") and her Inspector Guardian ("ISTJ") Pygmalion tactics, see *The Pygmalion Project, Volumes One* and *Two*.

pale and thin," and "who could paint and speak French, and
knew what algebra meant." Miriam eyes him wistfully,
attracted as Monastics often are by the delicacy—as well as
the dependency—suggested by physical infirmity:

> Then he was so ill, and she felt he would be weak....If she
> could be mistress of him in his weakness, take care of him, if
> he could depend on her, if she could, as it were, have him in
> her arms, how she would love him![47]

In *Please Understand Me*, Keirsey notes an interesting
contradiction in the Idealists' attitude toward dependency in
their loved ones. According to Keirsey, Idealists strive for
such deep sensitivity and soul-intimacy in their
relationships that at times they can make their loved ones
emotionally dependent on them; and when this occurs
Idealists can suddenly become irritable and demand that
their loved ones toughen up and "stand on their own two
feet."[48] As I hope to show in the next few pages, D.H.
Lawrence describes this abrupt reversal in Idealist behavior
quite accurately in *Sons and Lovers*, though he made an
important differentiation between Miriam and Paul in this
regard, and by implication between Monastic and Teacher
Idealists.

In Lawrence's hands, Miriam (the gentle, role-informing
Monastic) seems determined to make Paul spiritual to the
point of dependence on her; while Paul (the more critical,
role-directing Teacher) becomes quickly impatient with
Miriam's wish for soulful communion, and tries to make
her stand up for herself as an independent, flesh-and-blood
human being. Indeed, these two conflicting attitudes toward
interpersonal dependency form the bases of Miriam and
Paul's conflicting Pygmalion projects in *Sons and Lovers*,

---

[47]D.H. Lawrence, *Sons and Lovers*, p. 143.

[48]David Keirsey, *Please Understand Me*, p. 94.

as the two young people gradually fall in love and then struggle to reshape each other in their own image.

At first, however, Paul is barely aware of Miriam. He spends most of his time outside with her coltish younger brothers, or discussing ideas with her older brother Edgar, "a rationalist," as Lawrence calls him, "who was curious, and had a sort of scientific interest in life." And yet Paul also seems enthralled by the Monastic fervency inside the house, "this atmosphere where everything took on a religious value," and he soon falls under Miriam and her mother's spell: "There was something in the air," he feels, "something different, something he loved, something that at times he hated."

During these first months, Miriam seems to hide in the shadows, peering at Paul with eyes "which were usually dark as a dark church, but could flame with light." And her gaze, searching, almost pleading in its soulfulness, both awakens and frightens the young man. "She got so near him," Paul says of her naked stares, "it was a strange stimulant...as if his feelings were new." And yet, somehow, Paul feels he must guard his independence from Miriam, almost unconsciously resisting her hypnotic eyes: "always something in his breast," Lawrence says, "shrank from these close, intimate, dazzled looks of hers."

Miriam slowly approaches Paul, intrigued by his sketches— "Why do I like this so?"—and asking him shyly if he would tutor her in his schoolwork. As a Disciple, Miriam is far more comfortable being a devoted follower than a leader, and yet, as she grows closer to Paul, she feels she can share with him her deeply religious feeling for nature, eventually offering to show him her sacred wild-rose bush in the woods:

> Almost passionately she wanted to be with him when he stood
> before the flowers. They were going to have a communion
> together—something that thrilled her, something holy.[49]

Paul's reaction to Miriam's overtures is again ambivalent,
both fascination and resistance. In the first place, Miriam's
spirituality opens a whole new world for him. Paul has been
raised in a concrete Artisan-Guardian family, concerned
primarily with the work and worry of everyday life, and his
innate Idealism has never known such inspiring company.
Paul's Artisan father is a blustering, hard-drinking coal
miner, quite a peacock in his day, but now a broken man
and gruffly hostile to his son's intellectual and artistic
ambitions. His mother is just the opposite: she has borne the
burden of her hateful marriage and has tried to support her
beloved son Paul in her own dutiful Guardian way,
worrying about "himself and his achievement," and
showing Paul how to be "quietly determined" and
"unwearied" in his studies. But Miriam's Idealism lifts Paul
quite miraculously to a new plane of consciousness,
abstract, symbolic, and richly spiritual. "In contact with
Miriam," Lawrence tells us, "all his latent mysticism
quivered into life," and the contrast Lawrence draws
between Miriam and Mrs. Morel clearly differentiates the
abstract influence of the Idealist from the concrete influence
of the Guardian:

> In contact with Miriam he gained insight; his vision went
> deeper. From his mother he drew the life-warmth, the strength
> to produce; Miriam urged this warmth into intensity like a
> white light.[50]

It is a common experience for Idealists who grow up in
Artisan or Guardian families to feel somehow out of place

---

[49]D.H. Lawrence, *Sons and Lovers*, p. 159.

[50]D.H. Lawrence, *Sons and Lovers*, p. 158.

with other people, like "strangers in a strange land," unaware that there are other human beings like themselves who share their poetical, soulful way-of-being. The Idealists' first contact with other Idealists (or with Rationals, for that matter) is often a revelation, validating feelings they have long kept hidden, and awakening a hunger for abstract communication they have always had, but were only vaguely aware of. In Paul's case, Lawrence simple tells us, "his soul, hurt, highly developed, sought her as if for nourishment."

At the same time, Paul is warned off by the enveloping strength of Miriam's Monastic feelings: "her intensity," Lawrence tells us, "which could leave no emotion on a normal plane, irritated the youth into a frenzy." Thus, as Miriam humbly ponders the meaning of his sketches, Paul wonders at her unearthly seriousness, and he reproaches her: "Why are you always sad?" he demands of her; "you're never jolly, or even just all right." Again, when he tries to teach her algebra, Miriam seems "intensely supplicating" before the book, as if trying to absorb the mathematics with her feelings, and her slowness and reverence make Paul furious:

> "What do you tremble your *soul* before it for?" he cried. "You don't learn algebra with your blessed soul. Can't you look at it with your clear simple wits?"[51]

During Miriam and Paul's communion with the flowers, while Miriam "went forward and touched them in worship," Paul holds back, feeling "anxious and imprisoned" by the fervency of her spiritual quest. And, finally, after they part, while she walks home slowly, "feeling her soul satisfied with the holiness of the night," Paul feels nearly suffocated

---

[51]D.H. Lawrence, *Sons and Lovers*, p. 156.

by Miriam's ecstasy, and "as soon as he was out of the wood, in the free open meadow, where he could breathe, he started to run as fast as he could," as if to shake off and outdistance the heavenly host hovering around his head.

For years neither Paul nor Miriam acknowledges any romantic love growing between them—"he thought he was too sane for such sentimentality, and she thought herself too lofty." When Miriam waits for Paul to arrive at the farm she likes to picture herself as the immaculate "St. Catherine" in Veronese's painting, sitting "in the window, dreaming." On his side, when Paul's friends tease him about Miriam, he defends the innocence of his feelings:

> He would not have it that they were lovers. The intimacy between them had been kept so abstract, such a matter of the soul, all thought and weary struggle into consciousness, that he saw it only as a platonic friendship. He stoutly denied there was anything else between them.[52]

But as Paul and Miriam grow past adolescence what Lawrence calls their "chaste intimacy" begins warming to physical passion, and Lawrence's true genius as a novelist lies in his astonishing ability to describe this area of his characters' feelings with so much insight.

Like many young female Monastics, Miriam is deeply distressed by sexuality: "the faintest suggestion of such intercourse," Lawrence confesses, "made her recoil almost in anguish." Her father and brothers have to be especially careful around Miriam when they speak of the "birthing and begetting" on the farm, and in one symbolic scene Lawrence describes Miriam's odd discomfort when Paul discovers some nest-warm thrush eggs in the meadow— "blood heat" is how Paul explains the eggs' primal warmth,

---

[52]D.H. Lawrence, *Sons and Lovers*, p. 172.

and Miriam can barely bring herself to touch them.[53]
Moreover, Miriam has always thought of her love for Paul
as intellectual and spiritual—an "annunciation," she calls
it—and once she nearly blacks out in terror when Paul
asserts his physical strength and handles her too firmly on a
rope swing:

> She felt the accuracy with which he caught her, exactly at the
> right moment, and the exactly proportionate strength of his
> thrust, and she was afraid. Down to her bowels went the hot
> wave of fear. She was in his hands. Again, firm and inevitable
> came the thrust at the right moment. She gripped the rope,
> almost swooning.[54]

The day soon comes, however, when Miriam makes the
terrifying discovery that she has sexual longings herself.
One morning while dressing, as she listens secretly to
Paul's voice below in the stables (note that stable life is
"below" her), she suddenly wonders if her feelings for the
young man have changed. Tensing with fear, she searches

---

[53]In a similar scene, Miriam shrinks in "fear, and pain" from letting the
yard chickens peck seed corn from her hand, which is an even more
compelling symbol of her discomfort with her fertility. In his work on
temperament and madness, Keirsey notes the parallel between the high
incidence of *anorexia nervosa* in Idealist females and their peculiar
ambivalence about "seeds," "eggs," or ripe fruit of various kinds. It
appears likely that *anorexia* has much to do with the Idealist's rejection
of herself as the seed-bearing female. See Sheila MacLeod's *The Art of
Starvation* (New York: Viking Press, 1970) for a brilliant exposition of
the metaphorical function of anorexia.

[54]D.H. Lawrence, *Sons and Lovers*, p. 151. Later in this scene
Lawrence comments that Miriam "could never lose herself" in physical
action, an observation paralleled in *The Divided Self*, when Laing
describes the schizoid's fearful withdrawal from the world of real
experience into a severely controlled self:

> The [schizoid] individual is frightened of the world,
> afraid...of letting anything of himself "go"...of losing
> himself in any experience, because he will be depleted,
> exhausted, emptied, robbed, sucked dry (p. 83).

her heart for signs of a new passion, and to her humiliation she finds,

> there was a serpent in her Eden. She searched earnestly in herself to see if she wanted Paul Morel. She felt there would be some disgrace in it. Full of twisted feeling, she was afraid she did want him....Then came an agony of new shame. She shrank within herself in a coil of torture.[55]

Because they have so carefully sealed off from themselves what they think of as their "ugly, cruel" emotions, Monastics all too often experience this rush of shameful recognition when they come face to face with their normal erotic feelings. And Monastics can feel profoundly vulnerable, almost panic-stricken, in these moments of internal revelation, at least until they are able somehow to dissociate themselves from their sexuality and restore their sense of inner purity. In this scene, Miriam lives out a terrifying sequence of self-condemnation and repentance— a sudden, harrowing trial and punishment—so peculiar and so destructive to the Idealists. She "stood self-convicted," Lawrence tells us, "tied to that stake of torture," until she drops on her knees and prays fervently to keep her love purely spiritual:

> O Lord, let me not love Paul Morel. Keep me from loving him....But, Lord, if it is Thy will that I should love him, make me love him—as Christ would, who died for the souls of men.[56]

Paul is also an Idealist, and what Lawrence calls an "internecine battle" between his mind and his sexual feelings also begins in him. The touch of Miriam's skin, Lawrence tells us, "caused a violent conflict in him," Paul's flesh running "hot with friction" while his mind

---

[55]D.H. Lawrence, *Sons and Lovers*, p. 171.

[56]D.H. Lawrence, *Sons and Lovers*, pp. 171-172.

"writhed...with a feeling of humiliation." Lawrence appears to understand intuitively the schizoid defensive behavior of the Idealists, how prone they are to fragment or split off their thinking from their feeling, for he says that Paul's "consciousness seemed to split" as he attempts to deny his unexpected desire for the girl. Indeed, Paul's confusion grows more painful each time he is with Miriam, and Lawrence offers telling analysis:

> He did not know what was the matter. He was naturally so young, and their intimacy so abstract, he did not know he wanted to crush her on to his breast to ease the ache there....The fact that he might want her as a man wants a woman had in him been suppressed into a shame....And now this "purity" prevented even their first love-kiss. It was as if she could scarcely stand the shock of physical love, even a passionate kiss, and then he was too shrinking and sensitive to give it.[57]

The difference between Paul and Miriam's response to such internal conflict—and this is the key to their different Pygmalion projects—is that while Miriam prays to be delivered from the carnal side of her love, Paul wants desperately to overcome his own shyness and meet with Miriam in flesh as well as in spirit. This might be the difference, as I have suggested, between the Monastic and the Teacher Idealist, or perhaps even more fundamentally between the *female* Monastic and the *male* Teacher, at least as Lawrence views them. But in any event, as their relationship grows from the "lad-and-girl" courtship of their youth, Paul knows he cannot contain his "natural fire of love" much longer, whereas Miriam feels she can only love Paul if he is "made abstract first."

---

[57]D.H. Lawrence, *Sons and Lovers*, pp. 178-179.

Miriam's methods for keeping Paul gentle and abstract in his love are more timid even than Alyosha Karamazov's, but no less effective. Though Miriam tries to project into Paul her Monastic image of him, she does not "front-load" this role as aggressively as Alyosha does with his loved ones. On the contrary, she meets the growing urgency of Paul's physical passion with an attitude of silent, soulful patience, what Lawrence calls "the doctrine of the other cheek." This is not a generous patience that recognizes Paul's sexual needs and gives him time to bank the fires of his passion, but an agenda-laden patience that reproaches Paul's sexuality and smothers his passion with unrelenting meekness. "Feeling exalted, glad in her faith," Miriam vows to bring out "the good in the soul of Paul Morel" by showing him the spiritual beauty of self-denial. She will wait humbly for him to leave behind "his lesser self" and to rise to her idealized conception of him, to become again "her" Paul—"the real, deep Paul Morel"—who loves her only with his soul.

Again, the Monastics' Pygmalion projects are powerful because they seem so innocently to address the "the better angel" of our natures. And certainly Miriam's coercive saintliness holds Paul's desires in check, though at a terrible cost in frustration and bitterness. Paul knows full well Miriam's "deeply moved and religious" mood around him, her bowed, meditative look, as if she is "expecting some religious state in him"—and he confesses that he feels "impotent against it," "insubstantial," "almost bewildered and unable to move." Though Paul loves Miriam deeply, and "was mad to comfort her and kiss her," Lawrence tells us that something in the very nature of her innocence stymies him. "See," Paul tells her, "you are a nun...a holy nun," and he knows

his kisses were wrong for her....If he could have kissed her in
abstract purity he would have done so. But he could not kiss
her thus—and she seemed to leave no other way.[58]

Unable to approach Miriam physically, Paul's passion
explodes unexpectedly into a vengeful desire for other girls
("it served Miriam right," he grumbles), but also into
furious anger and accusation against Miriam. "You make
me so spiritual!" he rages at her, "and I don't want to be
spiritual." "You wheedle the soul out of things," he cries,
and begs her, "If only you could want *me!*"

Unfortunately, both Paul's flirtations and his railing against
Miriam result in no real independence, but in terrible guilt
and self-accusation. Such is the hold of Miriam's
Pygmalion project that the harder Paul fights against her
presumption of saintliness, the more corrupt and unworthy
he feels. After all, how can Paul struggle against such
innocent faith in his "better" side without demonstrating his
wickedness? Thus, unable to live up to Miriam's
expectations, but unable at the same time to fault Miriam
for her goodness, Paul comes to believe that "he was
inadequate. His own love was at fault, not hers." He feels
that Miriam's love "was too good for him"—"she so good,"
he confesses, "when I'm not good."

And, unavoidably, Paul's self-reproach turns back against
Miriam. Lawrence tells us that more and more Paul "hated
her, for she seemed in some way to make him despise
himself." "How he hated her!" Lawrence says again, though
both Paul's guilt and his love for Miriam overcome him
immediately: "and then, what a rush of tenderness and
humility!...[for] he knew he was as much to blame
himself." Finally, in one of those wonderfully lucid
passages that seem to simplify the most complicated
relationships in his novels, Lawrence summarizes Paul's

---

[58]D.H. Lawrence, *Sons and Lovers*, pp. 189, 188.

impossible situation, torn and shackled in Miriam's Pygmalion project:

> Half the time he grieved for her, half the time he hated her. She was his conscience; and he felt, somehow, he had got a conscience that was too much for him. He could not leave her, because in one way she did hold the best of him. He could not stay with her because she did not take the rest of him, which was three-quarters. So he chafed himself into rawness over her.[59]

Paul and Miriam both struggle with their divided feelings for several years, their "strong desire," as Lawrence describes it, "battling with a still stronger shyness and virginity." But eventually, when Paul is twenty-three and Miriam twenty-two, they realize that they must either break through their awkwardness with each other, or part and find a more complete mating. Although Paul longs for Miriam, he also dreads the step into sexual intimacy with her— "Why was there his blood battling with her?" he cries, "why must he ask for the other thing?" And yet he knows he cannot marry her on soul-tenderness alone: "If people marry," he has written her, "they must live together as affectionate humans, who may be commonplace with each other without feeling awkward—not as two souls." And so he presses Miriam even more openly to fight against what he calls their "fierce" and "perverse" purity, and to consummate their love, promising her that sex "was God's gift," and that "it would all come right if they tried."

Miriam is less optimistic. She is content to keep her relationship with Paul on a "higher" level, as a communion of souls, sharing only their Idealist "passion for understanding," and yet she knows in her heart that Paul will soon leave her if she does not lower herself and meet

---

[59]D.H. Lawrence, *Sons and Lovers*, p. 251.

with him sexually. At the same time, she worries that she can never satisfy Paul's physical passion. Miriam's deep-seated fear of sexuality (and I suspect this is true for many Monastics) is at least partly a fear of being sexually inadequate. So innately estranged does she feel from the physical world of her body, so intrinsically unsure of herself on what she calls Paul's "lower" animal level, that she fully expects to fail Paul sexually. Lawrence tells us that Miriam "did not believe in herself," that she "doubted whether she could ever be what he would demand of her," and that she fears "she could never be properly mated." Thus Miriam expects to lose Paul either way—if she does give in to his desires, or if she does not. Miriam hates the double-bind she is in and silently reproaches Paul for demanding more of her than she can give ("after all, he was only like other men, seeking his satisfaction"), but she feels she has only one possible escape. She will give Paul her virginity and hope this contents "his manly pride," even though she fully believes he "would be disappointed, he would find no satisfaction, and then he would go away."

Miriam justifies her decision in two characteristic Monastic ways. Her first move is to exalt her action onto the plane of religious passion. As we have seen, Miriam dissociated herself from her original sexual feelings for Paul by re-framing physical love as a Christ-like sacrifice. And now, as she broods and broods about actually accepting Paul, she struggles to believe what he has told her, that "there was something divine" in sex—for if there is, she decides,

> then she would submit, religiously, to the sacrifice. He should have her. And at the thought her whole body clenched itself involuntarily, hard, as if against something; but Life forced her through this gate of suffering, too, and she would submit.[60]

---

[60]D.H. Lawrence, *Sons and Lovers*, p. 284.

Let me point out that Miriam cares little about what people might think of her behavior. Her unconscious resistance is based not so much on a concern for social propriety (a Guardian's consideration), but on an acutely private guilt and fear—guilt that she will be violating her lofty ideal of love, and fear that she will disappoint Paul and lose him altogether. And let me suggest further that, in her own Monastic manner, Miriam takes a curious, martyr-like satisfaction in her suffering. Lawrence says again that Miriam sees little but "sorrow, and sacrifice ahead" with Paul, but he adds that

> in sacrifice she was proud, in renunciation she was strong, for she did not trust herself to support everyday life. She was prepared for the big things and the deep things, like tragedy.[61]

Miriam's decision has another basis as well, one more loving and perhaps more typically Idealist. Keirsey argues in *Please Understand Me* that, at times, the female Idealist can become so selflessly dedicated to her mate that his satisfaction becomes her most important consideration. Even in sexual matters, her own wishes become

> inconsequential compared to the pleasure of giving pleasure to her mate. What matters is that *he* is fulfilled and satisfied.[62]

Keirsey comments that this attitude of romantic self-sacrifice has changed a good deal with the sexual liberation of women in the past few decades, but in *Sons and Lovers* (set at the turn of the century) Miriam's devotion to personal relationships easily overshadows her concern for women's rights, even though Lawrence describes the early days of the women's movement in some detail in the novel, and shows Miriam timorously trying to participate.

---

[61]D.H. Lawrence, *Sons and Lovers*, pp. 215-216.

[62]David Keirsey, *Please Understand Me*, p. 92.

However, Miriam is no modern woman (and no Advocate), and she takes what must now be regarded as an unconscionable pride in her sexual submission to Paul, seeing it not only as a religious sacrifice, but also as a precious personal offering: "it would give him what he wanted," she sighs, which Lawrence tells us "was her deepest wish."

Whatever her reasons, Miriam resolves to have Paul, but she also clearly determines to carry her Pygmalion project with her into this new relationship. She will submit to Paul, open herself to his "lesser" desires, but she will not love him joyously, or spontaneously—or with the impersonality and independence that Lawrence saw as the basis of right sexual relations. She will lay with Paul, but she will remind him every moment, even with her bowed compliance, that she is waiting for a higher spiritual love, and that hers is the passion of self-sacrifice.

Inevitably, Miriam's renewed Pygmalion pressure on Paul produces just the tragedy she fears. Paul courts her now like a lover, hoping to ease her gripped spirituality, to help her become jolly and "ordinary" in their love, but whenever he approaches her, she stymies him with her soulful gaze: "her dark eyes," Lawrence tells us, "full of love, earnest and searching, made him turn away." Paul closes his eyes and caresses Miriam, trying to draw her out of herself, but always she must be serious in her love, always self-conscious, always "deep and meaningful"—and time and again she frustrates him:

> Not for an instant would she let him forget. Back again he had to torture himself into a sense of his responsibility and hers. Never any relaxing, never leaving himself to the great hunger and impersonality of passion; he must be brought back to a deliberate, reflective creature. As if from a swoon of passion

she called him back to the littleness, the personal relationship.[63]

Maintaining "the personal relationship": this is the Idealist's unique talent in life, a gift for sympathetic awareness, for uniting with the hearts and minds of their loved ones, that the other temperaments can only wonder at. But all gifts have their cost, and Lawrence's primary criticism of Idealists, and particularly of Monastics, is that their sexuality can be lost and stifled in the deep well of their sensitivity. Certainly Lawrence wants us to have tender and nurturing *personal* relations with our loved ones in our everyday lives; but his ideal, which he describes again and again in his novels, is that in making love we must be able to let go of our confining egos, lapse out of our "little" personal awareness, and surrender to the dark, warm—and essentially *impersonal*—forces of procreation. Thus, to mate properly, "Paul and Miriam" as individual personalities must let themselves be burned away in the ageless flame of passion; they must meet in each other's arms only as "male and female," powerful, independent beings identifying themselves with the blind instinct of their sexual natures.

For his part, Paul is fully ready to melt with Miriam into this erotic unconsciousness. When he first embraces her in the "thick darkness" of the rainy forest, he quickly loses all track of Miriam as "Miriam": "he seemed to be almost unaware of her as a person: she was only to him then a woman." Miriam, however, still clings to her self-consciousness, as if frightened to give herself up: "She was afraid," Lawrence tells us; "she did not want to meet him so that there were two of them, man and woman together."

---

[63]D.H. Lawrence, *Sons and Lovers*, p. 284.

Miriam clenches herself and accepts Paul under the dark, dripping firs, but the cruel impersonality of the experience appalls her—"this thick-voiced, oblivious man was a stranger to her"—and her only satisfaction comes in what Lawrence calls "the anguished sweetness of self-sacrifice." Afterwards, when Paul comes back to himself, he feels all the dreary burden of Miriam's surrender: "he realised that she had not been with him all the time, that her soul had stood apart." And then, in his remorse for what he has made her do, he becomes again tender and sad—just the Paul Miriam wants him to be—and as he holds her quietly, "again she loved him deeply."

This scenario repeats itself with fatal regularity over the next few weeks, Miriam submitting her body to Paul's desires, while keeping her delicate spirit intact, split-off, observing him from above with reverence but also with "a sort of horror." And the one-sidedness or "halfness" of the love-making, as well as the implicit message of reproach in Miriam's abstraction, drives Paul nearly to despair:

> He could hardly bear it. She lay to be sacrificed for him because she loved him so much. And he had to sacrifice her. For a second he wished he were sexless or dead. Then he shut his eyes again to her, and his blood beat back.[64]

Even more desperately now, given the power of his sexual feelings, Paul is torn between his higher, soul-love for Miriam and his physical passion. And as Lawrence describes Paul's terrible struggle with the two sides of his feelings, he articulates even more clearly the dilemma he sees at the heart of Idealist love:

> He had always, almost wilfully, to put her out of count, and act from the brute strength of his feelings. And he could not do it often, and there remained afterwards always the sense of

---

[64]D.H. Lawrence, *Sons and Lovers*, p. 290.

failure and of death. If he were really with her, he had to put
aside himself and his desire. If he would have her, he had to
put her aside.[65]

Lawrence seems to be saying that, in love, Idealists cannot
have it both ways. No matter how much they might wish it,
sexual love cannot sustain the Idealist's kindly "personal
relationship" on the one hand and achieve full sensual
satisfaction on the other. Love can be either thoughtful or
sensual, either meaningful or voluptuous, either gentle or
overpowering—but it cannot be both, at least not at the
same time. This conflict between the apollonian and
dionysian faces of love is the source of much anguish in
Lawrence's characters, and many of the relationships in his
novels seem unable to survive the incompatibility. Even
Lawrence's relatively liberated Idealists (like Connie
Chatterley[66]) must fight to find some fulfilling balance
between Apollo and Dionysus, while his troubled and
hobbled Idealists (like Miriam and Paul) either renounce
sexual love entirely, holding high their idealized
spirituality, or they taste failure over and over again trying
to combine personal sensitivity and animal passion in the
same experience.

But beyond this, Lawrence's depiction of Miriam addresses
a larger point about interpersonal coercion. Lawrence
suggests that Miriam's inescapable self-consciousness, her
ambition for a higher self, even her ardent sense of self-
sacrifice, are all aspects of a preoccupation with Self—a
fundamental "self-ishness" on her part—that blocks her
ability to love Paul fully. Lawrence once wrote that "The
opposite of love is not hate; the opposite of love is self."

---

[65]D.H. Lawrence, *Sons and Lovers*, p. 290.

[66]See *The Pygmalion Project, Volume One* for my discussion of the
Artisan-Idealist relationship in *Lady Chatterley's Lover*.

And what he meant was that "whole" love requires that we abandon "the self" as the primary object of consciousness. Love requires a faith in Life as well as in Self, a belief in the blood as well as in the intellect, a trust in the unconscious ways of the flesh as well as in what he calls Miriam's "endless psychological accounting." And the sometimes frightening paradox for Idealists is that only by letting go their conscious control, both of themselves and of their loved ones, can they achieve their most consciously professed goals. Idealists must lose themselves in order to find their "real" whole selves, and they must give up what Lawrence calls their "will-to-power" over their loved ones in order to join them in a more satisfying intimacy.

In the end, sadly, Miriam is too devoted to her Monastic ideal of a spiritual relationship—and too terrified of her body—to "let go" either of herself or of her Pygmalion project. She continues "gladly" to make her loving sacrifice to Paul, but the poisonous unspoken message that she is doing something *for* him, lowering herself because she wants him to be happy, continues to shame Paul and to deprive their love-making of all its living strength. In his own Pygmalion project Paul has urged Miriam to abandon her fear and claim him boldly:

> He wanted her to hold him and say, with joy and authority: "Stop all this restlessness....You are mine for a mate."[67]

But Miriam has her own Monastic ideas about mating, and she is more determined than ever to wait in silence until Paul has exhausted himself sexually and is ready to give himself up to her saintly embrace. And so, with the sense of interpersonal failure growing stronger and stronger, Paul decides that their partial love must come to an end. Paul

---

[67]D.H. Lawrence, *Sons and Lovers*, p. 418.

understands he must leave Miriam—he must free himself
from her Pygmalion project if he is to have any chance of
finding a wholly satisfying relationship. For he finally
accepts that, despite their years of mental and spiritual—
and even physical—intimacy, Miriam "was only his
conscience, not his mate," and that she has never wanted
him as an independent man, but only the "Christ in him."

*   *   *   *   *

This is certainly not to say that all Monastic relationships
are as inhibited as Miriam Leivers' or as anguished as
Alyosha Karamazov's. Literature tends to exaggerate the
Monastics into almost unnaturally spiritual human beings,
with impossibly exalted aspirations for their loved ones—
traits which can bring tragic complications to their mating.
Most Monastics make successful, even joyous marriages,
filled with deeply-felt love and insight, and yet the very
excessiveness of Miriam's and Alyosha's experience allows
them to illustrate with exceptional clarity the Monastic's
pattern of interpersonal rolecasting.

Monastics dedicate themselves to nurturing the soul of their
loved ones, the deep, spiritual center that they believe to be
the moral source of all our living. Monastics are vigilant in
their nurturing, sensitive to signs of shallow desire and
facile enjoyment, and they are gentle in their efforts to help
their loved ones rise above human weakness. Monastics are
wonderfully personal and sympathetic with their loved
ones, seeking always to please and to heal their
relationships, even though they can seem distant and moody
in their expressions of physical affection, as if on guard
against the unseen dark forces of their nature. And
Monastics are serious and faithful in their love, although

they can feel in conflict between their utter devotion to their mates and their inviolable sense of their own integrity.

Ironically, this integrity, this uncompromising desire to maintain purity and wholeness in their lives, is the basis of the Monastics' self-esteem, and also the source of their Pygmalion projects. For however benign their intentions, and however indirect their tactics, Monastics feel an almost religious obligation to instill their own passion for spiritual integrity in their loved ones, to put them in touch with what Miriam calls "the God...in everything."

Chapter 3

The
Advocate

Isabel, I will write such things...and show them
deeper secrets than the Apocalypse!
——Herman Melville[1]

While the shy, seclusive Monastics devote themselves
largely to cultivating inner purity, the high-spirited
Advocates (Myers's "ENFPs") turn their energies outward
to investigate the public world and to develop their social
awareness. Keirsey calls the Advocates "keen and
penetrating observers,"[2] who "can't bear to miss out on
what is going on around them."[3] And he has referred to
them both as "Apocalyptics" and "Heralds" because of their
fervent desire to spread the news of their experience of
good and evil.

---

[1]Herman Melville, *Pierre; or, The Ambiguities* (Grove Press, 1957), p.
381.
[2]David Keirsey, *Please Understand Me*, p. 173.
[3]David Keirsey, *Portraits of Temperament*, p. 109.

Brimming with life, Advocates live more spontaneously "in-the-flesh" than Monastics, and at first glance they can be rather easily mistaken for Artisans. But more than simply seeking the excitement of new experiences, Advocates are interested in understanding the significance of things, and more than simply taking people as they find them, Advocates care about nurturing ethical and sympathetic social relationships. To be sure (and unlike the impulsive Artisans), Advocates are serious and con-scientious in their relationships, wanting to nourish human potential and to awaken what they believe to be the latent morality in their fellow-men. In a word, Advocates are *romantic* in their relation to the real world, seeing high drama in their quest for life, and hearing an irresistible call to enlighten those around them.

Although Advocates are thus more public-minded than the Monastics, and more confident in dealing with people, they are only slightly more directive in their private interactions. Like all the Idealists, Advocates want harmony above all else in their personal relationships, and they are far more inclined to "re-form" their loved ones by presenting them with information than by giving them commands. Nevertheless, Advocates can be quite coercive in their role-informative style of defining relationships. Advocates delight in free discussions of current issues—they burn with convictions and bubble with meaningful details, yearning to unveil what they believe to be the "true story" of significant events. At times, Advocates will champion a cause with such zeal that they can be carried away with the rightness of their position, and find themselves preaching to their friends and loved ones, trying fervently to convince them of their point of view. Indeed, in their penchant for investigating and reporting "the truth," Advocates can quite easily strain their relationships by reading too much into their loved ones' behavior, by over-interpreting the hidden meanings in their loved ones' words, and by overstating their own romantic views as apocalyptic revelations.

Newland Archer

Edith Wharton sets the main action of her Pulitzer Prize-winning novel *The Age of Innocence* (1920) in genteel "old New York" of the eighteen-seventies, the fashionable, conservative, and largely Guardian high society she knew so intimately from her own youth. Wharton looks back at New York with some affection, picturing it as an innocent and elegant world of lawn parties and black-tie dinners, of spacious landau carriages and massive brownstone houses, a world secure in its old-fashioned institutions and aristocratic traditions. But she also remembers New York with a good deal of scorn as a hidebound world, intolerant of personal freedom and almost cruelly inimical to the spirit of imagination.

In her own young womanhood Wharton chafed against the well-starched proprieties and implacable rituals of this Guardian social system. Though her family assumed that she would make her social début, marry correctly, and settle into her privileged life, Wharton was oddly enamored of books and ideas, and she dreamed of exploring European culture and of living a more liberated "life of the mind." Most likely an Advocate herself, Edith Wharton invested all her own longings and ideals—and all her frustrations—into the tragic story of Newland Archer, a young New Yorker torn to his soul between two kinds of love: his "lawfully wedded" love for his Guardian wife, and his forbidden desire for a magnificent Artisan woman he wants hopelessly to make his own.

From the first, Newland Archer seems suspiciously out of step with the "carefully-brushed, white-waistcoated, buttonhole-flowered gentlemen" of New York society. His very name calls to mind images of far-reaching apollonian discovery, and not the "dim domestic virtues" (in Wharton's phrase) of his tightly-knit social world. Apollo was the "archer" god, remember, and Wharton tells us that, though only thirty years old, "New-land" had "read more, thought more, and even seen a good deal more of the world than any other man" of his Fifth Avenue set. Without a doubt, Archer's intellectual interests are widespread and ambitious for one of the idle rich. He reads literature and anthropology, science and law, though it must be admitted that his reading appears rather impressionistic and unsystematic, reflecting what Keirsey calls the Idealists' "global and diffuse" imagination.[4] In *Please Understand Me* Keirsey notes that the Idealist "can be an intellectual butterfly, flitting from idea to idea, a dilettante in his pursuit of knowledge,"[5] and Wharton sees a similar flightiness of mind in Archer, calling him several times in the novel an intellectual "dilettante."

But Archer does keep up with new ideas, and some of his "modern" attitudes are alarmingly irregular for his class. He ruffles "old-fashioned Episcopalian New York" by not attending church. He spends his vacations in Europe, attending art galleries and museums. He has friends among the out-at-the-elbows New York poets and novelists (the "fellows who write"), and he is also known to mix on occasion with musicians and painters at Bohemian clubs.

---

[4]David Keirsey, *Portraits of Temperament*, pp. 92, 104. Keirsey borrows this phrase from Shapiro's discussion of the hysteric personality in *Neurotic Styles*, p. 111.
[5]David Keirsey, *Please Understand Me*, p. 65.

He is quick to take the part of the "few black sheep" (inevitably Artisans) in his family, and when pressed he lashes out at "the inexorable conventions" that rule his world. Advocates love to be on the cutting edge of society and to champion avant-garde causes, and thus Archer shocks the "pleasanter sentiments" of his mother and sister Janey (both gossipy Guardians) by advocating divorce as a solution to a wretched marriage. "Well why not?" he demands, and the very mention of "divorce" fell "like a bombshell in the pure and tranquil atmosphere of the Archer dining room."

Just as earthshaking, Archer dabbles in politics. The official attitude in polite circles is that "a gentleman couldn't go into politics," but Archer is not at all satisfied with his leisurely practice of law, as a desultory junior partner in the eminent office of "Letterblair, Lamson, and Low." His Advocate's nature gives him a stirring, deep-seated sympathy with social "reforms and 'movements,'" and we learn that after his marriage, and at the urging of Governor Theodore Roosevelt, Archer spends one year in the New York State Assembly trying to bring a new integrity to government.

He is not re-elected (the "honest man in American politics," he finds, is apparently not "what the country wants") and he contents his Advocate's instincts by writing articles for "the reforming weeklies that were trying to shake the country out of its apathy."[6] But Wharton conveys the natural discipleship of the Advocate when she describes how

---

[6]Idealists in general have had little success in American politics, at least at the presidential level, a fact that Ray Choiniere and David Keirsey discuss at some length in *Presidential Temperament* (Prometheus-Nemesis Books, 1992), their study of temperament differences in the Presidents of the United States.

Archer "glowed" at Roosevelt's appeal, "how eagerly he had risen up at the call" of the "great man." And she tells us that, even though his contribution to political life was small, Archer never returned to "the narrow groove of money-making, sport and society" so characteristic of his generation and his class. He "had high things to contemplate," Wharton says, and in his life Archer becomes the epitome of enlightened public-spiritedness, offering his energy and guidance to "every new movement, philanthropic, municipal or artistic."

On matters of the heart, however, Archer seems at first a good deal more conservative. May Welland, his fiancée, is the picture of feminine innocence in the novel, "the young girl in white," as Wharton calls her. May is a pink-cheeked and white-gloved Protector Guardian ("ISFJ"), and she is also the delicate "May" flower of the New York social nursery, carefully tended "by a conspiracy of mothers and aunts and grandmothers." And without question May's blushing modesty (she is only twenty-two) has perfectly captivated Archer. As he watches her at the opera on the night of their engagement, sitting demurely in her grandmother's box and holding a bouquet of lilies-of-the-valley on her knees, Archer smiles with a "tender reverence" on her childlike purity. Later that night, at the gala ball, as he dances with May among the tree ferns and camellias, the "cup of his bliss" overflows, and he realizes that "nothing about his betrothed pleased him more" than her invincible maidenly "niceness," her blind determination to obey the New York "ritual of ignoring the 'unpleasant'" in every facet of her life.

Edith Wharton offers a number of penetrating explanations for Archer's surprisingly old-fashioned infatuation. First of all (and this is an important point about all the Idealists), she shows us that beneath his intellectual non-conformity Archer has quite a traditional sense of morality, particularly when it comes to the woman he plans to marry. As an Advocate, Archer might "strike out on his own" in art and literature, in religion and politics, but concerning his fiancée he feels a genuine "solidarity" with the New York standards of feminine innocence, and about women in general he has rather complacently adopted the Fifth Avenue "doctrine on all the issues called moral." Idealists, let me say, share with Guardians an innately moral nature—both temperaments base their behavior first on considerations of right and wrong, rather than utility or efficiency, like the pragmatic Artisans and Rationals. In addition, Advocates are the most chivalrous, even quixotic, of all the Idealists in their relations with women. And thus it is understandable for a young Advocate man, raised in a traditional, moralistic Guardian social system, to set aside his broader intellectual ideals and take on a conservative, in some ways medieval, attitude toward feminine purity.

Moreover, Wharton's irony makes it clear that she believes the starry-eyed Archer is idealizing May's moral delicacy into a vision of spiritual perfection, very much romanticizing her spotless propriety into purity of soul. Wharton remarks (with droll seriousness) that Archer feels "something grave and sacramental" in the first hours of his engagement, and that he imagines almost deliriously "what a new life it was going to be, with this whiteness, radiance, goodness at one's side." Archer also calls May his "dear and great angel!" and he pledges himself to keep not only the golden "essence" of their love "untouched," but "the surface pure too." Wharton understands all too well the Idealists' ability to attribute their own soulfulness to their loved ones, for she describes how Archer marvels at the "depths of [May's] innocently-gazing soul"—and how, as she sits staring absently into space, he believes her eyes are "distant and serious," and are surely "bent on some ineffable vision."

But Wharton knows as well that Archer feels a more physical attraction to May. She explains (and with some personal bitterness) that New York keeps a young girl so conspicuously virginal before marriage precisely to excite her future husband's desire for erotic conquest—"in order that he might exercise his lordly pleasure," as Wharton puts it, "in smashing [her] like an image made of snow." And certainly Archer is not above feeling this same "thrill of possessorship" when he pictures himself initiating May into the mysteries of sexuality. As a temperament, Idealists are creatures of strong passions, but Advocates are the most adventurously amorous of the group, and Archer (with his swollen "masculine vanity") is indeed charmed by May's "radiant good looks" and enticed by the promise of her virginity. "The darling," he beams with pride at the opera, "she doesn't know what it's all about," and he fantasizes what it will be like on his honeymoon, when he plunges May "overnight into what people evasively called 'the facts of life'"—though Wharton makes it clear that, in typical Idealist style, Archer is rather embarrassed at his own eagerness.

Wharton offers yet another reason, and this a more subtle insight: she suggests that May's appeal for Archer springs from her Guardian promise of safety and stability, no less than from her tantalizing innocence. Keirsey observes in *Please Understand Me* that the "warmly enthusiastic" Advocates are often drawn to the sober, trustworthy Guardians, who take responsibility for "keeping the ship on a steady course," and who pride themselves on "providing anchorage and safe harbor" for their impetuous mates.[7] And in this case Archer describes May in almost these same words, expecting their marriage to be a "safe anchorage" among the adulterous backwaters of respectable New York society, and likening May to a ship which can sail him "safe past the Siren Isle and [into] the haven of a blameless domesticity."[8] In addition, Archer often thinks of May as a vessel holding all the virtues of home and family-life. He calls her "straightforward, loyal and brave," and then again "generous, faithful, unwearied." He trusts that, in her eyes, the world is "a good place, full of loving and harmonious households." And he feels that May is just the girl to keep a rein on his rebellious imagination, putting him more securely in touch with the familiar New York world around him: "in spite of the cosmopolitan views on which he prided himself," Wharton tells us, "he thanked heaven that he was a New Yorker, and about to ally himself with one of his own kind."

Edith Wharton's understanding of Archer's feelings for May is thus extensive, but she also knows that, as an Idealist, Archer is "too imaginative" not to have disturbing doubts about what he is getting himself into—doubts that perhaps his marriage will be no safe anchorage at all, "but a voyage on uncharted seas." May's Protector simplicity is endearing on the surface, but Archer has his Advocate's intellectual aspirations, and he insists with some dismay that he "did not in the least want the future Mrs. Newland

---

[7]David Keirsey, *Please Understand Me*, p. 74.

[8]Wharton is notoriously candid in her novels about the sexual "scandals and mysteries that...smouldered under the unruffled surface of New York society." And she scatters throughout *The Age of Innocence* details of Archer's own affair some years before with a married woman—"a tragedy," as Archer describes it in his conscience-stricken Idealist way, "of which his soul would always bear the scar."

Archer to be a simpleton." Again, May's Protector innocence is precious, but Archer has his Advocate's inquisitiveness, and he confesses that "he did not want May to have that kind of innocence, the innocence that seals the mind against imagination and the heart against experience."

Most young husbands-to-be have second thoughts (as Wharton points out), but Archer's fears run deeper than most, and alone in his study a few days after the ball, he studies May's framed photograph "with a new sense of awe." May's placidly assured Guardian features (her "frank forehead, serious eyes and gay innocent mouth") make her appear to him now "like a stranger," and he wonders if "she was frank, poor darling, because she had nothing to conceal, [and] assured because she knew of nothing to be on her guard against." As his apprehension grows, Archer calls the entire New York matrimonial system into question: "What could he and [May] really know of each other?" he asks himself with a sinking heart;

> what if, for some one of the subtler reasons...they should tire of each other, misunderstand or irritate each other? He reviewed his friends' marriages—the supposedly happy ones—and saw none that answered, even remotely, to the passionate and tender comradeship which he pictured as his permanent relationship with May Welland. He perceived that such a picture presupposes, on her part, the experience, the versatility, the freedom of judgment, which she had been carefully trained not to possess; and with a shiver of foreboding he saw his marriage becoming what most of the other marriages about him were: a dull association of material and social interests.[9]

Of course, in his anxiety Archer is unfairly exaggerating his misgivings about May's character, and about their chances for happiness as man and wife. Although female Protectors

---

[9]Edith Wharton, *The Age of Innocence* (Scribner Library, 1948), p. 44. All quotations from *The Age of Innocence* are from this edition.

do concern themselves primarily with the "material and social" needs of marriage, they also make devoted, nurturing wives, and can be helped a long way toward developing the "tender comradeship" in marriage which Archer envisions.[10] And yet, with his Idealist's intuition, Archer does anticipate an important source of conflict for Advocates and Protectors: the difference between what he calls his own "freedom of judgment" (i.e., his ardent desire to discover the world around him), and what he sees now as May's "dull association" and lack of "versatility" (i.e., her emotional cautiousness and intellectual orthodoxy).

But this is only one side of the story. Archer's new-found criticism of May's character has another source as well, and one that he has barely admitted to himself: he is falling in love with another woman. Ellen Olenska is May's cousin, a darkly rumored countess who has fled a sexually abusive marriage on the continent (to the brutal Polish Count Olenski), returning home to nurse her wounds and begin a new life. Nearly thirty, she and Archer played together as children, when she wasn't roaming over Europe with her charming, footloose parents, or with her eccentric aunt Medora, all the while picking up an "expensive but incoherent education." Ellen had been a "fearless" child, Wharton tells us, fond of "gaudy clothes," and precocious in the "outlandish arts" of drawing, and of dancing and singing—a brilliantly pretty little girl of "high color and high spirits." From all indications Madame Olenska is a vibrant Performer Artisan (an "ESFP"), and indeed, when Archer sees her again after so many years, sitting "gracefully" next to May at the opera, dressed "rather theatrically" in a low-cut, blue velvet gown, he is almost

---

[10]See *The Pygmalion Project, Volume Two* for a discussion of the ways of Protector females in their relationships.

immediately enthralled by "something inherently dramatic, passionate and unusual in her." New York society, worshipping the austere Guardian gods of Taste and Form, is severely taken aback by her daring neckline, and by her regal "Josephine" headdress; but, as usual, Archer is of a different mind, seeing in her audacity a

> mysterious authority of beauty, a sureness in the carriage of the head, the movement of the eyes, which...struck him as highly trained and full of a conscious power.[11]

In nearly every way Ellen Olenska is the opposite of May Welland. If May is pale and fair-haired, Ellen is richly brunette. If May is modest and traditional in her choice of clothes, Ellen is daringly sexual: her décolleté opera dress looks to one appalled observer "like a nightgown," and another evening dress—a "bold, sheath-like" red velvet robe, with black fur trim and bare arms—raises eyebrows with its sensuality. If May is discretely sheltered by her family, Ellen is worldly and independent, choosing to live by herself in the dilapidated Bohemian quarter, in a peeling stucco house near Archer's literary friends. If May is socially and intellectually conventional, Ellen is decidedly original, deflating stuffy New York conventions "at a stroke," and scattering her quaint little parlor with fresh flowers, obscure Italian paintings, and avant-garde French novels. And if May is indeed content with "dull association," Ellen seems to court scandal, amusing herself of a Sunday evening at risqué "common" houses, where (it is rumored) there is "smoking and champagne," and where a woman "got up on a table and sang" as in Paris.

As Archer is thrown together with Ellen on a number of social occasions, and later on, as he visits her on family legal business, he finds himself more and more "deeply

---

[11]Edith Wharton, *The Age of Innocence*, p. 61.

drawn into the atmosphere" of her sensuous, impulsive Artisan way of life. He responds to her "perverse and provocative" clothing with an undeniably sexual intensity: he stares at her arms, "bare to the elbow," and when she brushes him with her plumed fan, "it was the lightest touch, but it thrilled him like a caress." He finds her little house full of "shadowy charm" and a "sense of adventure"—the very air seems somehow "intimate, 'foreign,' subtly suggestive of old romantic scenes and sentiments." Her free-spoken irreverence about "pompous" New York society delights him, and her radical taste in art and literature "whetted [his] interest." He even finds himself defending Ellen's "French Sundays" as innocent gatherings for "good music" on nights when, as he sees it, "the whole of New York is dying of inanition." More than anything, however, Archer is fascinated by Ellen's worldly, knowing Artisan eyes. Looking into her eyes, Archer can imagine that Ellen "had lived and suffered, and also—perhaps—tasted mysterious joys." And more darkly, Wharton tells us "it frightened him to think what must have gone into the making of her eyes."

Intrigued by Ellen's Artisan mystery and drama, and thrown dangerously off-balance by "the curious way in which she reversed his values," Archer struggles with his conscience to decide on a course of action. Keirsey observes that male Idealists often have a romantic or "storybook" idea of love, and that they must guard against "pursuing the dream" of perfect love from "relationship to relationship."[12] And Archer is clearly playing out this scenario in his imagination, even to the point of projecting Ellen's face into a romantic novel he is reading: "All through the night," Wharton tells us, "he pursued through

---

[12]David Keirsey, *Please Understand Me*, pp. 91, 95-96.

those enchanted pages the vision of...Ellen Olenska." At the same time, Idealists are exceptionally sincere and faithful in their closest relationships, "the most loyal of the types," Keirsey calls them, "when committed to a cause."[13] And so, feeling himself committed to May, not only as her fiancé in society but also as her "soul's custodian," Archer determines to put Ellen Olenska out of his mind and to dedicate himself to saving his engagement. Unfortunately, but quite predictably, his plans take the form of a Pygmalion project.

Archer's first concern (to help May become less "dull" and more "versatile") is to see if he can lift her concrete Guardian soul to his higher Idealist world of imaginative literature. Keirsey observes that Idealists are not at all hesitant about trying to inspire their loved ones with "poetry...and quotations,"[14] and apparently Archer hopes that "thanks to his enlightening companionship" he can develop May into his literary comrade. During their courtship Archer is proud of "the shy interest in books and ideas that [May] was beginning to develop under his guidance"—although he admits that, without his help, she struggles with poetry a good deal and could not yet "feel the beauty" of the more challenging poems of Tennyson and Browning. And he dreams of revealing the "masterpieces of literature" to May on their honeymoon: "We'll read *Faust* together," he promises himself, "by the Italian lakes." May tries her best to please Archer by being soulful and deep, but she cannot help approaching poetry in her simple Guardian way: she loves to hear Archer read "beautiful things" out of "his poetry books," and she is far

---

[13]David Keirsey, *Portraits of Temperament*, p. 101.
[14]David Keirsey, *Please Understand Me*, p. 91.

more interested in learning poems by heart than in understanding them or discussing their ideas.

Wanting also to inspire more "freedom of judgment" in May, Archer urges her to take a drastic step with him: he pleads with her to throw off social convention (New York's obligatory "two-year engagement") and marry him right away. But here again, though she is pleasant enough about the idea, May's conservative Guardian temperament is a formidable obstacle to overcome. May's first thought is one of girlish pride in Archer's always-surprising imaginativeness: "Newland," she sighs, "you're so original." But as the social implications of Archer's proposal slowly dawn on her, she grows distinctly uncomfortable with the prospect of "doing things so differently," and she sweetly digs in her heels:

> "Mercy—should we elope?" she laughed.
>
> "If you would—"
>
> "You *do* love me, Newland! I'm so happy."
>
> "Then why not be happier?"
>
> "We can't behave like people in novels, though, can we?"
>
> "Why not—why not—why not?"
>
> She looked a little bored by his insistence. She knew very well that they couldn't, but it was troublesome to have to produce a reason. "I'm not clever enough to argue with you. But that kind of thing is rather—vulgar, isn't it?" she suggested, relieved to have hit on a word that would assuredly extinguish the whole subject.
>
> "Are you so much afraid, then, of being vulgar?"
>
> She was evidently staggered by this. "Of course I should hate it—so would you," she rejoined, a trifle irritably.[15]

This conversation is altogether typical of Archer and May, and it illustrates in detail the unavoidable frustration of informative role-casting. Advocates and Protectors are two

---

[15]Edith Wharton, *The Age of Innocence*, pp. 83-84.

of Keirsey's "role-informing" types (as opposed to the "role-directing" types), and though Archer wants very much for May to *do* something quite dramatic for him, he cannot bring himself to order her straightaway. Instead, he tries to direct her indirectly, by offering her courteous options ("if you would"), and by asking her rhetorical questions ("why not be happier?" and "are you so much afraid?"), hoping to open doors for her imagination and show her the way through.[16] Similarly, May responds not with clear countermands that would dash his hopes, but with gently obstructing information about herself and their shared values ("We can't behave," "that is—vulgar," and "I should hate it—so would you"); and she answers each one of Archer's leading questions with tentative, cautioning questions of her own ("should we?" "can we?" and "isn't it?").

Edith Wharton describes this couched, oblique style of communication with some personal frustration in *The Age of Innocence*, calling it a form of incomprehensible "hieroglyphics," a language of "faint implication and pale delicacies" in which "the real thing was never said." Role-informative types often appear indecisive in urgent situations, when they must try to come to the point and determine anothers' behavior. And here, certainly, Archer is fully aware of the exasperating separation between the bold action he wants to bring about in May, and the diplomatic words he must use to motivate her—feeling all through their conversations that he and May were in a "deaf-and-

---

[16]Later in the novel, after Archer and May have married, this conflict takes the symbolic form of Archer always wanting to open the windows in their house to let in some fresh air, and May remonstrating about drafts and cold weather.

dumb asylum," as they "sat and watched each other, and guessed at what was going on."

In truth, May guesses more than Archer gives her credit for, and a few weeks after this interview she gathers her dignity about her and confides to Archer that she has felt a difference in him ever since the night at the opera, the night they announced their engagement. She worries if he still cares for her, and she even promises him quite majestically that, if there is "someone else," she will give him his freedom. May's "tragic courage" touches the young Idealist to the heart, and her simple article of faith—"I can't have my happiness made out of a wrong...to somebody else"—makes his own moral position inescapably clear. No matter how great his desire for Ellen Olenska (and it is almost overwhelming him at this point), Archer knows he cannot break his word and forsake someone as trusting and as innocently deserving as May. And so, when she hints that her parents might consent to an early wedding, he resolves again to meet "all his obligations." Ellen, he knows deep in his soul, is "the woman I would have married if it had been possible," but he will stand by May and stay on "the path that he was committed to tread."

Archer endures the elaborate ritual of the "nineteenth century New York wedding," with its soaring music, top hats, and banks of lilies. And he survives his wedding tour on the continent, three months of social calls and shopping, of hiking, theaters, and lawn tennis. Sincerely determined to accept his fate and love May as she is, Archer all but abandons his plans to make her more poetical and free-spirited, though it must be said that he gives up his Pygmalion project more out of disappointment than love. Taking the measure of May's "absence of imagination," he thinks better of his dream to read Goethe with her by the

Italian lakes: "on reflection," Archer confesses, "he had not been able to picture his wife in that particular setting." And he quickly learns a difficult lesson for Idealists: that Guardians such as May do not think of themselves as bound by conventions, but actually prefer the security of a ritualized way of life—"there was no use," he realizes, "in trying to emancipate a wife who had not the dimmest notion that she was not free."

Though a stray memory of Ellen Olenska troubles him on occasion, Archer does his best to keep himself focused on the finer "lines of [May's] character": her Protector's "simplicity," her "innate dignity," her "sweet-temper." And, in this way, by the time they return home to New York Archer believes himself quite secure in "all his old traditions and reverences" concerning married life, taking his pleasure in May's good looks, her "easy and pleasant" companionship, and regarding his "momentary madness" with Ellen as "the last of his discarded experiments" in romance.

However, as they settle into their new house on East Thirty-ninth Street, Archer also reveals a curious—and ominous—division of sympathies that can occur in even the most comfortable Idealist-Guardian marriage. On the one hand, Archer seems content to lead a traditional Guardian domestic life with May. He resumes his law practice ("the old routine of the office"), he comes home "every evening" to his charming wife, and he hopes for children to fill "the vacant corners in both their lives." To be sure, life with May fulfills the most conservative dreams of his bachelorhood, and his marriage quickly comes to satisfy his ideal of "peace, stability, comradeship, and a steadying sense of...duty."

But what of his more ardent dreams of poetry and adventure, the longings that Ellen Olenska brought to life at such an impossible moment? Archer addresses this question with strained indifference in the novel, mentioning casually that "his artistic and intellectual life would go on, as it always had, outside the domestic circle." Archer means this innocently enough: he will simply continue to pursue his Idealist interests (what he has referred to as his "narrow margin of real life") in private, reading his books in his study and visiting galleries on his own. But his remark carries a more disturbing implication for his marriage. Indeed, when an Idealist divides his married life into a social, domestic side, which he gives over to his Guardian wife, and a personal, imaginative side, which he reserves for himself alone, he drives a wedge deep into the heart of his marriage—into the Idealist's vital need for "soul partnership"—that weakens the relationship at the core and makes it vulnerable to the inevitable pressures of married life.

And so, as the months pass, and as Archer lives his "systematized and affluent" life with May, his imagination takes its own course, back into the romantic world of literature and art, and inevitably into thoughts of Ellen Olenska. At first, he thinks of Ellen with a kind of suppressed detachment, believing that "by force of willing" he can keep his distance and remember her abstractly, dispassionately, as "someone long since dead." But Advocates have helplessly romantic imaginations, and relatively little strength of willpower (a Rational forte); and after only one year of marriage, Archer's "carefully built-up" emotional fortress begins tumbling "about him like a house of cards."

Archer happens to catch sight of Ellen at her aunt's summer-house in Newport, and this glimpse of her standing below him on the dock, looking tragically at the bay, suddenly floods him with desire. Afraid of the force of his emotion, he keeps himself from going down to her, but his longing to renew their relationship becomes from that moment what Wharton calls "an incessant undefinable craving, like the sudden whim of a sick man for food or drink." Archer fights this hunger for weeks, and tries to visit Ellen only in his imagination, almost feverishly following "the movements of her imagined figure as he had watched the real one in the summer-house." But his feelings are far too strong for him, and "sick with unsatisfied love" he soon arranges a business trip to Boston to meet "accidentally" with Ellen, thus taking the first trembling step along a new path, one that will lead him into an extra-marital affair.

The events in Archer and Ellen's liaison over the next several months—the secret meetings and the stolen moments, the passionate tears and the sorrowful kisses—is unforgettable reading, all the more affecting because the love has such little room to grow, and is in fact never consummated. This crippling, typically nineteenth century dilemma—of two people loving one another and yet not able to be together[17]—works itself out to a haunting conclusion in *The Age of Innocence*, which I will describe in a few pages. But first I must discuss Edith Wharton's remarkable analysis of how Archer reconciles his forbidden love for Ellen with his Idealist's conscience.

---

[17]For a more cynical twentieth century version of this tormenting relationship, read Hemingway's *The Sun Also Rises*, in which a castrating war wound keeps two lovers apart. See *The Pygmalion Project, Volume One: The Artisan* for a discussion of this novel.

Needless to say, none of the four temperaments is safe from the temptation of an illicit affair, but the evidence of literature suggests that the four deal with their unfaithfulness in vastly different ways. Artisans typically think of their "flings" as part of the generous experience of a full life; they "play" or "fool" around impulsively, with their eyes wide open, and they forgive themselves rather easily, with their usual generosity.[18] Guardians are less ambitious and less joyous in their transgressions; they feel uncomfortably sinful until the episode is over, and then, after a short period of mortification, they accept their "straying" as a common worldly failing.[19] Rationals, in contrast, don't try to excuse their infidelities much at all; they either control themselves in the first place, or they deal with an affair pragmatically, as addressing an emotional or sexual need—though they can also reproach themselves severely for the weakness of their will.[20] However, in *The*

---

[18]See my discussion of Norman Dewers in *Volume One: The Artisan.* Norman's disarming explanation on several incriminating occasions is, "I just wanted to make her happy."

[19]See my discussion of Henry Wilcox in Chapter 5. Henry is "heartily sorry" for his unfaithfulness to his first wife Ruth, and is even ill for several days when the knowledge leaks out. But quite soon he tries to explain away his adultery by calling it simply a "crop of wild oats," and by placing himself in a long masculine tradition: "We fellows all come to grief once in our time." Further, and even more interestingly, he tries to justify his behavior to his new wife Margaret by invoking (in a series of typical Guardian maxims) the sanctity of the marriage vows:

> I am far from a saint—in fact, the reverse—but you
> have taken me, for better or worse. Bygones must be
> bygones. You have promised to forgive me. Margaret,
> a promise is a promise. (p. 248)

[20]See Hank Rearden in Ayn Rand's *Atlas Shrugged.* Rearden tells his mistress Dagny that he wants "no self-deception" about their purely sexual relationship, "no pretense, no evasion...with the nature of our actions left unnamed." But he also has a good deal of contempt for himself, not so much out of sympathy for his Guardian wife, but (in true

Age of Innocence Wharton shows us that, with Idealists, the issue is more complicated.

Let me begin by reiterating Keirsey's point that male Idealists can be rather easily swept up in the storybook *idea* of extra-marital love, "compelled to pursue the impossible dream of a larger-than-life...goddess, who will be madonna, mistress, lover."[21] But let me add that, of the four temperaments, Idealists are also the most torn by the double life of an affair. With their need for "oneness" in themselves and "wholeness" in their relationships, Idealists find that such intimate duplicity strikes deep into the soul, cleaving the very foundation of their self-esteem: their personal integrity. Adultery, indeed, is nothing less than the betrayal of that integrity, and if they act on their fantasies Idealists put themselves into agonizing ethical conflicts— between their sacred marriage vows, and their devotion to their lover; and also between their innate need for authenticity, and the lies they must tell to conceal their secret life. Trapped in such conflicts, wanting to be faithful and sincere to both spouse *and* lover, Idealists must take one of two courses: either they must find reasons for dissolving one of the relationships; or, if they persist in both, they must find irrational, even hysterical ways of convincing themselves that they are doing nothing wrong.

The first option is the moral course, and just as earlier in *The Age of Innocence* Archer tried to separate himself from Ellen, this time he begins turning away from May. Archer starts to dwell quite cruelly "on the things he disliked in her," becoming intensely critical of May's personality, as if

---

Randian fashion) for his betrayal of his own autonomy: "I've given in to a desire which...has reduced my mind, my will, my being, my power to exist into an abject dependence upon you." (Signet, pp. 242-243.)

[21]David Keirsey, *Please Understand Me*, p. 92.

to blame his hunger for Ellen on what he now considers to be his wife's unforgivable shortcomings. Archer begins to see May's "tranquil unawareness" no longer as masking depths of feeling, but as an expression of stately superficiality: she looks to him now like a marble statue of "Civic Virtue," gazing out at the world with a blank stare. Further, May's "dreamy silences" (into which, he admits, "he had read so many meanings") now annoy him as an absence of vital spirit, "a negation," he calls it, with "the curtain dropped before an emptiness," and he fantasizes that May's veins are filled not with Ellen's "ravaging" blood, but with "preserving fluid." Although he still feels the "glow of proprietorship" when other men admire May's swan-like beauty, he has grown privately dissatisfied with her sexual timidity—and with his traditional sexual duty: he confesses irritably that "he was weary of living in a perpetual tepid honeymoon, without the temperature of passion yet with all its exactions."

Archer's underlying (and longstanding) complaint against May is what he now regards as the "deadly monotony" of her life, and the terrible predictability of her mind, particularly in comparison with Ellen's Artisan impulsiveness and originality. Ellen once promised him warmly, "I live in the moment when I'm happy," but May, Archer concedes, is a young woman whose "point of view had always been the same." And now, having "gone the brief round of her" in the first year of his marriage, Archer sees her as utterly "incapable of growth," and his future with her as an "endless emptiness." Keirsey points out that, at times, when Idealists believe they "know all there is to know about" their loved ones, they can feel beset by "restlessness and a sense of boredom."[22] And in a key

[22]David Keirsey, *Please Understand Me*, p. 96.

passage, as Archer watches May at her needlework, he reveals all his disillusionment with her steadfast, conventional Guardian character:

> As she sat thus, with the lamplight full on her clear brow, he said to himself with a secret dismay that he would always know the thoughts behind it, that never, in all the years to come, would she surprise him by an unexpected mood, by a new idea, a weakness, a cruelty or an emotion. She had spent her poetry and romance on their short courting...[and] now she was simply ripening into a copy of her mother, and mysteriously, by the very process, trying to turn him into a Mr. Welland.[23]

Archer's last comment accuses May, in essence, of starting up a Pygmalion project of her own, but it also suggests how determined the young man is to find fault with his wife in this tormenting time. Although Protector Guardians can be masterly Pygmalions, they are not overtly manipulative in their personal relationships, and Archer himself admits that May's effect on him is "mysterious," part of "the very process" of her own development as a person. In all fairness, May does little more in *The Age of Innocence* than use her Protector's "niceness" to try and wear away at the edges of Archer's passionate Advocate nature—to settle him down into an ordinary, sedate Guardian husband—but even this subtle coercion intensifies his disaffection. May's Pygmalion chisel might be dull and her pressure light, but Archer, now with a desperate sensitivity, feels it "bearing on the very angles whose sharpness he most wanted to keep."

While Archer thus begins to separate himself from May, hoping to work himself up to leaving her, he also turns to the Idealist's second option, which is to re-frame the reality of his deceitful behavior. In essence, Archer must find a

---

[23]Edith Wharton, *The Age of Innocence*, p. 295.

way to give his immoral love for Ellen a moral justification, and so he romanticizes his affair into a "grand passion," trying to make himself believe the affair is not merely an "affair," but the soulful yearning for a higher and truer love. Indeed, on the train home from Boston, Archer sits in a "state of abstraction," his head swirling in a "golden haze" with thoughts of Ellen—"his imagination," as Wharton pictures it, spinning "on the edge of a vortex." And over the next few months he virtually enshrines Ellen in his imagination, crowning her in his fantasies, and offering her an introspective homage that only an Idealist could conceive. Wharton tells us he builds

> within himself a kind of sanctuary in which she throned among his secret thoughts and longings. Little by little it became the scene of his real life, of his only rational [i.e. mental] activities; thither he brought the books he read, the ideas and feelings which nourished him, his judgments and his visions.[24]

Notice that, as an Idealist, Archer considers his "real life" to be the inner life of the mind and the heart—of books and ideas, of feelings and visions—and not the outer life of society and propriety that May inhabits. In that outer life, as he well knows, his golden dream of love with Ellen is little more than a sordid and barely tolerated "hole-and-corner" affair; and on that social level, he feels a stinging guilt about his hidden meetings with Ellen, and the "precautions and prevarications" he must use with May. He confesses he feels "ashamed" when he thinks of "May, and habit, and honor, and all the old decencies." He blushes when someone mentions the word "mistress," he winces at casual gossip about "a wife deceived," and he describes his married life with a pounding self-recrimination as

---

[24]Edith Wharton, *The Age of Innocence*, p. 262.

> a smiling, bantering, humoring, watchful, and incessant lie. A
> lie by day, a lie by night, a lie in every touch and every look; a
> lie in every caress and every quarrel; a lie in every word and
> every silence.[25]

It is precisely to escape from such a relentless morality—
both social and personal—that Archer must rise into his
Idealist's imagination, envisioning that he and Ellen belong
to a higher realm of ideal love where "they were answerable
to no tribunal but...their own judgment," and where the
iron-clad distinctions between "mistress" and "wife" can be
forgotten. "I want—" he sighs to Ellen, groping for words
to express his yearning,

> I want somehow to get away with you into a world where
> words like that—categories like that—won't exist. Where we
> shall be simply two human beings who love each other, who
> are the whole life to each other; and nothing else on earth will
> matter.[26]

Keirsey comments that an Idealist's "real-life mate is not
always able to measure up"[27] to the romantic image of his
lover; and certainly May is too simple a person—too
intellectually and emotionally prosaic—ever to compete
with Archer's dream of Ellen Olenska. But with a moral
twist characteristic of her very best work, Wharton
describes for us how Archer's passionate illusion ends up
estranging him from the very object of his illusion—from
Madame Olenska herself.

As an Artisan, Ellen Olenska is a clear-eyed realist, with a
concrete sense of the world,[28] and though she loves Archer
dearly she has little sympathy with his lovesick "vision of
you and me together." Almost impatiently, she confronts

---

[25]Edith Wharton, *The Age of Innocence*, p. 305.

[26]Edith Wharton, *The Age of Innocence*, p. 290.

[27]David Keirsey, *Please Understand Me*, p. 92.

[28]See Keirsey's *Portraits of Temperament*, pp. 32.

him with hard facts and tries to convince him that they must look "not at visions, but at realities" in their relationship. She insists that, despite his romantic longings, they can never be together in New York society in any open or honest way: "there's no *us* in that sense," she warns him. Ellen knows from her own life in Europe the pain of dishonored marriages and the selfish pleasure of sexual intrigues, "the abominations you know of," she reminds Archer, "and all the temptations you half guess." And she knows that, in reality, Archer's dream of love can never be anything more than a sneaking, heartbreaking affair, with the two of them "trying to be happy behind the backs of the people who trust them"—and she recognizes that Archer is too moral ever to be content for long with such a relationship.

The Artisans' utter lack of illusion can make them seem at times coldhearted, and when Archer continues, almost in a trance, urging Ellen to come away with him and search for a place where they can love each other openly, she "burst into a sudden hard laugh" at his naiveté:

> "Oh, my dear—where is that country? Have you ever been there?" she asked; and as he remained sullenly dumb she went on: "I know so many who've tried to find it; and, believe me...it wasn't at all different from the world they'd left, but only rather smaller and dingier and more promiscuous."[29]

Archer groans in protest, "Ah, I'm beyond that," but Ellen's Artisan eyes can only "look at things as they are," and she bluntly corrects him:

> "No you're not! You've never been beyond. And *I* have," she said in a strange voice, "and I know what it looks like there....Ah, believe me, it's a miserable little country."[30]

---

[29]Edith Wharton, *The Age of Innocence*, p. 290.
[30]Edith Wharton, *The Age of Innocence*, pp. 290, 291.

Edith Wharton's larger point in this scene (and this is surely one of her finest insights in the novel) is that, given the inescapable sexual morality of the time, Archer's love for Ellen can never be more than a precious dream—indeed, a love as rare and other-worldly as Archer's can exist nowhere *but* in his imagination.

Sadly, Archer is not yet able to grasp the paradoxical truth that, as Ellen puts it, "We're near each other only if we stay far from each other." And with a growing emotional and sexual frustration he presses blindly for Ellen to be his mistress in reality—"come to me once," he pleads with her, hoping (as he has hoped so often before) that if he could hold her "in his arms" he might sweep "away her arguments." Ellen is finally moved by the force of Archer's love (for she is *not* coldhearted), and with what Archer believes is a "deep inner radiance" she promises to come to him and share his bed. But in fact she agrees sadly, fatally, as if knowing that this final step into sexual intimacy will destroy Archer's beautiful illusion, making their affair merely "like all the others," and dooming what little happiness they can share as friends.

However, as I have said, the consummation never takes place. Before this fateful tryst with Ellen can be arranged, May asks for a private moment and tells Archer in her timid way ("all dew and roses") that she is pregnant with their first child—and the news stuns him, and mocks him, and binds him irrevocably to his family responsibility. Archer might have been able to abandon his marriage for some imagined ideal of a more perfect woman, but the idea of forsaking his child is too much to bear, and with cold hands and a "sick stare" he strokes May's shining hair and accepts his fate. Ellen leaves immediately to live in Paris, and Archer resolves once again—and this time finally—to do his "dull duty" and become "what was called a faithful husband."

But Edith Wharton does not let her portrait of Advocate love end on this note of tragic surrender. In a poignant last chapter, set twenty-five years after the defining crisis of Archer's marriage, Wharton offers us one last glimpse into the romantic power of his imagination. The chapter begins as Archer pauses in his busy New York schedule and takes a long backward look at his life, lapsing into a state of mind rather typical of Idealists, a profound though wandering reverie of self-analysis and self-recognition. His three children are grown, and May has been dead for years, having given her life in admirable Protector Guardian style, nursing their youngest child through infectious pneumonia. Archer himself has practiced law, tried his hand at politics, accomplished great things in his social work—and scrupulously avoided Paris. In short, he has kept the "dignity of [his] duty" as a husband, a father, and a "good citizen," and as his memories unfold and reach gently back to the faded scenes of his life, "he honored his own past, and mourned for it."

At the same time, his Advocate's innate enthusiasm flares out against the stifled, starved life he has led: Archer realizes "the worst of doing one's duty was that it apparently unsuited one for doing anything else," and he wonders whatever became of "the magnificent fellow he had dreamed of being." In his years of quiet, devoted marriage, Archer had learned to think of Ellen Olenska "abstractly, serenely, as one might think of some imaginary beloved in a book or a picture." But now, at the age of fifty-seven, as he makes plans for a trip to Paris with his son, Archer ponders what might remain of his and Ellen's love, the cherished relationship he has often thought of as "the flower of life":

> For such summer dreams it was too late; but surely not for a quiet harvest of friendship, of comradeship, in the blessed hush of her nearness.[31]

In the last pages of the novel, then, Archer embarks on what he calls "his pilgrimage" through the streets of Paris to meet with Countess Olenska and discover what life has left him of his dream. He arrives at Ellen's building in the late afternoon, gazes up at her fifth-floor windows, his heart "beating with the confusion and eagerness of youth." But at this moment he mysteriously pauses below her balcony. Archer decides to rest for a few moments under the chestnut trees on the avenue—he wants to breathe the "rich atmosphere" of Ellen's world and to bask in the "golden light" of his imaginings. Over the years with May, Archer had frequently pictured to himself what Ellen's Artisan life in Paris would be like: "the theaters she must have been to, the pictures she must have looked at, the splendid old houses she must have frequented." And now, within a few minutes and a few yards of seeing her again, he strains to put aside his "youthful memory" and to imagine what she must look like now, and how she will greet him after "more than half a lifetime." "A dark lady, pale and dark," he envisions her, "who would look up quickly, half rise, and hold out a long thin hand."

And as Archer sits on his bench minute after minute, lost in his memories and imaginings, he comes to an extraordinary realization about himself as an Idealist. Keirsey tells us that the Idealists' fantasy of love is often so tenderly romanticized that they find "anticipation...more delightful

---

[31]Edith Wharton, *The Age of Innocence*, p. 357.

than consummation."[32] In just the same way, Wharton had observed early in the novel that, for a man such as Archer, "thinking over a pleasure to come often gave him a subtler satisfaction than its realization." And now, in this last scene, Archer all at once understands that he is more profoundly in love with his vision of Ellen than with whatever reality awaits him in her drawing room—and that by seeing her again he risks destroying the illusion of love that has sustained him most of his adult life:

> "It's more real to me here than if I went up," he suddenly heard himself say; and the fear lest that last shadow of reality should lose its edge kept him rooted to his seat.[33]

Archer never does go up to see the Countess. He stays below her windows for a long while, imagining every detail of the scene, then walks back to his hotel alone "in the thickening dusk." Some might criticize Archer's turning away from Ellen—and from life—in this scene as absurdly abstract, and as a sad waste of his and Ellen's last years. Wharton herself allows that Archer, after so many years of respectable Guardian marriage, "found himself held fast by habit, by memories, by a sudden startled shrinking from new things." But there is a more fundamental basis in temperament for Archer's withdrawal. We must remember that Archer has loved Ellen far too long and far too ideally to be content with anything less than his exquisite vision of her—and that he is an Idealist, for whom dreams can be incomparably more precious than reality.

Marya Alexandrovna

For Advocates, clearly, loving the two "real world" temperaments requires a sometimes unappreciated

---

[32]David Keirsey, *Please Understand Me*, p. 95.
[33]Edith Wharton, *The Age of Innocence*, p. 361.

compromise between their own Idealist dreams of love and their Guardian or Artisan mate's more down-to-earth sense of marriage and mating. Most often in these relationships, as Newland Archer shows us, Advocates manage to keep their fantasies of higher "perfect" love from overwhelming them, and they find their fulfillment in the social activities of their marriages, in the comforts of family life, or in their own private dreams of romance. With Rational mates, however, the Idealist's conflict and compromise are significantly different.

Rationals share with Idealists the abstract cast of mind, and so can offer them an intellectual companionship, a mutual love of ideas and imagination, even a similar fluency with metaphorical language, that bond these two temperaments in deeply satisfying ways. But the vivacious Advocates also want from their Rational mates an emotional responsiveness—a willingness to "open up" their hearts and share their feelings—that Rationals find quite foreign to their nature. Rationals typically have a reflective, self-controlled way about them, and while Advocates are initially attracted by such calmness (so different from their own effervescence), they often come to see it as a barrier in the relationship, an emotional wall to be broken down, or at least to be chipped at with Pygmalion's chisel. This fundamental conflict—the Advocate's need for emotional expressiveness, against the Rational's cool resistance to showing feelings—is described in literature no where more skillfully than in the love affair and marriage between young Marya Alexandrovna and her guardian Sergey Mikhaylych, in Leo Tolstoy's early novella, entitled, with a subtle irony, *Family Happiness* (1859).

Let me begin by explaining that Tolstoy presents *Family Happiness* as a remembrance of things past, narrated in the first person (the "I" voice) by a somewhat older and wiser Marya. This narrative strategy is particularly effective in portraying the Advocate personality, for by telling her story in her own words Marya is revealing the truth of herself to the reader, sharing her inner life and giving voice to her deepest feelings with a personal intimacy simply not possible in the most common kind of novel, narrated by an unknown, omniscient third person. Keirsey has said that Advocates have an innate desire to report on their experience of life—they are "eager to relate the stories they've uncovered"[34]—and in the very act of telling her own story Marya illustrates this point.

And yet, what is gained in authenticity with a first person narrator can sometimes be lost in objectivity, and we must always bear in mind when reading *Family Happiness* that Marya's views of herself, and of Sergey, are filtered through her highly romantic Advocate's imagination. Having said that, let me add that in all but a few instances Marya seems under remarkably few illusions about herself in the story, and that she describes Sergey (an "INTJ" MasterPlanner Rational) with great accuracy—in both cases Tolstoy's genius for portraying human personality seems evident behind the narrative. In this way, seeing with Tolstoy's remarkably clear eye, Marya reveals in her story many of the personal strengths and weaknesses of both the Advocate and the MasterPlanner personality, and she describes many of the extraordinary joys of their union, as well as the one nearly fatal disappointment.

Marya begins her tale of family happiness on a portentous note of family sadness. It is a "dark and sad winter," a few months after the death of her mother (her father having died

---

[34]David Keirsey, *Portraits of Temperament*, p. 109.

some years before), and she and her little sister Sonya and her governess Katya are living out the winter alone in the family's country house. Though the loss of her mother is a great grief to her, and though she suffers terribly from "the feeling of death that clung to the house," Marya remembers two other feelings that give us our first inkling of her Advocate's nature. Keirsey observes that Advocates typically want to "go everywhere and look into everything"[35] of importance in their world, and Marya admits to a curious fascination with her dead mother's locked and shrouded bedroom: every time she passes the door she feels a "strange uncomfortable impulse to look into that cold empty room." Keirsey also notes that Advocates, more than any other Idealists, are drawn to witness "the significant social events"[36] of their time, and Marya confesses to feeling helplessly stranded in the provinces, locked away from "what is going on" in the world around her. Marya is seventeen that winter, poised on the brink of life, and the significant events she longs to witness are to be found not in this deathly, snow-bound house, but in Petersburg society. And thus while she mourns her mother sincerely, she also cannot help feeling (somewhat guiltily) "that I was wasting [another] winter in the solitude of the country."

Bored often to the point of tears, Marya has only one event to look forward to all that dreary season: the appearance in early spring of Sergey Mikhaylych, a close family friend and neighbor whom her dying father had made the family legal adviser, and whom her mother had once held up to Marya as the kind of man "I should like you to marry." The thought of Sergey Mikhaylych as a husband seemed

[35]David Keirsey, *Portraits of Temperament*, p. 108.
[36]David Keirsey, *Portraits of Temperament*, p. 108.

ludicrous to Marya at the time; her own "ideal husband" she had always pictured as a sensitive, romantic young poet, "thin, pale, and sad," while she thinks of Sergey as a "middle-aged, tall, robust" man who merely manages the financial affairs of the family. However, Sergey's visit is the one possible ray of sunshine in the long winter of her discontent, and Marya finds herself fantasizing innocently, "What *shall* I do, if he suddenly wants to marry me?"

Sergey arrives wearing a new beard (Marya hasn't seen him in some years), but with his features much as she recalls them, "his honest open face, his bright intelligent eyes, his friendly, almost boyish smile." Nor is his manner much changed. He still has his "plain, decisive way" with others, as well as his seeming "indifference" to conventional behavior, a disinterest in social rituals that Marya now believes is not indifference at all, but an expression of what she calls the "sincerity" of his feelings. But Marya is only partly right. While Sergey does have sincere respect for the memory of her father, and while he takes very seriously his role as family guardian now that her mother has died, he is also unquestionably indifferent to social rituals. MasterPlanners (all Rationals, for that matter) are so focused on efficient problem-solving that they hate to waste their time on useless ceremonies and polite social protocols; and certainly in this case Sergey is far more concerned with addressing the needs of the living than with dutifully mourning the dead. Thus, though the house is draped in solemn black, Sergey strides into the parlor and stands before Marya, not at all like the other gloomy neighbors she has received that winter, but looking "straight into my eyes with the old firmness and cheerfulness in his face."

Sergey is clearly amazed at the new first bloom of Marya's womanhood—"Can this really be you?" he asks; "Is so great a change possible?"—but as a Rational he is also concerned with her intellectual development, and Marya remembers him quickly turning his attention to her education and her plans for the future: "he asked me...about my tastes, what I read and what I intended to do, and gave me advice." MasterPlanners are role-directive Rationals, and so more than giving advice, Sergey is not at all shy about sitting Marya down at the piano and instructing her to show him her skills in music. "Marya Alexandrovna, come here and play something," he orders her, and then, turning to the adagio of Beethoven's *Moonlight Sonata*, he insists, "play this...let me hear how you play." Though Marya likes what she calls his "friendly tone of command," she dreads his criticism of her playing, and she is "anxious about each word" she speaks, wanting to please Sergey and earn for herself the love he gives her as her father's child.

Rationals are uncomfortable praising others. If they praise at all, they tend to restrict themselves to highly qualified praise—accuracy is the thing, not warm feelings—and Sergey tells Marya only that her playing "was not bad; you seem to be musical," and that intellectually, "Yes,...there is something in you." Idealists, however, respond to praise, even moderate praise, like flowers opening to the sun, and Marya basks happily in what she fancies to be Sergey's "flattery" of her, quite forgetting her earlier insight about his plain words and sincere feelings.

Eager now to impress Sergey with her grown-up attitudes and accomplishments, Marya feels reproached when, later that night (after Katya has complained to him), Sergey confronts her about her winter's listlessness. "It is a bad thing" he begins, "not to be able to stand solitude"; and then he continues with more severity than he intends:

> I can't praise a young lady who is alive only when people are admiring her, but as soon as she is left alone, collapses and

> finds nothing to her taste—one who is all for show and has no resources in herself.[37]

As Keirsey points out, developing one's internal resources is a Rational point of pride, the very basis of their parenting style,[38] but here Sergey seems to be taking his role as guardian almost too seriously for some reason. Indeed, after weakening a bit as he studies Marya's radiant young face, he redoubles his effort to make her think about her long-range goals: "You ought not to be bored, and you cannot be," he lectures her,

> you have music, which you appreciate, books, study; your whole life lies before you, and now or never is the time to prepare for it and save yourself future regrets.[39]

Marya is moved by Sergey's strangely urgent words, but like most Idealists she responds even more sensitively to the unspoken nuances of his manner. Thus she is hurt that he sounds to her now "like a father or an uncle," which makes her feel that "he considered me as inferior to himself." At the same time, she is flattered (and, again, rather embarrassed) at the more than fatherly admiration in Sergey's "kind attentive look," while she also senses a strain in his words, an attempt to keep "a constant check upon himself" when speaking to her, as if uncertain whether to address her as a woman or a schoolgirl.

At all events, Sergey ends his visit in a perturbing state of ambivalence (being of two minds is particularly stressful to Rationals), and he goes off to set the family's affairs in order, promising to look in on Marya again that summer.

---

[37]Leo Tolstoy, *The Death of Ivan Ilych and Other Stories* (Signet Classic, 1960), p. 12. All quotations from *Family Happiness* are from this edition.

[38]David Keirsey, *Portraits of Temperament*, pp. 71, 82.

[39]Leo Tolstoy, *The Death of Ivan Ilych and Other Stories*, p. 12.

Marya, on the other hand, has been miraculously transformed by Sergey's unmistakable interest in her. She pledges to herself to read and to study and to practice her music, and she gives up her selfish longing for Petersburg society, filling her nights instead with restless and incoherent dreams of nature, moonlight visions of the beauty of spring (nightingales and lilac blossoms) which she remembers years later as almost unbelievably "strange and...remote from life."

Sergey returns at the end of May, riding over to the house nearly every day, and though Marya believes she still hears some "constraint latent in his voice," he seems to most appearances to have settled his own mind along with the family business. Whatever confusing romantic stirrings he felt before, Sergey now appears content to keep a kind of sexless intellectual distance with his ward: "he treated me like a boy whose company he liked," Marya remembers with distaste, "asked me questions, invited the most cordial frankness on my part, gave me advice and encouragement, or sometimes scolded and checked me." Sergey has decided, clearly, to be nothing more than Marya's mentor, a safe enough relationship with a beautiful, blooming young girl; but even this apparently objective interest in her welfare has unforeseen consequences, and creates an unintended intimacy.

Advocates are so suggestible (and can be so "desperate to please"[40]), that Marya soon begins to identify with Sergey's personality, adopting his likes and dislikes, and taking on some of his Rational views of life as her own. For example, Marya notes Sergey's "complete indifference [to] my personal appearance" (a typical Rational attitude), and so

---

[40]David Keirsey, *Portraits of Temperament*, p. 103.

she decides to stop dressing up for him, assuming instead an "affectation of simplicity" in her clothes which she hopes will win Sergey's approval. Marya's identification with Sergey occurs in more significant intellectual areas as well, and Tolstoy describes this subtle, internal metamorphosis—utterly spontaneous with the Idealists—in amazing detail. "Most of my former tastes and habits," Marya remembers,

> did not please him; and a mere look of his, or a twitch of his eyebrow was enough to show that he did not like what I was trying to say; and I felt at once that my own standard was changed. Sometimes, when he was about to give me a piece of advice, I seemed to know beforehand what he would say. When he looked in my face and asked me a question, his very look would draw out of me the answer he wanted. All my thoughts and feelings of that time were not really mine: they were his thoughts and feelings, which had suddenly become mine and passed into my life and lighted it up. Quite unconsciously I began to look at everything with different eyes.[41]

Tolstoy here shows a wonderful grasp of the Idealist personality. As Keirsey tells us, the Idealists' powerful empathy and sensitivity to suggestion make them natural mind-readers, able quickly to anticipate what others will say—and what they want to hear—about a given subject.[42] And when Idealists wish to please someone, or create a sympathetic bonding with another, they will often reshape themselves intuitively to mirror the other person, unconsciously altering their own personality for the sake of acceptance or rapport.[43]

---

[41]Leo Tolstoy, *The Death of Ivan Ilych and Other Stories*, p. 21.

[42]David Keirsey, *Portraits of Temperament*, p. 105.

[43]We must be careful here to differentiate between the Idealist's unconscious and benevolent change of manner, and the Artisans' often calculated talent for impressing or exploiting another. Idealists attempt to give *others* what they want or need in life—to make them feel loved,

Such innate ability to introject another's point-of-view, to see with another's eyes, makes the Idealists (and particularly the Disciple Idealists) exceptionally responsive students, and Marya feels positively transformed as a person by her impersonation of Sergey. "Without wishing to deceive him, I did deceive him," she confesses, "and I became better myself while deceiving him." But whatever the benefit, Marya's emphasis on her *deception* of Sergey suggests that this changing into the other can call into question the Idealist's own integrity of self; Keirsey even points out that, "on occasion, [the Disciples'] identification with another is so complete that they feel in danger of losing their own identity."[44] At this early stage of her love—of her infatuation, really—Marya's Idealist dilemma of "becoming" Sergey versus "being" herself is not a significant problem for her, though soon will be.

If Marya is striving to appear intellectually serious and sophisticated for Sergey, her effect on him is just the opposite, freeing him to rediscover a youthfulness and playfulness he had nearly put out of his life. Though only thirty-six, Sergey has long thought of himself as "too old...to marry," calling himself an "old worn-out man who only wants to sit still" in life with his books and business matters, and telling himself that he is "quite comfortable since the matter was settled." MasterPlanners in particular tend to settle into fixed patterns in their emotional lives. Once they have resolved their feelings about a personal

---

or effective, or admired—in order to avoid conflict and animosity in their relationships, and to be loved or admired in return. Artisans also have an ability to "read" other people, and will "act" to fulfill the other person's expectations; only Artisans are far more cunning about imitating others, and have been known to try and flatter others into giving the Artisan what he or she wants.

[44]David Keirsey, *Portraits of Temperament*, p. 100.

problem (especially a problem they believe they have no control over, such as not being loved), they are reluctant to tamper with a mind-set that works for them and open themselves up to potentially disconcerting variations.

Marya, however, is a new and disturbing factor in Sergey's equation. Sergey's instinct as a Rational (and as a man twice Marya's age) is to control his feelings and not be swept into a relationship he expects will be a waste of time—and very likely humiliating and painful for him. And yet Keirsey tells us that MasterPlanners are particularly attracted by the Advocate's "enthusiastic...and apparently spontaneous enjoyment" of life—"the very antithesis of [their own] careful, thoughtful exactitude."[45] Indeed, Marya's beauty, though even more her enthusiasm and eagerness to learn about the world, cast a spell on Sergey despite his better judgment, and he finds himself letting his imagination go and dreaming dreams he believed would never come true in his life.

Marya remembers one particular game Sergey played more and more that summer, in a mood she calls "wild ecstasy." Hat off and "radiant with high spirits," he would try to surprise her and Sonia in the dell (with Katya asleep in the grass), tiptoeing toward them, biting his lip, "just like a schoolboy playing truant; his whole figure...[breathing] content, happiness, and boyish frolic." And when Marya (or "Masha" as he has begun to call her) laughs and asks "is it 'wild ecstasy'?" Sergey winks and flashes a smile, "Yes...I feel just like a boy of thirteen—I want to play at horses and climb trees."

Yet for all his merriment (and make no mistake, Rationals can have a great sense of fun), Sergey is afraid to let Masha

---

[45]David Keirsey, *Please Understand Me*, p. 73.

see the real strength of his feelings for her. Rationals do not expect to be liked by others, let alone loved, and Sergey instinctively mistrusts Masha's interest in him, cautioning himself, "Heaven knows what wishes are fermenting in that heart of [hers]." He even nearly convinces himself that Masha is only toying with him, that she "wants amusement, and I want something different." At the same time, Masha is straining to penetrate Sergey's heart of hearts and find there the deeper love she is certain he is "hiding...under a mask of raillery." Rationals and Idealists often play emotional hide and seek in this way, and Tolstoy portrays Sergey and Masha's game in a simple but richly symbolical little scene characteristic of his best writing.

One afternoon in the meadow, after playing "wild ecstasy" behind Katya's back, and clumsily sitting on Sonya's dolls, Sergey promises gallantly to fill Masha's bowl with cherries. The orchard is locked, but Sergey climbs the wall and slips in under the netting, while Masha promises to run for the key. But Advocates, as Keirsey tells us, are "inclined...to look into everything,"[46] and so Masha hangs back with an irresistible curiosity: "suddenly I felt that I must see what he was doing there and what he looked like—that I must watch his movements while he supposed that no one saw him."

Masha climbs up quietly and peers over the wall, and what she sees and overhears bears out all her most romantic fantasies: Sergey has climbed into a "gnarled old" tree, amidst heavy clusters of the ripened fruit, and is tenderly muttering "Masha! Darling Masha!" Masha feels a kind of reeling, illicit joy in her eavesdropping, and when she reaches for her balance, Sergey suddenly notices her and his

---

[46]David Keirsey, *Portraits of Temperament*, p. 108.

face flames up, first with shock and embarrassment, and then with a flush of happiness. The "old man" playing boy and the "ripe" young woman stare at each other for a naked, complicated moment, speechless with relief and regret, until Sergey regains his composure and resumes his "cold paternal" role: "You had better get down," he warns her (again symbolically), "or you will hurt yourself." And then, trying to hide his confusion, Sergey admonishes Masha with a line that expresses what MasterPlanners often find incomprehensible about Advocates: "What foolish things you do!"

Although this scene ends in frustration for Masha, and some self-reproach, it is a turning point in her life. For a precious moment, she has clearly glimpsed the human heart behind Sergey's Rational self-control, and this insight immediately focuses her intentions. "He had ceased to be the old uncle who spoiled me or scolded me," she knows; "he was a man on my level, who loved and feared me as I loved and feared him." Once committed to an idea, Idealists can become quite obstinately single-minded in their beliefs, and there is no question in Masha's mind that Sergey does indeed care for her: "I know that he loves me," she tells herself again and again, pacing back and forth in the garden, "and all his endeavours to seem indifferent will not change my opinion." And so, from this moment, Masha dedicates herself to nurturing the more expressive, emotional side of Sergey, an effort that will bring her considerable happiness, but that will also involve her in a more and more convoluted Pygmalion project.

Feeling "an irresistible desire to upset his composure again," Masha's first goal is to break through Sergey's intellectual reserve and make him admit he loves her. After the compromising scene in the cherry orchard, Sergey becomes even more shy, and almost scientifically skeptical, about expressions of love. When the snoopy Katya asks him if he has ever told a woman he loves her, Sergey bristles and (eyeing Masha) insists the words "I love you" are little more than self-deception, or worse, a deception of the loved one—"no change at all takes place" in the lovers, he scoffs; "their eyes and their noses and their whole selves remain exactly as they were." Masha is convinced otherwise, naturally; as an Idealist she believes that love mysteriously transforms "the world of the possible," and that she and Sergey are poised to step through a "magic wall" into an enchanted garden of love—if only he will speak. And thus she cannot understand why he "thought it necessary to hide his feelings and pretend coldness" around her:

> "Only why does he not tell me plainly that he loves me?" I thought; "what makes him invent obstacles and call himself old, when all is so simple and so splendid? What makes him waste this golden time which may never return? Let him say 'I love you'—say it in plain words; let him take my hand in his and bend over it and say 'I love you.' Let him blush and look down before me; and then I will tell him all. No! not tell him, but throw my arms round him and press close to him and weep."[47]

Pondering his course of action, Sergey stays away all the week of Masha's birthday, returning at the end of August to congratulate her—and to tell her, with calm resignation, that he is going away to Moscow on business. Advocates are the most emotionally spontaneous of all the Idealists, and Masha knows she must confront Sergey now or lose him forever. And so, after dinner, on the veranda, surprised at her own coolness and determination (feeling as if "something independent of my will was speaking through my lips"), Masha asks him why he is going: "I ask this

---

[47]Leo Tolstoy, *The Death of Ivan Ilych and Other Stories*, p. 33.

question," she fixes him with a stare, "because I *must* know the answer."

MasterPlanners, on the other hand, proceed quite deliberately in their relationships, moving upon well-considered lines of action, and Sergey answers only that "I have thought much about you and about myself, and have decided that I must go." Masha will not let Sergey off that easily, however, and with her heart beating faster she demands, "you must tell me, in God's name." Sergey realizes regretfully that he cannot escape giving some account of his feelings—at best a disagreeable exercise for Rationals—and therefore, with an intensity that "might have shown either perfect calm or strong emotion," he begins an explanation that captures the Rational cast of mind perfectly.

When cornered into expressing their emotions, Rationals often turn to an impossibly abstract and theoretical, almost algebraic, mode of rhetoric, and here Sergey voices all the Rational's embarrassment and stiffness—and desire for coherence—when dealing with the most incoherent of subjects. "It is a foolish business," he begins, "and impossible to put into words, and I feel the difficulty, but I will try to explain it to you." (Tolstoy describes him "frowning" as he says this—a common Rational trait—"as if in bodily pain.") Sergey then withdraws into his mathematical abstraction: "Just imagine," he urges Masha,

> the existence of a man—let us call him A—who has left youth far behind, and of a woman whom we may call B, who is young and happy and has seen nothing as yet of life or the world.[48]

---

[48]Leo Tolstoy, *The Death of Ivan Ilych and Other Stories*, p. 40.

Sergey continues in this hypothetical manner, trying to de-
personalize the most personal conversation of his life: he
describes "A's" growing love for "B," and how he "forgot
that B was so young, that life was all a May-game to her";
he tells of "A's" fear of destroying their "old friendly
relations," and how in leaving her "A" behaved badly, "but
it all came to an end and they parted friends." Masha has to
restrain herself throughout this story, furious with Sergey's
"pretence of indifference." She longs to know, simply, "Did
he love her or not?" and she finally breaks in with a wail:
"This is horrible! Is there no other ending?" "Yes there is,"
Sergey continues, trying to keep his voice steady and to
remain systematic; "there are two different endings. But, for
God's sake, listen to me quietly and don't interrupt":

> Some say that A went off his head, fell passionately in love
> with B, and told her so. But she only laughed. To her it was all
> a jest....[49]

The second ending is even more painful for him, and more
farsighted:

> The other story is that she took pity on him, and fancied, poor
> child, from her ignorance of the world, that she could love
> him, and so consented to be his wife. And he, in his madness,
> believed it—believed that his whole life could begin anew; but
> she saw herself that she had deceived him and that he had
> deceived her.[50]

Masha can hold back no longer and frantically cuts Sergey
off, trying any way she can to make this fateful
conversation more personal and emotional. "It is wrong!"
she all but screams, choking with anger, "you have been
pretending, not I"; and then she bares her own soul with a
low, wild cry that strangely frightens her: "I have loved you
since the first day we met, loved you." Rationals might

---

[49]Leo Tolstoy, *The Death of Ivan Ilych and Other Stories*, p. 41.
[50]Leo Tolstoy, *The Death of Ivan Ilych and Other Stories*, p. 41.

seem shy and uncomfortable when expressing their emotion, but they are people of mighty passion, and once Masha has declared her love Sergey's eyes fill with tears, he kisses her hands—"My God! if I had only known"—and within minutes the news of their engagement is being proclaimed throughout the house.

The couple now meet every day, Sergey staying after dinner, often until midnight, and their relationship develops quickly along its earlier lines of convergence. Masha soon glows with feeling herself "entirely his equal," no longer frightened of his judgments; while Sergey seems not so much "a grown man inspiring respect and awe but a loving and wildly happy child." From the height of their intellect, Rationals (especially Rational men) often appear removed from everyday life, "above" mere mortals, but now Masha realizes "how mistaken I was about him; he is just such another human being as myself!"

However, in spite of Masha and Sergey's moving closer and closer together (Masha feeling older and more confident, Sergey younger and more human), Tolstoy reminds us that they are strongly separate individuals, and that several differences need to be worked out in their relationship. In the first place, while Masha fills herself with the romance of Sergey's attentions, Sergey (like most Rationals) regards courtship as bothersome and taxing, and wants to get through it as efficiently as possible. Moreover, although they spend a great deal more personal time together, Sergey is still not physically demonstrative enough for Masha. Keirsey points out that a "public display of emotion or affection is particularly repugnant"[51] to a Rational, and indeed Sergey's outward show of passion

---

[51]David Keirsey, *Please Understand Me*, p. 86.

seems to have spent itself in the stormy scene of his betrothal. "Until the day of our marriage," Masha remembers with disappointment, almost with disbelief,

> he did not even kiss my hand; he did not seek, but even avoided, opportunities of being alone with me. It was as if he feared to yield to the harmful excess of tenderness he felt.[52]

But most tellingly, though he now loves Masha to distraction, and has no intention of ever giving her up, Sergey has nagging doubts about the wisdom of a man of his age and temperament marrying such an eager, inquisitive young girl. In a serious moment, Sergey describes for Masha his vision of their future life together:

> a quiet secluded life in the country, with the possibility of being useful...then work which one hopes may be of some use; then rest, nature, books, music...such is my idea of happiness. And then, on top of all that, you for a mate, and children, perhaps—what more can the heart of man desire?[53]

And yet Sergey knows that this is a middle-aged man's dream of happiness, and let me add that it is also very much a Rational's, with its emphasis on calm intellectual pursuits, quiet family life, and "useful" occupation. Always trying to anticipate trouble, Sergey wonders whether such a life will be enough for Masha: "you have youth and beauty," he tells her, looking far into her eyes, and then he thoughtfully predicts, "life is still before you, and you will perhaps seek happiness, and perhaps find it, in something different."

Masha contradicts him (Idealists seem to contradict Rationals reflexively), promising, "You are wrong; I have always desired just that quiet domestic life and prized it." We know, of course, that this is not true, for just the past winter Masha had felt exiled in the country, cheated of her

---

[52]Leo Tolstoy, *The Death of Ivan Ilych and Other Stories*, p. 43.

[53]Leo Tolstoy, *The Death of Ivan Ilych and Other Stories*, p. 45.

chance at real life. In this instance, again, Masha is identifying with Sergey, adopting his Rational views as her own, trying to be the woman he wants. And yet the truth of his words—"So you think, my dear; but that is not enough for you"—strikes deep into her soul, and Sergey's compelling, hypnotic gaze causes her very nearly to hallucinate that he is invading her consciousness and taking over her identity. "I did not reply," Masha recalls, "and involuntarily looked into his eyes," when

> suddenly a strange thing happened to me: first I ceased to see what was around me; then his face seemed to vanish till only the eyes were left, shining over against mine; next the eyes seemed to be in my own head, and then *all became confused*— I could see nothing and was forced to shut my eyes, in order to break loose.[54]

Masha closes her eyes to escape from the disturbing truth Sergey offers her: that her youth and beauty—and her Advocate's nature—have their own needs perhaps not easily satisfied by an older man of his temperament. Blinding herself to this unwanted reality, Masha clings to her Idealist illusion that she and Sergey are perfect for each other—that his dreams are her dreams, his hopes her hopes, and "his character...how congenial to my own." Tolstoy has criticized Masha in the novel for seeing in life only "what [she] wished to see," and now he shows us how foolishly she insists to herself that Sergey's vision of the future "agreed...perfectly" with her own—that

> our life would be endlessly happy and untroubled. I looked forward, not to foreign tours or fashionable society or display,

---

[54]Leo Tolstoy, *The Death of Ivan Ilych and Other Stories*, p. 46 (italics are mine). Keirsey notes that Idealists characteristically "defend themselves by acting as if confused" (*Portraits of Temperament*, p. 108).

but to a quite different scene—a quiet family life in the country, with constant...mutual love.[55]

Almost immediately, however, Masha's experience of life begins to wake her from her dreams. For example, she expects her wedding ceremony to be the final, glorious step in love's transformation of her character. "Shall I become from today someone that I myself do not know?" she wonders the morning of the wedding; "and is a new world, that will realize my hopes and desires, opening before me?" But the garden that day shows the first signs of the "bareness of autumn," and the footpath to the church leads not through the magic wall she had once dreamed of, but through the real-world "brownish stubble...over a hollow to a distant leafless wood." And then the ceremony itself, which she had expected to crown her love, "found no echo" in Masha's romantic young heart. She remembers saying the prayers with Sergey mechanically and receiving the priest's blessing, but in her soul, she confesses,

> I was only frightened and disappointed: all was over, but nothing extraordinary, nothing worthy of the Sacrament I had just received, had taken place in myself. He and I exchanged kisses, but the kiss seemed strange and not expressive of our feeling. "Is this all?" I thought.[56]

Dismissing a frivolous honeymoon trip, Sergey settles Masha quietly into his house, Nikolskoe, run "like a clock" by his strict, humorless Monitor Guardian mother. And for the first two months Masha ignores her wedding-day misgivings and does all she can "to realize his conception of me": she reads to Sergey, plays his favorite pieces on the piano, and "sometimes even talks philosophy" with him. Sergey for his part delights in making plans with Masha, and he plays "wild ecstasy" at times, banding together with

---

[55]Leo Tolstoy, *The Death of Ivan Ilych and Other Stories*, p. 37.
[56]Leo Tolstoy, *The Death of Ivan Ilych and Other Stories*, p. 49.

her late at night to raid the pantry, smothering giggles and hiding from his mother's watchful eye. But all too often Sergey maintains his MasterPlanner's calm, purposeful demeanor in the house, going to his study to work for a little while, and refusing "to betray...signs of emotion" to his young wife, or to upset the "solidity and order" of his mother's regime—and Masha recalls that, more and more, his "apparent indifference to everything annoyed me, and I took it for weakness."

Indeed, as the snows of winter begin to fall, Masha's dissatisfaction becomes a heavier burden to bear. Sergey begins to devote more of his time to business, and to expect from his wife and his homelife only a tranquil, comfortable stability, what Tolstoy calls "a calm course of existence," much coveted by introverted Rationals. On the other hand, Keirsey tells us that Advocates "can become bored rather quickly with both situations and people, and resist repeating experiences,"[57] and in almost the same words Masha soon starts "to feel lonely, that life was repeating itself, that there was nothing new in either him or myself"—and she confesses that such a life of "unbroken calmness provoked me." Masha is sure she loves Sergey as much as ever, "and was as happy as ever in his love," but she also comes to realize a fundamental truth about herself, (and true for many young Idealists), namely, that for her "to love him was not enough...after the happiness I had felt falling in love."

Ashamed of her unrest, Masha searches inside herself, hoping to find that "my uncomfortable feelings were my own fault," but what she finds growing in her heart is an honest "feeling of youth and craving for movement, which found no satisfaction in our quiet life." Masha is an

---

[57]David Keirsey, *Please Understand Me*, p. 174.

Advocate, after all, the type according to Keirsey who see "life as an exciting drama, pregnant with possibilities for both good and evil."[58] And to be sure Masha imagines how "outside" in the real world "there was noise and...excitement, and hosts of people suffering or rejoicing," while in her marriage, as the snow deepens in the meadow, she fears that "custom was daily petrifying our lives into one fixed shape."

Although Rationals are inventive and unconventional in their approach to "business" (which is, in essence, problem-solving), they do tend to let their personal lives, and their personal relationships, fall into fixed routines. As I have said, once Rationals have found an emotional or interpersonal methodology that works for them, they see no reason to change it. Such consistency might be reassuring, even endearing, to some mates, but to a young Advocate, who desires "feeling to be the guide of life, and not life to guide feeling," the effect is very nearly maddening. Indeed, as the winter drags on, Masha begins to suffer from what Tolstoy calls "her nerves"—bouts of desperate boredom, and then "fits of excessive tenderness and high spirits"— swinging to further and further romantic extremes in her feelings for Sergey. Masha chafes against her husband's "steady passionless course" of life, longing for more "excitement and danger" in her marriage, and she also fantasizes about love's "torment" and "sacrifice":

> I wanted, not what I had got, but a life of struggle....If only I could go with him to the edge of a precipice and say, "One step, and I shall fall over—one movement, and I shall be lost!" then, pale with fear, he would catch me in his strong arms and hold me over the edge till my blood froze, and then carry me off whither he pleased.[59]

---

[58]David Keirsey, *Please Understand Me*, p. 173.
[59]Leo Tolstoy, *The Death of Ivan Ilych and Other Stories*, p. 59.

Keirsey argues that the Advocates' histrionics under stress are involuntarily tactical, unconsciously designed to "extort recognition"[60] from their loved ones, and Sergey certainly gets the message loud and clear. He immediately "realized my state of mind," Masha remembers, and he calmly proposes a practical solution to the problem, offering to take his young wife to visit Petersburg and let her spread her wings a bit in society.

But Masha no longer sees herself as the problem in the marriage, and she wants no reasonable solution from Sergey—a solution that would make her feel even more like a frantic child, and more dependent on his judgment. Why, she demands, must he "humiliate me by his magnificent composure, and always be in the right against me"; and she asserts her own Advocate's point of view: "but I too am in the right when I find things tiresome and trivial, and I do well to want an active life rather than to stagnate in one spot and feel life flowing past me." Masha has decided that *Sergey* is the problem in the marriage—his lethargy and lack of emotional responsiveness—and she contemplates her own solution: "he need not take me to town," she works it out,

> he need only be like me and not put compulsion on himself and regulate his feelings....That is what is the matter.[61]

Tolstoy puts his finger on several important points in Masha's statement. Rationals *are* compulsive in much of their behavior,[62] and they do endeavor to control their feelings as much as possible[63]—and without question such seemingly arrogant self-control is the source of much

---

[60]David Keirsey, *Portraits of Temperament*, p. 108.

[61]Leo Tolstoy, *The Death of Ivan Ilych and Other Stories*, p. 59.

[62]David Keirsey, *Portraits of Temperament*, pp. 73-4, 86.

[63]David Keirsey, *Portraits of Temperament*, pp. 68, 79.

misunderstanding in their marriages.[64] More significantly, however, Tolstoy also identifies in Masha's words the fundamental source of Pygmalion projects in all human relationships, the naive attitude that the other person "need only be like me" for problems to be solved. Notice that Masha has swung completely away from her earlier attempts to identify with Sergey, and has now convinced herself that *he* must become more like *her* for their love to right itself. Sadly, at this stage in her life Masha cannot recognize that there is a third option: simply to let herself and Sergey be who they are, Idealist and Rational, and to appreciate the union of their differences.

Nevertheless, Masha is determined to elicit some sort of passionate response from her husband, and if it cannot be loving then let it be painful. She goes about the house tearfully, forcing Sergey to notice her and to inquire, "Masha, are you out of sorts?" and she remembers replying "with a cold look, as much as to say, 'You are very polite, but what is the use of asking?'" The core of Masha's complaint is that Sergey excludes her from what she thinks of as his "real" life and his serious feelings, treating her like "a delightful child who must be humored and kept quiet"— and she flares angrily: "but I don't want to be quiet and calm; that is more in your line, and too much in your line." Sergey's eyes narrow with "intense attention" (Masha confesses "I found it so pleasant to break down his composure"), but he collects himself and advises her that excitement always leads to anger and foolish words—"I have learnt that from the experience of life." Masha is "vexed again by his calmness and coolness," and answers contemptuously, "You are always in the right." Sergey knows full well that Masha is dangerously dissatisfied with

---

[64]David Keirsey, *Please Understand Me*, p. 86.

him, but when he begins to question her feelings he cannot (as a Rational) keep from trying to correct her thinking:

> Masha, what is the matter? The question is not, which of us is in the right—not at all; but rather, what grievance have you against me? Take time before you answer, and tell me all that is in your mind...let me understand what I have done wrong.[65]

To Sergey's amazement, his very fairness and thoughtfulness only irritate Masha further, making her feel again that "I stood before him like a child, that I could do nothing without his understanding and foreseeing it." Masha cannot put her grievance into words—in a sense, her complaint is that Sergey is too reasonable—but her show of distress has its desired effect. As the depth of his wife's unhappiness becomes clear to him, Sergey's eyes sag with anguish, and Masha realizes, "I had gained my object: his calmness had disappeared, and I read fear and pain on his face." In an instant Sergey understands that "the happiness of our lives is at stake," and with his Rational efficiency he immediately begins making plans to take Masha to Petersburg.

"Society in itself is no great harm," Sergey believes, "but unsatisfied social aspirations are a bad and ugly business," and so his strategy is to take his young wife to Petersburg, introduce her to a few important relations, escort her to a fashionable ball or to the opera, and get this dangerous restlessness out of her system. Masha agrees: she is sure she wants to see only enough of society "to get thoroughly sick" of it, and she expects "to be ready to come home before Easter." But neither she nor Sergey is prepared for the effect the social world has on her, nor she on it.

---

[65]Leo Tolstoy, *The Death of Ivan Ilych and Other Stories*, p. 61.

Looking back on that pivotal time, Masha remembers that "I found myself at once in such a new and delightful world, surrounded by so many pleasures and confronted by such novel interests, that I instantly, though unconsciously, turned my back on my past life and its plans." At the same time, Masha's beauty and freshness delight this badly jaded *haut monde*, and almost immediately she becomes the belle of the season, sought after by every scheming society matron and ambitious courtier. And she pursues this new infatuation with a self-deception sadly typical of the Idealists. Whereas she was once confused and blinded to the truth by her love for Sergey, she now confesses, "I was utterly blinded by this sudden affection which I seemed to evoke in all our new acquaintances, and confused by the unfamiliar atmosphere of luxury, refinement, and novelty."

Masha's fascination with fashionable society is a curious turn for an Advocate. Though Advocates are the most social of all the Idealists, and though Keirsey emphasizes their weakness for "extravagant luxuries" and "novel" experiences,[66] they are usually too non-conformist in nature, and far too creative, to find much satisfaction in the fawning and frivolous world of high society. Tolstoy recognizes this inconsistency in Masha's character—she cannot believe her own shallowness and vanity at this time in her life—but Tolstoy also understands that there are several compelling reasons for her uncharacteristic behavior.

First, at only eighteen, Masha is an innocent country girl (and also an impressionable Idealist) whose head can be all too easily turned. Second, feeling like an inferior child in her marriage, she finds "a new sense of pride and self-satisfaction" in the admiring eyes of these sophisticated

[66]David Keirsey, *Please Understand Me*, p. 175.

Petersburg aristocrats, and she finds she can stand up to Sergey "more independently than before." (As Advocates grow in confidence, they often demand what Keirsey call a "fierce independence"[67] in their relationships.) But most importantly, Masha's fabulous social success gives her, she believes, just the leverage she needs in her Pygmalion project to make Sergey a more passionate and responsive husband. Masha has dreamed of frightening Sergey into snatching her from the brink of disaster, and this is in effect what she attempts to bring about in Petersburg society.

Thus, all that winter—and for two years more—Masha throws herself into society with a strangely purposeful abandon. She attends balls, dinners, and receptions for foreign nobility; she goes on elaborate hunting parties and sightseeing expeditions abroad; she is admired by princes, ambassadors, and in particular by a sensual Italian marquis. "Fashionable life," Masha looks back,

> which had dazzled me at first by its glitter and flattery of my self-love, now took entire command of my nature, became a habit, laid its fetters upon me, and monopolized my capacity for feeling.[68]

As we have seen, Idealists tend to blame their uncontrolled behavior on influences outside of themselves, believing their will can be taken over by malevolent forces embodied in seductive people, in foreign ways of life, even in unwanted feelings.[69] And yet Tolstoy seems to know that, on some level at least, Masha is in control of herself, behaving with a darkly romantic intention to "test my power over" Sergey. Thus Masha might feel seduced by the

---

[67]David Keirsey, *Please Understand Me*, p. 174.

[68]Leo Tolstoy, *The Death of Ivan Ilych and Other Stories*, p. 75.

[69]In his game theory of madness, Keirsey refers to the Idealist's most characteristic hysterical game as playing "Puppet."

pleasures of "fashionable life," or dominated by what she calls "some evil feeling in my soul," and yet Tolstoy points out that she has her eye ever on her husband, gauging his reaction: "What will he say?" she wonders, and "Will he...forgive me?" In one scene she actually puts herself in Sergey's way, trying to force him to respond to her:

> I went into the middle of the room, so that he had to pass close to me, and looked at him. I thought, "He will come and clasp me in his arms, and there will be an end of it."[70]

Sergey's reaction, unfortunately, could not be more Rational, and is not at all what Masha wants. Sergey is appalled by the Masha he sees in Petersburg, and knows that what he calls his "true relation" with his wife will be lost unless she comes to her senses. Rationals, however, believe firmly in their mates' personal autonomy—that they are "responsible," as Keirsey puts it, "to themselves alone to develop in their own direction"[71]—and so they seldom if ever step in to interfere with their loved ones, even to save them from their most grievous errors. And here Sergey, holding fast to the principle (as he phrases it himself) not "to put compulsion on others," chooses merely to observe Masha's behavior, looking on as if from a distance, "undisturbed and indifferent," or at most catching his wife's eye across a banquet table or from the edge of a ballroom floor, studying her "with a serious attentive gaze."

To Masha, intent on her Pygmalion project, Sergey's impassive observation could not be a more galling response. Feeling so proud of her social success, and wanting so much to make Sergey melt and take her in his arms, Masha cannot bear his "old expression of sagacity, penetration, and patronizing composure." Sergey "would

---

[70]Leo Tolstoy, *The Death of Ivan Ilych and Other Stories*, p. 69.
[71]David Keirsey, *Portraits of Temperament*, p. 71.

not show himself to me as a mere man," Masha fumes, "but had to be a demi-god on a pedestal." And she mistakenly believes that "he was hiding his real self from me," not realizing that such coolness under stress *is* a Rational's real self.

Although Masha accuses her husband, "you never lose self-control," Rationals are not made of ice, and such seemingly aloof objectivity is difficult to maintain, especially for role-directive MasterPlanners like Sergey. In the face of Masha's more and more foolish behavior, Sergey must fight to keep his composure, and Masha often hears the "tone of suppressed irritation" in his voice. At one point, indeed, he loses control (for a Rational) and expresses his disapproval, though even here he tries to keep to his unemotional, professorial tone, and his conditional ("if...then") style of argument:

> "Do you not understand yet?" he asked.
>
> "No, I don't."
>
> "Then I must explain. What I feel, and cannot help feeling, positively sickens me for the first time in my life." He stopped, evidently startled by the harsh sound of his own voice.
>
> "What do you mean?" I asked, with tears of indignation in my eyes.
>
> "It sickens me that the Prince admired you, and you therefore run to meet him, forgetting your husband and yourself and womanly dignity; and you wilfully misunderstand what your want of self-respect makes your husband feel for you."[72]

Sergey continues his scathing criticism in this extraordinary scene, growing more grimly furious as he vents his feelings, and coming finally to the only words of regret he ever utters to Masha, "I was a fool, when I..." However, Keirsey notes that it is deeply distressing for Rationals "to verbalize any

[72]Leo Tolstoy, *The Death of Ivan Ilych and Other Stories*, pp. 69-70.

disappointment or dissatisfaction" with their marriages,[73] and here Tolstoy tells us Sergey "refrained with a visible effort from ending the sentence."

Such an outburst, precise and restrained though it is, costs Sergey a great deal emotionally, and seems to decide something momentous in his attitude toward his wife: "From that day," Masha remembers, "there was a complete change in our life and our relations to each other." Far from the passionate interaction she had once dreamed of, far even from the "calm indulgence...which used to provoke me," Masha now sees Sergey draw back into himself quietly but remorselessly: "there were no further scenes or quarrels between us," she admits, but neither is there any further sense of intimate emotional involvement. Keirsey tells us that Rationals, more than any other temperament, have the ability to disengage emotionally from their loved ones' manipulations—to refuse to play destructive games after a point[74]—and Sergey now turns away from Masha and her Pygmalion project with a deadly finality: his eyes, Masha notices, which were once so penetrating and expressive, now "merely looked—they said nothing, and a veil seemed to cover them from me."

This is not to say that Sergey turns his back on Masha entirely. On the contrary, Sergey's emotional withdrawal seems to calm hostilities on both sides, and soon "good, friendly relations" between husband and wife are restored—there is even a child born the next year in Petersburg. "I tried to satisfy him," Masha remembers, "he carried out all my wishes, and we seemed to love each other." But there is a terrible difference. Masha now seeks

---

[73]David Keirsey, *Please Understand Me*, p. 87.
[74]David Keirsey, *Please Understand Me*, p. 90.

her pleasure by losing herself in the social whirl, while Sergey happily spends more of his time with his baby son, but in their rare moments alone Masha "felt something wrong and some pain at my heart, and I seemed to read the same story in his eyes." They now live together cordially, as ordinary husband and wife, with Masha conscious "of a limit to tenderness, which he seemingly would not, and I could not, overstep." And Masha realizes that now, instead of hanging breathlessly over the "edge of a precipice," waiting for Sergey to save her, there is merely an awkward "gulf between us"—"both of us knew where [it] lay, and seemed afraid to approach it."

Ironically, fashionable life itself pushes Masha to the edge of the abyss. On a summer junket to the hot springs at Baden, the Italian marquis (an Operator Artisan ["STP"]) boldly makes his play for Masha, approaching her with his "liquid blazing eyes, right up against my face," his importunate hands squeezing Masha's "harder and harder," and his parted, breathing lips "coming nearer and nearer." Keirsey describes how Idealists, like Apollo, are often secretly torn between "the urge to...spirituality and sacredness" and the powerful "desire to plumb the profane,"[75] and in this vividly sensual scene Masha's mind is flooded with thoughts of her baby and the "noble serenity" of her husband, but she also responds with all her frustrated passion to the marquis's ardent kiss: "he was utterly repugnant and alien to me," she confesses,

> and yet the excitement and passion of this hateful strange man raised a powerful echo in my own heart; I felt an irresistible longing to surrender myself to the kisses of that coarse handsome mouth, and the pressure of those white hands with their delicate veins and jewelled fingers; I was tempted to

---

[75]David Keirsey, *Please Understand Me*, p. 66.

throw myself headlong into the abyss of forbidden delights that had suddenly opened up before me.[76]

As I have argued extensively in my portraits of D.H. Lawrence's characters, Idealists in times of abnormal stress often yearn to throw off their heavy burden of self-consciousness and escape into the oblivion of sensuality.[77] But suddenly, at this moment of irrevocable yielding, Masha's Idealist conscience seizes her, and burning with "the shame of that kiss" she pulls herself away from the marquis. That evening, sick with repentance, and moving "with feverish haste," Masha takes the train back to Sergey, and then pleads with him to take her home to Nikolskoe "and settle there for ever." Sergey knows something has happened, but is understandably skeptical—"spare us these sentimental scenes, my dear." And yet, since their money is running low, he consents to return to the country and reopen the house, even though he promises Masha somewhat sarcastically that "the notion of stopping there 'for ever' is fanciful."

All that winter in the country Masha and Sergey are "coldly friendly to each other," going about their separate lives and feeling distant and alone in each other's company. Masha mourns inwardly "for what I had lost" (felt even more keenly in the familiar surroundings), and Sergey shyly avoids any frank discussion of their estrangement, "evidently suspecting me of insincerity," Masha feels, "and dreading the folly of any emotional display." At times, Masha is convinced that Sergey is "only pretending to be like that, in order to hurt me," as if he "were punishing me and pretending not to be aware of it." Rationals rarely try to

---

[76]Leo Tolstoy, *The Death of Ivan Ilych and Other Stories*, p. 80.

[77]See my portrait of Miriam and Paul in Chapter 2, as well as my portrait of Connie Chatterley in *Volume One: The Artisan*.

punish their loved ones, however, and they almost never punish emotionally, although over-sensitive Idealists often accuse their Rational mates of such devious behavior. Eventually Masha seems to understand that her husband is harboring no grievance against her—there is nothing she must "ask pardon for"—and she appears to accept, simply, that the heartfelt love he once shared with her is no longer there, "as though he had no longer a heart to give." The house at Nikolskoe might come alive again, but Masha concedes that "much of the past was dead beyond recall."

And yet, while Masha's romantic dreams of marriage have thus brought her little more than "an oppressive, difficult, and joyless life," she has not really given up her Pygmalion project, and as spring comes round (and she recovers from the birth of her second son) she longs to feel again "all that once blossomed in my heart," and also to call forth "the old feeling" of boyish love in her husband. Staying at her childhood house on a visit, she sits on the old veranda one evening and wets her hair in a spring shower, wondering why, though her own "visions of youth" have dimmed, so little in nature has changed since her marriage:

> all remained the same—the garden, visible through the window, the grass, the path...the same song of the nightingale by the pond, the same lilacs in full bloom, the same moon shining above the house.[78]

When Sergey wanders out to join her, Masha turns and cautiously begins the crucial conversation of her marriage. Sergey looks out at the rain in the darkening garden and mentions how "perfectly happy" he is, and Masha ("full of vague unsatisfied longing") asks him timidly if he has no "yearning for the past." Guessing her meaning, Sergey

---

[78]Leo Tolstoy, *The Death of Ivan Ilych and Other Stories*, p. 84.

assures her, "I don't ask for impossibilities," and then he concisely differentiates their attitudes:

> you envy the leaves and the grass their wetting from the rain, and you would like yourself to be the grass and the leaves and the rain. But I am content to enjoy them.[79]

Tolstoy here quite beautifully makes Keirsey's point that Idealists have a transformational or metaphorical consciousness: in their imaginations, at least, they can *become* other things.[80] Rationals like Sergey, however, while they greatly appreciate the Idealists' romantic fantasies, have far more structural imaginations, and know that nature is shaped by physical laws and "not," as Keirsey puts it, by "human desires."[81] This distinction is lost on Masha, however, and "confused and baffled," she asks again, "Would you not like to have it back...would you not alter the past?" And Sergey reiterates, and this time more coldly, "No; I might as well wish to have wings. It is impossible."

Advocates have a natural facility for forgetting (or repressing) their painful memories (Keirsey sees them in the extreme as "Amnesic Hysterics"[82]), and Masha longs to escape from time, erase the folly of Petersburg, and start her marriage over again. But Sergey is of a different nature. As a Rational, Sergey considers the past "dead and gone," of interest, as Keirsey argues, only as a guide to the future, to avoid "a repetition of errors."[83] Moreover, Sergey believes with the Rationals (and with the existentialists) that we sculpt the statue of our own lives, and that each chisel

---

[79]Leo Tolstoy, *The Death of Ivan Ilych and Other Stories*, p. 88.

[80]David Keirsey, *Portraits of Temperament*, p. 104.

[81]David Keirsey, *Portraits of Temperament*, p. 66.

[82]David Keirsey, *Portraits of Temperament*, p. 108.

[83]David Keirsey, *Please Understand Me*, p. 55.

stroke remains indelibly etched in our character, brilliant strokes or blunders, but each stroke our own individual responsibility. In the same way, Keirsey describes Rationals as uncompromising individualists, refusing to ignore the consequences of their actions, and holding themselves rigorously accountable for their errors.[84] For these reasons, Sergey is not willing to forget the mistakes of the last three years and accompany his wife on a symbolical—and what he sees as a delusional—return to the past. Unfortunately, Masha takes his well-reasoned refusal as one more proof that he no longer loves her: "I cannot believe," she cries, "when I think of the past, that you still love me."

Sergey is stung by his wife's accusation, and in a "cool and dry" voice he attempts to explain his side of the story. First he clarifies the issue—"If you mean that I don't love you as I once did..."—and then he admits, "time is to blame for that, and we ourselves." Let me emphasize that Sergey's almost cruel aloofness to Masha since he lost his temper in Petersburg is the behavior of a Rational who has been deeply hurt. Indeed, Keirsey suggests that, at times, MasterPlanners appear "cold and unresponsive" because "in fact [they] are almost hypersensitive to signals of rejection from those for whom they care."[85] But Sergey knows Masha is now in pain herself, and he decides to describe for her the inexorable—and irreparable—changes he went through in Petersburg, as he tried to survive his all but crushing disappointment:

> Shall I tell you the whole truth, if you really wish for frankness? In that summer when I first knew you, I used to lie awake all night, thinking about you, and I made that love myself, and it grew and grew in my heart. So again, in Petersburg and abroad, in the course of horrible sleepless

[84]David Keirsey, *Portraits of Temperament*, pp. 71, 67.
[85]David Keirsey, *Please Understand Me*, p. 182.

> nights, I strove to shatter and destroy that love, which had come to torture me. I did not destroy it, but I destroyed that part of it which gave me pain. Then I grew calm; and I feel love still, but it is a different kind of love.[86]

Sergey's explanation, with its Rational emphasis on self-determination ("I made that love myself") and efficient problem-solving ("I destroyed that part of it which gave me pain"), does little to soothe Masha. On the contrary, she feels even more accused and guilty, and she defends herself by breaking into tears and angrily blaming Sergey for her unhappiness:

> Listen to me!...I must once for all say out what has long been torturing me. Is it my fault that I knew nothing of life, and that you left me to learn experience for myself? Is it my fault that now, when I have gained the knowledge and have been struggling for nearly a year to come back to you, you push me away and pretend not to understand what I want? [87]

Sergey listens intently, and remains silent a good while after Masha has finished crying, as if determining carefully how to proceed. As I have said, Rationals insist on their loved ones' autonomous personal development (as distinct from their intellectual development, which a Rational will more actively direct), and Sergey now ventures a defense of his Petersburg strategy. "All of us," he tells Masha in his categorical Rational way,

> must have personal experience of all the nonsense of life, in order to get back to life itself; the evidence of other people is no good....So I let you go through it alone, feeling I had no right to put pressure on you....Personal experience was necessary, and now you have had it.[88]

Masha dries her eyes as she listens to her husband's thoughtful justification, and she responds quite elegantly, I

---

[86]Leo Tolstoy, *The Death of Ivan Ilych and Other Stories*, p. 90.

[87]Leo Tolstoy, *The Death of Ivan Ilych and Other Stories*, p. 89.

[88]Leo Tolstoy, *The Death of Ivan Ilych and Other Stories*, p. 91.

believe, for the many Idealists who have dealt with Rationals in matters of the heart:

> There was much calculation in all that...but little love.[89]

Clearly, Tolstoy (an Idealist himself) is questioning Sergey's autonomous and impersonal Rational style in his marriage. Tolstoy suggests that Sergey might indeed have given his wife "a freedom for which [she] was unfit," and that if he had involved himself more closely and supportively in Masha's time of "growing up" in Petersburg he might have kept from diminishing their love. Sergey does not give in at this point, but he does grasp the truth of Masha's words and, as Rationals do, he quickly blames himself[90] for causing their unhappiness: "Yes, it is true," he sighs, losing himself in the implications; "I ought either to have kept myself from loving you at all, or to have loved you in a simpler way."

But the apparent tragedy of *Family Happiness* is that, even though Sergey has now begun to understand his error with Masha, the knowledge comes too late. MasterPlanners are relentlessly, some would say inflexibly, decisive in their lives, particularly in their emotional lives, and they do not easily reopen doors they have closed, nor wounds they have healed—"once [they] have made a decision" about their relationships, Keirsey tells us, "a change of heart is not likely to occur."[91] Thus, though Sergey now admits, "I was wrong when I said that I did not regret the past," he knows he cannot change what has happened inside him, and can

---

[89]Leo Tolstoy, *The Death of Ivan Ilych and Other Stories*, p. 91.

[90]In *Please Understand Me*, Keirsey notes that Rationals are "not apt to hold mates responsible for discord: usually the burden of doing whatever needs to be done will be seen by NTs as their own responsibility" (p. 87).

[91]David Keirsey, *Please Understand Me*, p. 87.

promise only to look on and "weep for that past love which can never return." And thus, though Masha implores him once again to let love banish time—"Let all be as it was before...surely that is possible?"—he can only "smile calmly" and remind her, "Why deceive ourselves? Don't let us try to repeat life. Don't let us make pretences to ourselves."

Tolstoy's story is about family "happiness," however, and in the final paragraphs Masha comes to her own higher understanding of love that lifts her marriage above this tragic impasse. Sergey has counseled her wisely that "each time of life has its own kind of love," but Masha seems ready to embrace Keirsey's wider idea, which I might paraphrase as "each *style* of life has its own kind of love." Thus, even as Masha begs Sergey passionately to let their love be reborn, she realizes that he cannot comply, and that her Pygmalion project cannot succeed: Sergey's eyes are "clear and calm" as he listens to her, and Masha knows deep in her heart that "my wishes and my petition were impossible." Masha understands that she must give up trying to relive "the old emotions and excitements" she felt while falling in love; Sergey was not then, and cannot be now, the emotional and poetical young husband she wants him to be—"the past feeling," she knows, "like the past time itself, was gone beyond recall." And with this insight, she relaxes her unconscious Pygmalion stance in the marriage: "suddenly"—and quite miraculously—Masha's "heart grew light," and it seems to her "that the cause of my suffering had been removed like an aching nerve."

That evening Masha learned the most important lesson of her marriage: that family happiness is achieved not by coercing others with your own selfish preconceptions, but simply by accepting, and respecting, your loved ones as they are. And as she closes her narrative she promises us "clearly and calmly" herself that

> the old feeling...became a new feeling of love for my children and the father of my children [which] laid the foundation of a new life and a quite different happiness; and that life and happiness have lasted to the present time.[92]

*   *   *   *   *

Masha finally finds her family happiness with Sergey, much as Newland Archer does with May Welland in *The Age of Innocence*, and both Advocates rightly take pride in their accomplishment. But the lesson in these stories for all Idealists is that Masha and Archer do not become content in their marriages without a long Pygmalion struggle, and without some profound sense of regret in having compromised their romantic ideals. Thus, even as she declares her "new feeling of love" for Sergey, Masha confesses somewhat sadly, "That day ended the romance of our marriage." And though Archer quietly "honored his own past," he cannot help feeling that, throughout the long years with May, "he had missed...the flower of life."

Indeed, compromise is not an easy thing for Idealists, particularly in their intimate relationships, and most particularly for Advocates, who long so fervently to realize their ideals in the social world—and in the people—around them. Advocates who can accept their mates as unique, valuable individuals, perhaps even learning to love them for their differences, will be able to outlive their regrets and nurture long and deeply satisfying relationships. But Advocates who trap themselves in the fantasy of finding a perfect love—believing "what *might be* is always more

---

[92]Leo Tolstoy, *The Death of Ivan Ilych and Other Stories*, p. 93.

fascinating than what *is*"[93]—run the risk of abandoning their loved ones in the name of romance, turning with all their wondrous enthusiasm and imagination to another lover, or perhaps to a series of lovers, and all too often dooming themselves to what Edith Wharton called, out of her own bitter experience, "the poverty, the miserable poverty, of any love that lies outside of marriage, of any love that is not a living together, a sharing of all."[94]

---

[93]David Keirsey, *Please Understand Me*, p. 174.
[94]Quoted in R.W.B. Lewis's brilliant biography of Edith Wharton, pp. 317-318.

Chapter 4

The Counselor

> JAMES: I guess it...feels good to help people.
> SARAH: And that's why you want to make me over in your image.
>
> ——Mark Medoff[1]

Mentor Idealists ("NFJs") are no more manipulative than Disciples ("NFPs"), and yet their greater sense of decisiveness with their loved ones might make them appear more coercive. While Disciples, as we have seen, rely for the most part on tacit and oblique Pygmalion maneuvers, Mentors are what Keirsey calls "role-directive" in their relationships, which means they are quite comfortable telling their mates how they ought to behave, and even suggesting what kind of person they should be. Mentors are so enthusiastic about personal development, and they are so swift and definite in their judgments of behavior (both of one's outward actions and unconscious attitudes) that they

---

[1]Mark Medoff, *Children of a Lesser God* (Peregrine Smith Books, 1980), pp. 20- 21.

seem almost unable to resist stepping in and advising others what to do, or be, or want, or feel.

Mentors, I should point out, have no wish to dominate their mates, and seem virtually unaware of their powerful directiveness. Like the Disciples, Mentors prefer harmony and cooperation in their relationships, and they see themselves as doing nothing more than benevolently enlightening their loved ones with their personal insights. Indeed, Keirsey remarks that Mentors are "surprised and nonplused when others balk or accuse them of being pushy, since they tend to see themselves as facilitative rather than directive, as catalysts rather than commandants."[2] For all their desire for smooth relationships, however, Mentors have a sometimes impatient sense of command about them, and for all their love of harmony, they have a judgmental cast of mind—and both of these traits distinguish them quite clearly from the Disciples

Not that this directiveness is always overt. The seclusive Mentors, the Counselors (Myers's "INFJs"), are exceptionally shy, sensitive people, with a complicated internal world—and with very nearly an aversion to interpersonal confrontation. And yet, while they might appear timid (and perhaps flustered) in public, Counselors work quite intensely in their closest relationships, exerting their influence on an intimate, often unconscious level. With their uncanny feel for the emotional lives of others, Counselors try to shape their loved ones from the inside out, with personal projections and attributions, with meaningful silences, as well as with any number of ethical directives or "should" statements.

---

[2]David Keirsey, *Portraits of Temperament*, p. 88.

Konstantin Levin

Fully half of Tolstoy's monumental *Anna Karenina* (1877) tells the story of an adulterous love affair between two Artisans, the beautiful, sensual Anna and the more shallowly impulsive Count Vronsky. However, the book as a whole is a much more far-reaching and balanced study of male-female relations, and especially of married life. "The main, basic idea" of the novel, as Tolstoy told his own wife, is "the idea of a family,"[3] and he carefully interweaves Anna's ruinous extra-marital affair with the fates of three related marriages in the novel: Anna's own hateful marriage with her Monitor Guardian ("STJ") husband; the strained marriage between Anna's libertine brother Stepan Oblonsky and his long-suffering wife Dolly (another brilliantly portrayed Artisan-Guardian relationship); and, as the main counter-plot in the novel, the hard-won happiness of Stepan's sister-in-law Kitty, and her husband Konstantin Levin, the Counselor Idealist who in many ways is Tolstoy's autobiographical[4] hero in *Anna Karenina*.

Konstantin Levin is a thoughtful and "highly energetic" young man, thirty-two years old, massively broad-shouldered, and with a full, curly beard—but also with the familiar naiveté of the Idealist: he is "strong as a horse," the rakish Oblonsky calls him, "and fresh as a twelve-year-old girl." The orphaned son of Moscow nobility, Levin (after graduating from the university) turned his back on the luxury and superficial sophistication of the great city to take

---

[3]Quoted in the diary of Tolstoy's wife Sophie, March 2, 1877.

[4]Tolstoy did almost nothing to conceal the similarities: Levin looks like Tolstoy, has almost identical family background and traits of character, and displays the same intellectual interests; Tolstoy also put passages out of his personal notebooks into Levin's speeches, and even Tolstoy's first name "Leo" is spelled "Lev" in Russian.

up a secluded life of farming and cattle-breeding on his family's eight thousand acre country estate. Levin joined in the healthy hard work on the land, and came to love the simple "bread and cheese" life of the peasants; but he also began spending more and more of his time reading Plato and the German Idealists,[5] and in dreaming up theories of agrarian reform. Despite his university studies in the physical sciences, and despite looking "more like a barge hauler than a philosopher," Levin has always had a contemplative nature, and in the country he finds himself wrestling mightily with abstruse philosophical issues, not only with schemes of social justice, but also with metaphysical questions "concerning the meaning of life and death."

Ane yet (like Tolstoy himself as a young man), Levin has very little of the soulful Monastic ("INFP") or the socially active Advocate ("ENFP") about him. At this early point in the novel, Levin is interested far more in "scientific questions" than in fashionable "spiritualism"—more in theories of "electricity" than in what he calls "table rapping"—and his embryonic religious thinking strives to combine somehow "the basic principles of the natural sciences" with what he believes is an instinctive "life force" for good over evil. Moreover, he is sharply critical of liberal social movements aimed at the "general good," and he has withdrawn his support from the newly-organized rural county councils. Levin wants fervently to revolutionize Russian society, but he intends to do so by writing a scholarly book about the character of the Russian peasant,

---

[5]Much later in *Anna Karenina* Tolstoy catalogues Levin's choice of philosophers, mentioning that he "reread Plato, Spinoza, Kant, Schelling, Hegel, and Schopenhauer, the philosophers who explain life other than materialistically" (p. 779).

and not by taking part in what he considers to be corrupt political experiments.

Nor, certainly, is Levin a charismatic Teacher Idealist ("ENFJ"). When he must come up to Moscow he is reticent and ill-at-ease in society, particularly when asked to defend his "new ideas" about the inherent morality of rural life. Levin is so shy in the limelight, in fact, that his most passionately held ideas soon vanish into boyish incoherence. Tolstoy points out that, though Levin seems obstinately "single-minded" in his views, his mind is also "full of contradictions," and that in the heat of discussion he easily grows over-excited and often finds himself "going off at a tangent" from his original ideas, or, even worse, "changing his former opinions and formulating new ones" quite at odds with his argument. And sometimes, when caught in his inconsistencies, "convicted of contradicting himself" (and feeling vulnerable and embarrassed at being so scattered), he will "stammer" angrily, or show a nervous "twitching...in his left cheek,"[6] and then he will blush with painful intensity:

> not as grown-up people blush, lightly and without noticing it themselves, but as boys blush, conscious that they are making themselves ridiculous by their shyness and in consequence feeling ashamed and blushing still more, almost to the point of tears.[7]

In this way, swinging almost uncontrollably between his ardent intellectual enthusiasm and his inhibiting self-consciousness, Levin shows us quite clearly the unique

---

[6]Keirsey points out that Mentor Idealists typically "defend themselves by acting as if confused," and that such nervous twitches are common in the "Seizure Hysterics" (*Portraits of Temperament*, p. 96).

[7]Leo Tolstoy, *Anna Karenina* (Signet Classic, David Magarshack trans., 1961), p. 35. All quotations from *Anna Karenina* are from this edition.

internal struggle of the Counselor Idealist, between what Tolstoy calls Levin's "childlike, rapturous" delight in ideas, and his "irritable bashfulness" at having to articulate them logically or publicly.[8]

Whatever the case, Levin's private reading and pondering start him on a long inward journey in *Anna Karenina* toward his own (and, again, Tolstoy's) personal religion—a humanistic and altruistic philosophy which elevates the instinctive morality of the loving human heart above both spiritualist dogma and what Levin finally comes to call the "stupidity of intellect." At the same time, Tolstoy is perhaps unequalled among novelists in his ability to interweave such philosophical themes with the realistic events and details of his characters' personal lives. And thus Tolstoy describes how Levin's solitary existence on his estate turns his thinking outward as well, sending him also on a lengthy *inter*personal journey: Levin begins to yearn for marriage, and for young Kitty Shcherbatsky, the girl of his dreams.

When we first meet Levin in the novel, he has just arrived in Moscow, trembling with nerves, but with the "firm intention" of proposing to Kitty and marrying her. Levin had courted Kitty feverishly the previous winter, throwing himself into Moscow society in order to be near her; but after two months "in a dazed condition" he had lost his confidence (and his patience with fashionable life), and abruptly retreated to the country, hoping to get clear of his feelings. Instead, as you might expect, absence made his heart grow fonder, and Tolstoy tells us that (like all the Idealists) Levin's imagination "wrapped" the object of his love "in some mysterious poetic veil," so that "Kitty

---

[8]Keirsey observes in *Portraits of Temperament* that, though Idealists' are primarily "enthusiastic" in their outlook, "they are also easily irritated" (p. 91).

seemed to him to be perfect in every respect, a being incomparably above all other human beings." And thus, after two tormenting months of helpless desire, feeling his love for Kitty like a "force outside me which has taken possession of me," Levin takes his heart in his hands and returns to Moscow to resolve his fate.

Levin's rather fitful decisiveness, first in fleeing Kitty and then in storming back to ask for her hand, is typical of the Mentor Idealists (both Counselors and Teachers), and offers a significant point of contrast with the Disciples. Disciples can seem remarkably patient in their relationships, far more comfortable *responding* to their loved ones' overtures than *initiating* action themselves. Mentors, however, cannot rest for very long with such an indefinite state of affairs and feel they must act swiftly to determine the direction of their lives. For Levin, love is not a vague romantic dream, it is the "the chief thing in life on which its whole happiness depended," and thus he seems driven, almost hounded, by his longing for Kitty, confessing that

> this feeling did not give him a moment's peace; he could not live without having settled the question whether or not she would be his wife.[9]

In other words, if Disciples seem in no hurry to close their options during courtship, Mentors quickly develop what seems an almost mortal urgency to decide their destiny one way or another. "You must understand," Levin insists to Oblonsky, who is heartening him about his chances with Kitty,

> that for me it's a question of life and death....I have struggled with myself and I can see now that I can't go on living without [her]. And it has to be settled.[10]

---

[9]Leo Tolstoy, *Anna Karenina*, p. 39.
[10]Leo Tolstoy, *Anna Karenina*, pp. 53-54.

Levin's desire to "settle" his future once and for all reflects the Mentors' need for closure in their lives,[11] but it also opens for discussion a larger characteristic of the Mentor style. As I have argued in the two previous chapters, the Disciples' ideal of love (like all their ideals) tends to be unfocused and all-embracing, reflecting their "global and diffuse" style of consciousness, and perhaps this accounts in part for their relative sense of uncertainty with their loved ones. But, in Levin, Tolstoy shows us that Mentors have far more well-defined and demanding ideals, at least in their closest relationships. Thus, though Levin's parents died when he was very young, Tolstoy explains that their marriage has become "the ideal of perfection" to him, and it is a remarkably clear-cut picture of idyllic family life "which he dreamed of restoring with a wife and family of his own." In the same way, Tolstoy says that Levin's shadowy memories of his mother have provided him with an "enchanting and sacred ideal of womanhood," and it is a portrait he has built in his imagination into an exacting ideal of which "his future wife was to be a repetition."

Tolstoy even points out that Levin is quite discriminating, even somewhat categorical, in his feelings of love. Mentors will draw lines of distinction (a Rational preoccupation) far more quickly than Disciples, and Levin speaks knowingly about the two "kinds of love"—spiritual and physical—which "Plato defines in his *Symposium*." And he further describes his ideal love for Kitty by dividing all of womanhood into "two classes," though his categories are so subjective and disproportionate that they render the notion of categories useless:

> one class included all the girls in the world except her and all
> of them had all the human weaknesses, and all of them were

---

[11]David Keirsey, *Please Understand Me*, p. 23.

> very ordinary; the other class included Kitty alone, a girl who had no weaknesses of any kind and who was above the rest of humanity.[12]

This is certainly not to say that Mentors are narrowly predisposed in their choice of spouse. Compared with the Organizer Rationals ("NTJs"), for example, who often keep mental lists of the features they want in a mate, Mentors are still somewhat "global and diffuse" in their affections. In spite of Levin's rather strictly conceived images of wife and family, Tolstoy says that the young man enjoys a romantic "aura of mystery" about his love for Kitty, and that at times tantalizing "pictures of his...future family rose up disconnectedly in his imagination." Nevertheless (and though it seems contradictory), Tolstoy also observes that Levin fully believes he can "only fall in love with" a certain kind of "beautiful...and exceptional" woman, and he cites the curious fact that, before Kitty, Levin had been similarly in love with both of her older sisters, because the Shcherbatsky females fit his "elevated" ideal of womanhood so precisely.

As with his social and religious ideas, however, no matter how determined and structured Levin is in his views of love, he becomes just that timid and muddled in reality. The idea of actually meeting Kitty again (knowing what he must ask of her) grips him with the Counselor's overwhelming confusion of "joy and terror," and when he locates Kitty at a Moscow skating rink he can barely bring himself to look at her. To Levin, Kitty is like some goddess, as blindingly radiant as "the sun," and Tolstoy tells us he "nearly went away, so terrified was he." Levin tries to quiet his heart— "You mustn't get excited!" he commands himself again and again, "You must keep calm!"—but it is not until Kitty

---

[12]Leo Tolstoy, *Anna Karenina*, p. 53.

recognizes him and reassures him with a welcoming smile that he can overcome his agitation and approach her for a turn on the ice.

As they skate together, with Kitty securely on his arm, Levin regains some composure and ventures to speak of his feelings. "I have confidence in myself when you lean on me," he begins, but he immediately remembers his purpose and becomes "frightened at what he had said, and blushed." Looking at him closely, and slowly grasping "the reason for his confusion," Kitty shrinks back almost imperceptibly, and tries to guide the conversation to a harmless social level, inquiring politely, "Are you going to stay here long?" But Levin knows

> that if he gave in to her tone of calm friendliness, he would again go away without having settled anything, and he decided to make a fight for it.[13]

And so he answers breathlessly, "I don't know....It all depends on you"—though once again "he was terrified at his own words." Pretending not to hear, Kitty stumbles and then pushes away to her governess, leaving Levin wild with regret: "Good lord, what have I done?" he cries to himself, and then skates off violently, "describing rings within rings."

Levin is indeed chasing in circles at this point in *Anna Karenina*, for no matter how resolved he is in his own feelings, Kitty is unable to return his love. As a beautiful eighteen-year-old, whose winter début was a huge success, Kitty is far more interested in making her way in fashionable society than in giving herself to a man who (in her mother's words) has such "strange and uncompromising opinions," and who exhibits such "awkwardness in

---

[13]Leo Tolstoy, *Anna Karenina*, p. 47.

society." Furthermore, as a gregarious Guardian (she is a Provider ["ESFJ"]), Kitty little appreciates the shy intensity of Levin's Idealist romantic style. Kitty has known Levin since she was a little girl (he frequently stayed with the Shcherbatskys during his student years), and she has always had a "natural and untroubled" affection for him, "as if he were her favorite brother." Even now, as he strains to win her heart, she thinks of Levin with "pleasure and tenderness"—"how sweet and nice he is," she smiles—and his obvious love for her "was flattering and made her feel happy." But Tolstoy also suggests that Kitty (again like her Guardian mother) "neither understood nor wished to understand" Levin's abstract, philosophical turn of mind, nor his seclusive nature. Although the thought of marrying Levin brings Kitty a "peculiar poetic charm," she is a concrete, social-minded young Guardian, and she worries not only that Levin's plans for his future "appeared rather misty," but also that she would be "bored in the country in winter."

And yet, the most immediate reason for Kitty's coolness to Levin is that her heart is glowing with love for another admirer, the dashing regimental officer (and Operator Artisan ["STP"]), Count Vronsky. Vronsky, who has not met Anna Karenina at this early point in the novel, has all the social graces and connections that Levin lacks, and that a young Guardian girl might dream of: he is charming and good-natured (though notoriously conceited); he is wellborn, wealthy, and highly placed as an aide-de-camp to the emperor—he is, by all accounts, what Tolstoy calls "the gilded youth of Petersburg." Moreover, Vronsky displays the intriguing sense of insouciance that Guardians so often fall for in Artisans, an impulsive, devil-may-care attitude toward life that Tolstoy sums up in one brilliantly descriptive sentence: in Vronsky's view, "the main thing was to be elegant, handsome, generous, daring, gay, giving oneself up unblushingly to every passion and laughing at everything else."

In many ways, Vronsky is a carefully devised opposite or "foil" for Levin in the novel, but no more so than in his view of marriage and family. Though he has pursued Kitty boldly ever since Levin left for the country, Vronsky has engaged in many such meaningless flirtations over the years and he had "no intention of marrying" Kitty—indeed,

> marriage had never presented itself to him as a possibility. Not only did he dislike family life...but he regarded the family and particularly a husband as something alien, hostile, and above all, ridiculous.[14]

Tolstoy makes it clear that Vronsky means no harm to Kitty or her family with his dalliance; he simply enjoys "the seduction of a girl" so much that he gives no thought to the consequences. But Kitty is completely misled by his suave, self-assured style with women, and even though she notices "a sort of insincerity" in Vronsky's attentions, she need only think of her gallant young officer and "a dazzling perspective of happiness rose before her."

For all these reasons, when Levin comes to a party at the Shcherbatskys', arriving early to meet with Kitty and make his fateful proposal, she cannot find it in her heart to accept him. Levin is barely able to speak, so frozen is he with anxiety and emotion: "What I wanted to say was...What I wanted to say...You see, what I have come for is to ask you to be my wife!" And though Kitty is "overwhelmed with rapture" at having this imposing man declare his love, she

---

[14]Leo Tolstoy, *Anna Karenina*, p. 72.

"remembers Vronsky" and gently refuses him: "I'm afraid it cannot be. I'm sorry...."

In their hunger for closure in their lives, Counselors accept their most awful disappointments with a sense of tragic destiny, and Levin resigns himself to defeat with an "aching heart" but without a word of protest: "It couldn't have been otherwise," he says quietly to himself, as if already pulling away from Kitty and the life he cannot have. When hurt (and they are hurt rather easily[15]), Counselors often withdraw emotionally, both to protect themselves and, indirectly, to punish the other person. This can be a chilling experience for the Counselor's loved ones—a barrier of ice suddenly falls—and, here, almost the instant she refuses Levin, Kitty is stung to see "how distant and what a complete stranger she had become to him now."[16]

Levin slips away from the party as soon as he can, then takes the train home in the morning, and Tolstoy's portrait of his wounded state of mind offers an important insight into the Counselors' way with people. As a temperament, Idealists strive to treat others always with kindness—or, as Keirsey puts it, "they would be of goodwill to all, even their enemies, suppressing their...enmity as best they can."[17] On the other hand, with their demand for perfection[18] and with their quick, critical view of people, Counselors under stress can come to judge others—and also themselves—rather harshly. In just this way, Tolstoy has described Levin in the novel as naturally inclined to see "only the good" in people,

---

[15]David Keirsey, *Please Understand Me*, p. 172.

[16]Keirsey notes that, in the extreme case of hysterical withdrawal, Mentor Idealists are liable to become cataleptic or catatonic in order to punish their loved ones.

[17]David Keirsey, *Portraits of Temperament*, p. 91

[18]David Keirsey, *Please Understand Me*, p. 170.

even in his rival Vronsky; but he has also pictured him
nervously "despising" effete Moscow officials, and as
utterly "outraged" by loose foreign women. And now he
shows him turning the same disgust on himself over his
wretched failure with Kitty. "Yes," Levin confesses,
walking the streets late that night,

> there is something repugnant and repellent about me....It is my
> own fault. What right had I to think that she would be willing
> to unite her life with mine? Who am I? What am I? A nobody,
> wanted by no one, and of no use to anyone.[19]

Though, clearly, Levin's self-reproach has a good deal of
self-pity in it, Counselors do not feel sorry for themselves
for very long. As quickly as they lash themselves when
things go wrong, Counselors turn around and dedicate
themselves to living a new and more perfect life. The next
day, slumped in the train, reliving the humiliating scene of
his proposal, Levin is again "overcome by [a] confusion of
ideas, dissatisfaction with himself, and a vague sense of
shame." But then he squares his shoulders and resolves to
change his life—to renew himself in his beloved
countryside. Wanting fervently "to be better than he had
been before," Levin plans to curb "his temper" with his
servants and to "work harder" on his estate; he pledges to
allow himself "still less luxury," even to deny himself the
guilty pleasure of "low passion" with peasant women; and
he also decides—and here's the sore point—to humble his
expectations of love and give up forever "looking for any
extraordinary happiness such as marriage."

In the midst of emotional or moral turmoil, Counselors
often try to take control of their inner lives in this manner,
believing they can regenerate themselves morally with a

---

[19]Leo Tolstoy, *Anna Karenina*, p. 98.

slate of saintly resolutions.[20] And indeed by the time Levin arrives at his estate he is "feeling greatly uplifted by this hope of a new and better life." Tolstoy, however, understood from a lifetime of his own experience that such renewal is more difficult than it appears—that all of one's established patterns of living weigh heavily against personal change—and he dramatizes the Counselor's internal struggle quite effectively in this scene. Though Levin (with all the Idealists) takes as an article of faith that "one can make what one likes of oneself," he immediately feels the stubborn pull of his familiar attitudes and associations. As he enters his house, all the "traces of his old life," Tolstoy tells us,

> seemed to seize hold of him, saying, "No, you won't get away from us, and you're not going to be different; you're going to be just the same as you've always been with your doubts, your everlasting dissatisfaction with yourself, your vain attempts at reform, your falling from grace, and the constant expectation of the happiness you have missed and which is not possible for you."[21]

These two voices of resolution and doubt—resolution to become a virtuous man, and doubt that he can overcome his shameful weaknesses—contend in Levin throughout *Anna Karenina*, as the young Counselor pursues that elusive dream in the lives of the Idealists, what Tolstoy calls Levin's "ever-present desire to perfect himself."

Levin's and Kitty's paths diverge for a long while at this point in the novel. As a glorious spring unfolds, Levin (trying not to dwell on his disappointment) resumes his solitary life in the country. He is full of ideas for reforming

---

[20]Tolstoy in his diaries repeatedly made lists of rules for his self-improvement and moral reform. See the excellent recent biography, *Tolstoy*, by A.N. Wilson (W.W. Norton & Co., 1988).
[21]Leo Tolstoy, *Anna Karenina*, p. 107.

the estate, he begins his book on socio-agronomic theory, and though many of his personal resolutions fall by the wayside, he has a good deal of success observing "the main thing—purity of life," by which he means gaining some control over his tormenting sexual drive.

On her side, Kitty has a harder time of it. When, without a word, Vronsky leaves her for Anna Karenina, Kitty suffers a mild depression (a particularly Guardian response to stress which her doctor calls "morbid irritability"), and is taken to a German spa to regain her interest in life. There she comes under the spell of a ministering, self-sacrificing Christian Pietist (and Monastic), one Mademoiselle Varenka, who devotes herself to nursing the sick, and who believes that one need only "forget oneself and love others to be at peace, happy, and good." Although, for a while, Kitty feels inspired to follow Varenka, she undergoes no lasting spiritual transformation in this brief friendship: Tolstoy says that, for all her would-be soulfulness, Kitty finally "realized that she was deceiving herself." Even so, by trying to emulate Varenka's altruism Kitty does gain some idea of how shallow and self-serving Vronsky's attentions had been, and how badly she had misjudged Levin's heartfelt if clumsy devotion.

By mid-summer Levin has grown ashamed of his "wearisome, idle, and artificial" life of books and theories, and he longs to renounce his class privileges and his education for what he has romanticized as "the simplicity, purity, and integrity" of peasant life. Counselors are forever considering themselves, mulling over means of personal transformation, and one night Levin roams outdoors until dawn lost in thoughts of "how to bring about this transition from his old life to the new": should he join a "peasant commune"? should he "marry a peasant girl"? At the very least he decides his "old dreams of married life were nonsense," and as the sun rises in the cool, gray morning sky, he congratulates himself on an apollonian "victory of light over darkness." At this moment, however, events conspire to reunite Levin and Kitty. Levin hears a carriage rumbling by on the highroad, and when he glances inside he recognizes Kitty's "bright and thoughtful" face—and all his plans for a peasant wife and a "simple life of toil" vanish into the misty air. There in the disappearing carriage, he realizes, was the "one being in the world who was able to concentrate for him the whole world and the meaning of life."

Although, as Keirsey notes, Idealists often find the "meaning of life" in their loved ones' eyes and make them "the center of [their] world,"[22] as a Counselor Levin is so bashful that he cannot bring himself to see Kitty again socially. Home from Germany, Kitty is staying with her sister Dolly no more than twenty-five miles from Levin's estate, and Dolly (another Provider Guardian ["ESFJ"]) quickly comes to Levin to arrange a meeting, promising him that Kitty now realizes how foolish she has been, and hinting that she would welcome a renewal of his offer of marriage. While Levin is longing to see Kitty, he refuses to call upon her—the idea of such a staged meeting is odious to him—and here his Idealist's need for authenticity[23] is unyielding. Had they met on the road "accidentally," Levin feels, "then everything would have come to pass naturally"; but he is too sincere a man, and still too deeply hurt, merely to ignore the past and act the part of the compassionate

---

[22]David Keirsey, *Please Understand Me*, p. 91.

[23]Keirsey observes that all Idealists "suffer feelings of shame if they are phony, insincere, or fake. Even a joking reference to their lapses in genuineness may occasion a quick and irate response" (*Portraits of Temperament*, p. 91).

lover: "to stand before her," as he imagines it, "in the role of one who forgives her and graciously consents to offer her his love...it is impossible, impossible!"

Finally, however, after months spent travelling abroad trying to avoid Kitty, Levin's longing overcomes his self-consciousness, and he accepts an invitation to a dinner party at the Oblonskys'. Levin knows "deep inside him" that he will meet Kitty among the guests, but Idealists are especially adept at hiding from unwanted realities, and Tolstoy tells us "he tried to persuade himself that he did not know it." Nevertheless, when he hears Kitty's name at the party, "he was suddenly filled with such joy and, at the same time, with such terror that it took his breath away." And then when he sees Kitty, and hears the "appeal for forgiveness" and the "tender and timid" promise of love in her voice, he feels "as if he had grown a pair of wings" and can "fly upward...quite independent of his body." Wrapped in what seems a "mysterious communion," Levin and Kitty draw off from the other guests, and with much blushing and smiling (what Tolstoy calls "blissful confusion") they soon come to an understanding.

The next morning, after an excruciating sleepless night, Levin returns to Kitty's side and receives her parents' grateful blessing on their marriage. (I say "grateful" because Tolstoy tells us that lurking in the mother's Guardian heart—and also in Kitty's—is "the terror of the humiliation of remaining an old maid.") But though Levin is graciously welcomed as a fiancé and a son-in-law, and though he himself is very nearly overcome with happiness, he begins almost immediately to have problems with the traditional, aristocratic Guardian world he is entering.

First of all, as a Counselor, Levin had hoped for an unpretentious courtship, reflecting the purity of love in his heart—a "courtship," as he imagines it, "unlike any other." But he is met straightaway with a host of "artificial but affectionate" friends and relatives, and with elaborately trivial instructions about what is "expected of him" socially: buying sweets, for example, and worrying about flowers, and arranging to pay for presents. Levin is "uncomfortable and bored" with these Guardian details and rituals, and not a little irritated at being told what to do at every turn ("I'd advise you to get your flowers from...."). But his Idealist predisposition is, as Tolstoy puts it, "never [to] think ill" of others, and so he goes along with the conventions and the advice, refusing at this point to let them dampen his spirits.

A far more serious problem arises, however, concerning Levin's lack of orthodox faith. With the preparations for the formal Guardian church wedding all but completed ("all the customs," Tolstoy observes, "being strictly observed"), Levin is dismayed to learn that he must produce "a certificate to show that [he has] received Communion," or else the church will not sanction the ceremony. Since, as I have suggested, Levin's religious feeling is more humanistic than supernatural, and more personal than social, such an urgent need to satisfy Kitty and her family's Christian conventions places him in a difficult moral dilemma. Though an "unbeliever" himself, strictly speaking, Levin is a profoundly ethical man who "respects the beliefs of others," and thus the idea of either *saying* he has had Communion or of going to church quickly and *pretending* to take the sacrament "was not only painful to him, but seemed utterly impossible." He had "either to lie or to commit sacrilege," Tolstoy summarizes, "and he felt incapable of doing either."

Levin decides to go to church, hoping perhaps he can revive there the "strong religious feeling" he had experienced for a short time as a teenager. When this doesn't work, he tries to take a more detached (and essentially Rational) view—"to look upon it all as a meaningless, empty custom"—and so dismiss the holy service from his conscience altogether. But Levin is even less able to be skeptical than devout, and Tolstoy describes his deepening predicament with a good deal of sympathy:

> He could not believe, and at the same time he was not firmly convinced that it was all untrue. And therefore, being both unable to believe in the significance of what he was doing and to regard it with indifference as an empty formality, he felt uncomfortable and ashamed all the time he was getting ready for the sacrament, doing something he did not understand and therefore, as an inner voice told him, something that was false and wrong.[24]

Tolstoy observes Levin's Idealist "inner voice" again and again in *Anna Karenina*, what he calls the young man's implacable "consciousness that it would be wrong" ("it" being almost any misthought or misdeed), and also the terrible "remorse he felt" at his slightest interpersonal errors. In this case, trapped in a double-bind, wrong if he does believe and wrong if he doesn't, Levin struggles helplessly in the grip of his conscience, feeling "more than ever...something vague and unclean in his soul."

Levin also feels unclean in his body, especially when compared with the Guardian Kitty, whom he has placed high on a pedestal as a "pure, innocent being," and before whom he "morally bowed." As an Idealist, Levin seems temperamentally bound, as Tolstoy puts it, "to do everything with passion," but, sadly, he finds his towering sexual passion an endless source of shame. Believing they

---

[24]Leo Tolstoy, *Anna Karenina*, pp. 442-443.

should be able to control their bodies with their intellect and their moral decisiveness, Counselors often erect impossibly high standards of chastity for themselves, trapping themselves in a degrading vicious cycle of intended virtue and inevitable failure, followed by redoubled pledges of abstinence and even more shameful surrenders. Certainly, Levin is proud of his intellectual devotion to "platonic love...clear and pure," but he also knows all too well his trembling desire for almost any pretty girl he sees, and then "the feeling of shame which usually tormented him after a lapse," a shame so crushing that for days he can hardly "look people...in the face."

Now, when faced with enfolding Kitty's "dovelike purity" in his arms, Levin is horrified at his past wantonness with prostitutes and peasant women, and in a flurry of conscience he rushes to Kitty and urges her to read his personal diaries. Although strait-laced in their public morality, Guardians can be remarkably matter-of-fact about private sexual needs, and indeed Kitty does not know quite what to make of the spiritual depth of Levin's shame. Guardians suffer prostrating shame for failing in their duties or responsibilities, and Kitty cannot understand Levin's nearly hysterical self-punishment when he has broken no rules and violated no vows. "You won't forgive me," he whispers hoarsely, "you can't love me," but Kitty (overcome with pity) calms him, and forgives him, and though she finds the diaries truly "dreadful, dreadful!" she reassures him that "it's better, after all" to know him at his worst.

These several points of contrast with Kitty and her Guardian world build in Levin to a moment of troubling intuition about his choice of mate. At his "stag" wedding dinner, Levin is being roundly teased about losing his bachelor's freedom, when he astounds his mostly Artisan companions with the singular view that "it is this loss of freedom that I am so glad of." As I have explained, Counselors do not care so much about keeping their romantic options open as about having their relationships securely decided; indeed, they can hardly wait to settle the question of matrimony and get on with their lives. (Thus, Levin is sure "that real life would only begin after marriage.") Beyond that, however, Counselors typically see marriage not as a closing off of life—as a prison cell—but as a mysteriously expansive merging of souls, a giving up of personal freedom in order to gain a greater freedom in the relationship, and Levin thinks grandly to himself, "Happiness consists only in loving and desiring, in wishing her wishes, thinking her thoughts." But then, suddenly, a voice inside him asks, "But do you know her thoughts, her wishes, her feelings?" and the smile quickly drains from his face, and he is "overwhelmed by fear and doubt, doubt of everything."

Levin goes to Kitty again with his misgivings, and she comforts him at the very last minute, promising him tearfully (though erroneously) that "she loved him because she completely understood him." Though he is soothed and the wedding ceremony begins, Levin's "strange feeling" of disunion—that he does not know what is going on inside Kitty—comes over him again at the altar. Levin is, as usual, almost petrified with emotion during most of the service, scarcely "able to understand what was said to him"; but when the priest joins his and Kitty's hands and begins extolling their symbolical "union in love," Levin's mind clears and he understands "how profound those words are, and how they fit with what one feels at this moment!" But then Levin suddenly wonders, "does she feel the same as I do?" and he looks at Kitty with searching, loving eyes—and contents himself that she does.

Tolstoy knows better, however, and he interrupts the scene to caution the reader, "But that was not so." Kitty is not being transported by the mystery of spiritual union, Tolstoy tells us, but is coming to grips with the enormous and irrevocable changes taking place in her social and family life. Of all the temperaments, Guardians observe their social ties most seriously, and thus Kitty is terribly worried about "the complete rupture with her former life" being consecrated in the priest's words. Kitty's every Guardian instinct tells her to cling to what she calls "the old life"— the "things, habits, and people who had loved and still loved her"—and while the thought of marriage brings her a growing "feeling of joy [and] full fruition," she is also horrified at the "completely new, different, and quite unknown life" she is about to begin. And who is this Levin, this strange man she had accepted only six weeks before? Kitty admits now honestly that he is "one man, whom she did not understand," and that she is bound to him "by a feeling she understood even less than the man himself, a feeling that attracted her to him, and at the same time repelled her."

Levin and Kitty move rather shakily through the rest of the ceremony, Levin divided by his spiritual exaltation and his nascent uncertainty, and Kitty utterly confused by the "radiant joy" swelling in her heart despite her sense of insecurity. And their inherent separateness—Idealist and Guardian—becomes even more apparent in the first days and weeks of the marriage. Kitty has refused a fancy honeymoon (Guardians can have a rather spartan outlook on holidays), so the newlyweds retire directly to Levin's estate to start their married life, a life which Levin the

Idealist expects to be "merely the enjoyment of love...from which no petty cares should distract"—and surely nothing like the trifling, commonplace marriages he has heartily condemned in his friends.

But almost immediately Kitty begins to reveal her Guardian ways in running the house, and Levin is amazed, and devastated, to see how "his poetic, lovely Kitty...could think, remember, and worry about tablecloths, furniture, spare-room mattresses, a tray, the cook, the dinner, etc." Levin watches his bride selecting furniture, hanging curtains, fitting out the guest room—happily absorbed in a thousand "petty preoccupations," as he calls them—and he cannot quite believe that something as insignificant as housekeeping has such an "irresistible attraction to her." Tolstoy, in his wise narrator's voice, sums up the essence of the Guardian's concern for homemaking (and not at all a petty concern), explaining that Kitty "instinctively felt the approach of spring, and knowing that there would be foul weather, built her nest as well as she could." And Levin, in turn, does his best to overcome his expectations of an "elevated happiness" and to appreciate his wife's bustling domesticity: he tries to think of Kitty's interests as "charming," as "new enchantments" in her character, or, at the very least, as merely "the fault of her upbringing, which was too superficial and frivolous."

By the third month of the marriage, however, Levin's underlying anger at the frivolousness of Kitty's existence (all embroidery and sweet pudding, as he sees it) boils over into bitter reproach: "she has no serious interests," he fumes, "no interest in my work, in running the estate, in the peasants, in the music...or in books." Although he recognizes that Kitty is quite busy with her household duties, Levin seethes that "she does nothing and is quite content." Again, Tolstoy tries to defend Kitty with a broader perspective on the archetypal Guardian way of life: Levin, he explains,

> did not realize that she was preparing herself for the period of activity which must come to her when at one and the same time she would be wife to her husband, mistress of the house, and bear, nurse, and bring up his children. It never occurred to him that she knew it instinctively and, preparing herself for this great task, did not reproach herself...while gaily building her nest for the future.[25]

Although Tolstoy recognizes Kitty's Guardian virtues at this point in the novel, Levin certainly does not, and he has passed the point of hoping she will deepen her interests on her own. Kitty's brother-in-law once chided Levin about his readiness to impose his own values onto others:

> Well, you see, you are a thoroughly earnest and sincere man. This is your strength and your limitation. You are thoroughly earnest and sincere and you want all life to be earnest and sincere too.[26]

And in just this way Levin quietly (and all but unconsciously) begins a Pygmalion project to instill some "serious interests" in his wife, or at least to admonish her for what he regards as her trivial pursuits. I have said that Counselor Idealists are role-directive, but also that they are are reticent and non-confrontational, and so Levin turns initially to a coercive tactic quite natural to the Counselors, what Keirsey has called "mute withdrawal."[27] In other words, Levin makes up his mind that if Kitty is happy in her trifling household duties, and takes no interest in *his* more serious and philosophical matters, then he will keep

---

[25]Leo Tolstoy, *Anna Karenina*, p. 489.

[26]Leo Tolstoy, *Anna Karenina*, p. 57.

[27]David Keirsey, *Portraits of Temperament*, p. 97.

strictly to himself and go about his business alone, all but excluding her from the significant parts of his life.

As a young, outgoing Guardian from Moscow, Kitty is especially susceptible to feeling isolated and abandoned in the country, and indeed, Levin's silent exclusion is the basis of the couple's first quarrel. Having stolen away one morning to tour a new farm, Levin returns home late, and Kitty meets him at the door with a scolding sarcasm— "You're having a nice time...."—followed by a flood of "reproaches, senseless jealousy, and everything else that had been tormenting her." Levin receives Kitty's outburst like "a sudden blow," and, bristling, is on the verge of voicing his criticisms of her superficial life, when he realizes how much he cares for his young wife, and how much further damage he might inflict in an open argument. It costs Counselors a great deal to vent their negative feelings in personal confrontation; they would rather act the peacemaker with their loved ones, and Tolstoy analyzes Levin's moment of decision with great insight:

> His first impulse was quite naturally to justify himself and explain that she was in the wrong; but to show her that she was in the wrong meant to exasperate her still more and to widen the breach which was the cause of all this trouble. One impulse quite naturally drew him to shift the blame from himself and lay it upon her; another much more powerful feeling drew him to smooth over the breach and prevent it from widening.[28]

Idealists (unlike many Rationals) are more interested in maintaining what Keirsey calls "sympathetic rapport"[29] with their loved ones than in pinning down who is right and wrong in a disagreement. But such emotional capitulation— such giving up of one's rightful feelings—can frustrate an

---

[28]Leo Tolstoy, *Anna Karenina*, p. 485.
[29]David Keirsey, *Portraits of Temperament*, p. 90.

Idealist's sense of justice, and can fracture his already fragile sense of identity. Thus, in this scene, Levin swallows his complaints, and makes up with Kitty to all appearances; but Tolstoy tells us that living with so "unjust an accusation was painful" to him, and also that repressing his anger gives Levin an "agonizing feeling of division into two parts."

Furthermore, differences never expressed never become resolved, and in a few weeks the same quarrel surfaces more hurtfully. Receiving word that his older brother Nikolai is dying in a rural hotel (he has been wasting away from consumption for years), Levin plans immediately to go to his side. Just as before, he offers Kitty almost no explanation for the journey he must undertake—no more than "Nikolai is dying. I must go." And feeling again shut out Kitty proposes to accompany him and help him in his hardship. Levin won't hear of it, however, explaining politely that he wants to spare Kitty the ordeal of the journey, the foulness of the sickroom, and the impropriety of meeting his brother's pock-marked mistress. But his tone is actually quite condescending—"Kitty, really!...It's impossible"—and this is because, deep down, he believes she is not sincere in her offer, but is childishly jealous of his company, afraid of being "bored without me here"—and "such an excuse at so grave a juncture," Tolstoy discloses, "made him angry."

Sensing his disapproval, and offended by his unwillingness to take her seriously, Kitty protests that she won't be in the way—"Why is it impossible?" she demands, "wherever you can go, I can too." Tolstoy observes of Levin that, "as always, interference made him feel vexed," and so, when Kitty obstinately *refuses* to stay at home, he can no longer resist returning the blow from their previous quarrel, though he disguises his criticism at first with a conciliatory tone: "don't be angry," he counsels her, as if trying to soothe a little girl,

> but just think. It's such a grave matter and it hurts me to think that you should get it mixed up with your weakness, your dislike of being left alone. If you feel bored alone, well, go to Moscow.[30]

If Levin ever seriously intended his words to calm the waters, the coercive forms they take have exactly the opposite effect. In his role-directive style, he brackets his message with commands, opening with "don't be angry" and "just think," and ending with the final, icy, "go to Moscow." At the same time, he insults Kitty in a curiously blameless way, by consoling her for her anger, her "mixed up" motives, her "weakness," and her shallow need for people. Levin is using a negative form of front-loading here, trying to shame Kitty by commiserating with her helplessness, sounding genuinely concerned for her welfare, but actually attributing to his wife the most trivial and selfish reasons for wanting to make the journey.[31]

And yet, in his desire to punish Kitty, Levin badly misjudges both her Guardian motives and her Guardian character. Kitty might have spent the first few months of her marriage building her nest, but her desire to share her husband's burden in this deathwatch is indeed serious (preparing for winter is Demeter's role, after all), and she knows she must once and for all throw off the "spoiled child" role into which he has so subtly cast her. And so, feeling trapped in Levin's false sympathy, she lashes out first at his assumptions about her: "There," she cries, "you

---

[30]Leo Tolstoy, *Anna Karenina*, p. 491.

[31]Shapiro notes that, in general, "projection [deals] with the intentions of others, their motives, thoughts, feelings" (*Neurotic Styles*, p. 70).

always attribute mean and contemptible motives to me."
And then she expounds her true Guardian intention:

> There's...no question of any weakness, nothing....I simply feel
> that it is my duty to be with my husband at a time of sorrow,
> but you want to hurt me on purpose, you purposely don't want
> to understand.[32]

Kitty's response here is exceptionally skillful (reflecting, I
suspect, Tolstoy's own intuitive grasp of communication
games), and it quickly turns the tables. The attribution of
motives, either good or bad, is typically an Idealist tactic for
gaining interpersonal advantage; but when Kitty calls Levin
on his front-loading, and then accurately accuses *him* of evil
motives (i.e., of wanting to hurt her, and not wanting to
understand), she beats him at his own game and takes
control of the argument. Of course, relinquishing his power
in the relationship frustrates and aggravates Levin to his
soul: Kitty's stubbornness, he cries (almost beside himself),
makes him feel like "a sort of slave." But he no longer
holds the high moral ground in this battle—which, like all
marital battles, is fought to see who's in charge—and he
can no longer refuse to let her join him.

Kitty thus accompanies Levin to Nikolai's deathbed, and it
is a good thing, for when he sees what has become of his
brother Levin is virtually paralyzed with emotion. Nikolai
is little more than a skeleton of a man, lying in filthy
bedclothes and racked with pain, and Levin is so overcome
with the horror of his brother's suffering—and with the
larger *idea* of death—that he almost swoons. Keirsey points
out that Idealists are liable to become "confused" and
"immobilized"[33] in fearful or critical situations; they

---

[32]Leo Tolstoy, *Anna Karenina*, p. 491.
[33]David Keirsey, *Portraits of Temperament*, p. 96, *Please Understand Me*, p. 172.

find their emotional circuits often so overloaded...that they
cannot deal with the emotional experiences of
others...particularly when experiences involve conflict and
hurt.[34]

And, here, Levin is so stunned by the enormity and
inevitability of death that he can barely bring himself to
touch his brother, or to comfort him, or even to stay in the
sickroom. As a Counselor, Levin can contemplate mortality
as an intellectual or spiritual abstraction; indeed, Tolstoy
tells us that Levin goes off from his brother and ponders the
meaning of life and death "with all his heart and soul." But
in the room with death Levin is in such self-conscious terror
that he "did not know what to say, how to look, how to
walk," and he anxiously "kept coming in and going out on
all sorts of excuses, incapable of remaining alone."

Kitty, on the other hand, brings all her Guardian practicality
to Nikolai's bedside and, undaunted by the hopelessness
and the squalor, swings promptly into action to care for
him. "When she saw the sick man," Tolstoy explains,
drawing a pointed contrast with Levin,

> she was filled with pity for him. And pity in her woman's
> [read "Provider's"] heart aroused a feeling not of horror or
> repulsion, which it had aroused in her husband, but a need for
> action, a need to find out all the details of his condition and to
> remedy them.[35]

And so Kitty sends quickly to the doctor and the chemist's,
orders the maid to sweep and scrub the room, and prevails
("with gentle insistence") upon the surly waiter to hurry up
and serve them a meal. She rolls up her own sleeves and
begins washing and rinsing, and (ignoring the other guests
in the corridors) she runs to fetch "clean sheets,
pillowcases, towels, and shirts." She even remembers the

---

[34]David Keirsey, *Please Understand Me*, p. 95.
[35]Leo Tolstoy, *Anna Karenina*, p. 496.

comforts of religious ritual: she succeeds, Tolstoy points out, "besides all her cares about linen, bedsores, and cooling drinks...in persuading the sick man of the necessity of receiving Communion and extreme unction."

When a haggard Levin looks in later, he sees the room entirely changed: the air scented with vinegar, the medicine and water pitcher and candles neatly arranged, and Nikolai "washed and combed" and propped up in a clean nightshirt, looking at Kitty with new hope. And Kitty? As a Provider Guardian, she is not in the least exhausted from her labors; on the contrary, she "was more active than usual," Tolstoy tells us, "even more animated," as if brought alive by this exercise of responsibility and devotion. Nor is she at all burdened by Levin's deep and self-conscious questions about the meaning of life and death; "she had no time to think of herself," Tolstoy remarks, for

> she was thinking of Nikolai all the time....She smiled, sympathized, petted him, mentioned cases of recovery, and everything turned out well; so she evidently knew.[36]

Sadly, and despite Kitty's tireless Guardian efforts, Nikolai sinks lower and lower, and finally passes away; but the entire episode gives Levin a new respect for his wife, and rekindles his love. Kitty has managed it all so well, he knows, and he tells her (shyly), "and—er—I must admit I'm very, very glad you came." The experience has given Levin no meaningful answers to his philosophical questions; in fact, Tolstoy confesses "he felt even less able than before to apprehend the meaning of death, and its inevitability appeared more terrible than ever to him." But his wife's gift for nursing the sick, her simple devotion to

---

[36]Leo Tolstoy, *Anna Karenina*, p. 499. Keirsey, by the way, calls Provider Guardians like Kitty "the most sympathetic of all the types" (*Please Understand Me*, p. 193).

caring for life no matter how wretched and hopeless it is, teaches him perhaps a more important lesson: now, "in spite of death," Tolstoy tells us, Levin "felt the need for living and loving"; now, "thanks to his wife's presence...he felt that love saved him from despair."

His more deeply felt love for Kitty—and his thoughts for their coming child—now bring Levin more satisfaction in his domestic life than he has ever known. But such closeness leaves Levin vulnerable to an emotion that torments Idealists perhaps more than any other temperament—jealousy. Idealists have an understandable weakness for feeling jealous. They are so passionate in their own lives, and often (especially the introverts) so insecure in their own attractiveness. Moreover, they see such significance in the slightest human interactions, in a tone of voice, for instance, or a glance, that their spouses' most innocent attention to someone else can pierce them to the heart. And so, the next summer, when Kitty's young "man-about-town" cousin Veslovsky arrives unannounced for a stay in the country, and when he kisses Kitty's hand a little too warmly and teases Levin that "you're wife and I...are very old friends," Levin begins a slow burn. He welcomes his uninvited guest outwardly, but inside, Tolstoy explains,

> he disliked Kitty for having allowed herself to succumb to the gay tone of that young bounder...and he was particularly displeased with the special smile with which she returned his smile.[37]

Levin moves brusquely to leave the drawing room, and Kitty can tell that something is bothering him; but Levin has again chosen to play "mute withdrawal" with his wife, and avoiding her eyes he hurries outdoors.

---

[37]Leo Tolstoy, *Anna Karenina*, p. 570.

At dinner, and even though Kitty is conspicuously pregnant, the handsome Veslovsky is even more flirtatious, and Levin (at the other end of the table, seemingly occupied with other guests) can only watch as Kitty listens raptly to her cousin and blushes at his animated conversation. Almost sickened now by his jealousy, Levin interprets this harmless scene "in his own way," imagining all sorts of evidence for his worst fears.[38] Though Levin is able to maintain his public role as polite host (Tolstoy describes as well "his fear of hurting anyone's feelings"), in his heart he is contemptuous of Veslosvsky—and furious with Kitty. Again, however, Counselors hate to initiate personal confrontation, and so later that night, after Veslovsky strolls off tipsily to sing love songs under the lime trees, Levin confronts Kitty in his own way: he comes to her bedroom and sits "scowling in an armchair...obstinately refusing to answer her questions as to what was the matter with him."

"Mute withdrawal" is attractive to Idealists because it initiates confrontation without appearing to do so, and here Levin accuses Kitty without actually accusing her—by pointedly saying nothing—which pressures Kitty, in a sense, to accuse herself: "was there something," she asks at last (and timidly), "you didn't like about Veslovsky?" Once *Kitty* has raised the issue, Levin can contain himself no longer and pours out all his suspicions; but even as he "told her everything" (with his "eyes flashing terribly under his knit brows") he finds himself deeply ashamed of his jealousy. Throughout *Anna Karenina*, Tolstoy describes Levin's desperate "sense of shame" whenever a "bad

---

[38]Levin's jealousy here is another example of the Idealist "projecting" his own anxiety onto the external world, or what Shapiro describes as the paranoid's "biased, quasi-empathic, interpretive cognitions of that person's glance, his look, an ambiguous phrase, or other small piece of behavior" (*Neurotic Styles*, p. 71).

feeling" sneaks by his internal monitor—indeed, this ever-lurking guilt for their darker feelings is very likely what makes Counselors turn to "mute" tactics in the first place.[39] But in this scene, Levin has opened up and said too much, and "straining every nerve to keep himself under control," he tries to take back his words by awkwardly denying that he is jealous: "Please, understand," he begs his wife,

> I'm not jealous—that's a horrible word. I can't be jealous and believe that....I'm sorry I can't say what I feel, but it is dreadful....I'm not jealous, but I'm offended and humiliated that anyone should dare to think—should dare to look at you with such eyes.[40]

Kitty is hurt by her husband's mistrust, and sorry that she must be denied such "innocent diversion" in her meager social life (for she admits to herself that she did rather enjoy the "superficial pleasure" of Veslovsky's gallantries). But Kitty is also touched by Levin's obvious suffering, and by the force of his love for her, and she does her best to convince him of his foolishness: "But, darling, you're exaggerating," she assures him, and then explains that she blushed only in embarrassment at her cousin's too-familiar manner. Thus, not quite certain why she is to blame, but knowing that she cannot bear to give her husband such pain, Kitty decides not to argue the point; instead, she works ever so gently to restore Levin's confidence in her, nursing him past this fever of jealousy much as she comforted his brother Nikolai in his illness.

---

[39]Guardians, in contrast, judge behavior (and primarily *others'* behavior) by a more external monitor—rules, laws, commandments, etc.—though they too will resort to a "silent treatment" to manipulate their loved ones (see my portrait of Rose Sayer from *The African Queen* in *Volume Two: The Guardian.*)

[40]Leo Tolstoy, *Anna Karenina*, p. 574.

In essence, Levin's jealousy springs from an imagined violation of his hallowed ideal of love and marriage: "you are my holy of holies" he vows to Kitty, "and now, when...we are so happy, so particularly happy, this rotter...." As I have argued throughout this book, such vexing disparity between "the ideal" and "the real" plagues all of an Idealist's relationships, and near the end of *Anna Karenina* it forms the basis of Levin's last great interpersonal crisis in the novel, the birth of his son Mitya.

For Levin, as an Idealist, the birth of his child is more than a happy, or even a joyous, prospect; it is an event of "immense and therefore impossible happiness," and in a more abstract sense it is a "mysterious" phenomenon he likens (in a great apollonian metaphor) to the passing on of "some sacred fire" of life. "So extraordinary" indeed is the idea of birth that Levin regards the family's arrangements for Kitty's confinement in Moscow—questions of diapers and doctors and apartments—as not only "trivial," but "scandalous and degrading to him," as if preparing merely "for something ordinary, something human beings themselves were responsible for." The birth of his child raises for Levin no such practical questions, but the higher Idealist questions of the meaning of life and death—the same questions he agonized over during his deathwatch with Nikolai: "Both that sorrow and this joy," he recognizes, were

> equally beyond the ordinary conditions of life. In this ordinary life they were like openings through which something higher became visible. And what was happening now was equally hard and agonizing to bear and equally incomprehensible, and one's soul when contemplating it, soared to a height such as one did not think possible before and where reason could not keep up with it.[41]

---

[41]Leo Tolstoy, *Anna Karenina*, p. 707.

Nonetheless, in spite of (or perhaps because of) the soaring significance he has given his son's birth—so overarching that he forgets his agnosticism and prays to God for strength—the reality of the baby is inevitably a let down. Levin might ponder the abstract "idea" of his child— "Whence and why had he come? And who was he"?—but after the delivery, "having returned to the world of reality," Tolstoy tells us, Levin looks down at this "tiny, pathetic" newborn in its red, wrinkled flesh and he "sighed with disappointment":

> What he felt about the little creature was not at all what he expected. There was nothing happy or cheerful about it; on the contrary, there was a new distressful feeling of fear. It was the consciousness of another sphere of vulnerability. And this consciousness was so painful at first, his fear that this helpless creature might suffer was so strong, that it completely submerged the strange feeling of unreasonable joy and even pride he felt when the baby sneezed.[42]

Once again, Tolstoy captures the divided feelings evoked in the Idealist by virtually all the significant experiences of life, that mixture of joy and fear which seems always to complicate their consciousness, robbing them of the very thing they want most, a simple authenticity of living.

Levin eventually finds a truer love for his son, and in the process comes to a last, profound understanding about his Counselor's way in life and marriage. When Kitty and the baby are caught in a howling storm, Levin, battling the rain and the thrashing trees, rushes through the forest to find them, again forgetting himself and praying to God to spare His fury: "Dear Lord, dear Lord, not on them!" The storm has nearly passed when he comes upon Kitty and Mitya sheltering under an old lime tree, but his horrible panic and dread—as well as the epiphany-like flashes of lightning in

---

[42]Leo Tolstoy, *Anna Karenina*, p. 712.

the forest—seem to have worked some change in his soul and galvanized his paternal feeling. Paradoxically, his "fright during the storm" helps Levin break through his stifling fear for his son's vulnerability; his storm fear makes Levin feel just how precious little Mitya is to him, and how his lack of love was due to his own impossibly romantic expectations. That night, in the nursery, Levin admits to Kitty that "during the storm I realized I loved him," and he confesses that all this time he was not "disappointed...in him, but in my feeling. I had expected more."

Does the story thus end with Kitty and Mitya safe, and Levin filled with new-found love for them both? This outcome is what Levin would like, no doubt, and he imagines that now, in the wisdom of his loving heart,

> there won't be that lack of sympathy there used to be...there will be no disputes; with Kitty there will be no more quarrels; I shall be nice and kind to the visitor, whoever he may be, and the servants...—it will all be different.[43]

But, again, Tolstoy knows his "divided" Counselors far too well to leave Levin with such a simple and comforting sense of resolution. In the storm scene, Tolstoy describes a "great tree"—what he calls a "familiar oak"—in the middle of the forest that had been splintered by lightning, and this sundered oak tree might well be a metaphor for Levin's own great but divided Idealist spirit. For at the same time that Levin comes to find his love for his son, he finds himself raging at his wife for exposing herself and Mitya to such peril: "You ought to be ashamed of yourself," he roars at her; "I can't understand how anyone can be so careless!" And it is this violent, and certainly familiar, split in his feelings that leads Levin to his final personal revelation. Levin quickly apologizes to Kitty for his angry outburst—

---

[43]Leo Tolstoy, *Anna Karenina*, p. 791.

"I'm sorry, I don't know what I am saying"—but his guilt gnaws at him until, that night, leaving the nursery, he stops on the terrace to look at the lightning flashing on the horizon, and his heart quietly opens to a new "understanding of good and evil" in his nature.

Like so many Idealists, Levin has struggled all of his life trying to transform himself into a perfectly good human being, believing that self-esteem is possible only for the ideal man, and that devotion to "God and goodness" is "the only life that is worth living and the only life that we prize." But his violently contradictory emotions after the storm— his rush of love *and* of anger—give him pause and force him to consider a more tolerant basis for self-regard. Levin must confess that, for all his desire to banish his human flaws, for all his dreams of being a purely benevolent and loving man, he is no more than human and will likely continue to deal with others in his shy, intense, and passionately critical Counselor way. He finally admits to himself with a smile of recognition that, despite his saintly intentions,

> I shall still get angry...I shall still argue and express my thoughts inopportunely; there will still be a wall between the holy of holies of my soul and other people, even my wife, and I shall still blame her for my own fears and shall regret it.[44]

Importantly, Levin recognizes "this new feeling" of self-acceptance not as the miraculous personal transformation he has sought for so long: it "has not changed me," he says, "has not made me happy and enlightened me all of a sudden as I dreamed it would." On the contrary, Levin seems to have become "joyfully aware" only of his own, inescapable limitations as a human being—as an Idealist—and he seems to have embraced the idea that we find a higher and

---

[44]Leo Tolstoy, *Anna Karenina*, p. 807.

"incontestable" feeling of goodness when we forgive ourselves for being ourselves.

It is not too simple to say that, in the course of *Anna Karenina*, Levin has learned to love both his wife and his son despite their all too human weaknesses—and that at the very end of the novel, after his storm of emotions, he finds the "joy and tranquility" of understanding and accepting himself as well.

Jane Eyre

Charlotte Brontë also uses a lightning-riven tree as a metaphor in *Jane Eyre* (1847), but it suggests not so much Jane's divided Counselor nature as the wrenching, searing separation she must endure from the man she loves as her soul's mate, the indomitable FieldMarshal Rational ("ENTJ") Edward Rochester. On the night Rochester asks Jane to marry him, a fierce storm suddenly unleashes its fury, drenching the lovers, and driving them indoors from the garden. The wind wails and the thunder crashes for two hours, and in the morning Jane finds that "the great horse-chestnut at the bottom of the orchard had been struck by lightning...and half of it split away." Of course, *Jane Eyre* is one of the most well-loved novels in English literature, and thus the shocking discovery that Rochester is already married—a revelation that will tear Jane from his side on their wedding day—is familiar to most readers. But the larger story of Jane's stormy romance with Rochester, of the powerful forces of personality underlying their attraction, their sudden breaking apart, and their eventual reconciliation, is in its own way a striking exposition of the problems and the joys of Idealist-Rational love.

After an unforgettably cruel and damaging childhood,[45] and
after six "disciplined and subdued" years as a student (and
two more as a teacher) at a charity-school, young Jane Eyre
finds that her spirit has suddenly undergone a "transforming
process," and she feels growing in her heart the need to
seek a wider "knowledge of life" along what she envisions
as "the white road" of her future.[46] This desire to pass
through the doors of life is more characteristic of the
outgoing Teacher Idealists than the seclusive Counselors,
and indeed as a child Jane had been a "solitary...shy little
thing," and had satisfied her restless imagination by closing
herself off with her favorite books and stories, looking at
pictures of "shadowy" foreign lands and reading tales of
"fairies" and "genii." But now, at eighteen, and despite

---

[45]The first fifth of *Jane Eyre* presents a deeply disturbing portrait of
exactly how *not* to raise a shy, imaginative Counselor child. Both in
her strict Aunt Reed's house, and in Lowood, the poor charity-school
she is shunted off to, Jane is harshly punished for being a passionate
and fantasy-filled child—for being "like nobody" around her, "opposed
to them in temperament, in capacity, in propensities." Trying to make
Jane show "a more sociable and childlike disposition," her cousin
bloodies her with a blow, her aunt locks her repeatedly in a dark "red"
room, and the school manager starves and publicly shames her. All of
this ill-treatment results in a frightened and love-starved little girl, but
also a rageful and vengeful one who resorts to a number of familiar
Idealist defensive symptoms: "frantic anguish," "rising hysteria,"
"stifling breath" and "constricting throat"—and who collapses at one
point in "a species of fit" so nerve-shattering that the adult Jane insists
"I feel the reverberation to this day."

[46]The etymology of the name "Eyre" provides a remarkably fruitful
study in Idealist character traits. The American Heritage Dictionary
indicates that the root of "Eyre" is from the Latin "ire" which translates
as "to go" and also "to travel" (as in knight-"errant"). In an extended
form ("ya") "ire" was the root of the Latin words "janus" ("archway")
and "Janus," the Roman god of doors and passages—a god Keirsey uses
to characterize the Mentor Idealists in *Portraits of Temperament* (p. 96).
And, finally, one Sanskrit variant of "ya" ("yanam") is translated as
"way," particularly in the Buddhist sense of "mode of knowledge."

knowing that "the step was contrary to my nature," Jane overcomes her Counselor's innate reserve—as well as what Brontë calls the "chaos" of her thinking—and she advertises for a position somewhere in "the real world...of hopes and fears."

Jane answers her one inquiry and (dressed in her "Quakerish" plainness) she embarks on what she hopes will be a new life in the "busy world," becoming governess for a little French girl named Adèle, who lives as a gentleman's ward in a handsome though slightly run-down manorhouse known as Thornfield Hall. Jane throws herself into her new duties with her usual enthusiasm, but within only a few months the ordinariness of the real world has proven a terrible disappointment to her. Adèle, she finds, has "no great talents...no peculiar developments of feeling"; Mrs. Fairfax the housekeeper is but a "placid-tempered, kind-natured woman"; and Thornfield is no more than a "pleasant" estate, with no "fairy place" on the grounds, and apparently "no legends or ghost stories" haunting the manor.

Keirsey points out that Counselors have perhaps the most "vivid imaginations" of all the Idealists, sometimes amounting to a kind of "genius" which enables them to write "poems, plays, and novels,"[47] and Jane clearly turns to something like a novelist's imagination to help her endure her "uniform and too still existence" at Thornfield. Jane describes how she seeks out the "silence and solitude" of the manor's dim third story, pacing the narrow hallway ("like a corridor in some Bluebeard's castle"), and opening her

---

[47]David Keirsey, *Please Understand Me*, p. 171.

> mind's eye to dwell on whatever bright visions rose before
> it...[and] my inward ear to a tale that was never ended—a tale
> my imagination created, and narrated continuously; quickened
> with all of incident, life, fire, feeling, that I desired and had not
> in my actual existence.[48]

Happily for Jane, two mysterious personages do manage to rouse her starved imagination. The first is a long-time family servant named Grace Poole, a sewing-woman who keeps to herself on the gloomy third floor, and who seems to be the source of a low and "mirthless" peal of laughter Jane hears echoing at times from a lonely chamber down the hall. Mrs. Fairfax quickly ruins the suspense, however, by introducing the woman to Jane, who feels almost embarrassed for the inkling of superstitious fear the laughter had stirred in her. Grace Poole turns out to be a plain, "square-made" woman, somewhat eccentric perhaps, but Jane blushes that "any apparition less romantic or less ghostly could scarcely be conceived."

The other figure intriguing Jane is her long-absent employer, Mr. Rochester. Jane has never seen Mr. Rochester (he only rarely visits Thornfield), and she eagerly

---

[48]Charlotte Brontë, *Jane Eyre* (Signet Classic, 1960), p. 112. All quotations from *Jane Eyre* are from this edition. Brontë, a Counselor Idealist herself, followed much the same method in writing her fiction. One critic described Brontë's writing process as "trance-like": "she writes rapidly, with her eyes shut, describing in detail the scene before her 'mind's eye.'" And Brontë herself said that her characters—those creatures of her imagination—become so vivid to her that "like Pygmalion's statue, they appeared to have a life beyond that of their creator" (Christine Alexander, quoted in the Norton Critical Edition of *Jane Eyre*, p. 409). Curiously, Brontë tried to make *Jane Eyre* appear not to be a work of fiction at all, having Jane tell her story in her own words, as a first person narrator, and publishing the first edition of the novel anonymously as "An Autobiography" prepared by an "Editor." Perhaps this was because, as a young writer, Brontë actually frightened herself at times with she called her "morbidly vivid realizations."

sounds out Mrs. Fairfax about what sort of person he is—not what he looks like, nor what he does in life, but with her typical Counselor interest in the inner person, she wants to know "what...is his character?" Good Mrs. Fairfax is a sturdy, capable Guardian, a down-to-earth Conservator ("SFJ") who has, Jane sees, "no notion of sketching a character," although she struggles to do her best: Mr. Rochester is "clever," she hints to Jane, but "rather peculiar," hastening to add that he is a "a very good master." Jane is even more enticed by such vagueness—"in what way is he peculiar?" she asks quickly—and when Mrs. Fairfax tries to frame her answer, she shows just how easily the ironical manner of the Rational can bewilder a straightforward Guardian. "I don't know—" Mrs. Fairfax ventures,

> it is not easy to describe—nothing striking, but you feel it when he speaks to you: you cannot be always sure whether he is in jest or earnest, whether he is pleased or the contrary; you don't thoroughly understand him...at least, I don't.[49]

Mrs. Fairfax shakes her head and goes about her housework, and Jane must content herself that, simply, "Mr. Rochester was Mr. Rochester in her eyes; a gentleman, a landed proprietor—nothing more." And yet, to Jane, the mystery of her employer's personality has deepened irresistibly, and she resolves in her Counselor's way "to gain a more definite notion of his identity."

Jane's wish is soon granted, for one cold January evening, as she is walking in the hills above Thornfield, she accidently startles a speeding horse and rider, throwing them off-balance on the icy road, and causing a serious fall. The "tall steed" is unharmed, but the "dark, strong, and stern" traveler has sprained his ankle—though when Jane

---

[49]Charlotte Brontë, *Jane Eyre*, p. 108.

gathers her courage and offers to run for help, he gruffly stops her. The man pulls himself to his feet, and (furrowing his brow and looking "ireful and thwarted") he asks Jane to bring him his horse. The animal, however, is as "spirited" and defiant as his master and will not let Jane catch his bridle; and the stranger, now grimacing in pain, knows he must bow to practical necessity and turn to this slender young girl for support. "Necessity compels me to make you useful," he informs her, and leaning his heavy hand on Jane's shoulder he hobbles to his horse—then springs into the saddle, and rides off into the night, vanishing, as Jane pictures it in her poetical imagination, "Like heath that, in the wilderness,/The wild wind whirls away."

Jane has no idea who this dark-faced, broad-chested man might be, nor does she know that this accidental meeting on the road foreshadows the course of her future relationship with Mr. Rochester. As she walks back to Thornfield the incident seems to Jane "of no moment, no romance" beyond the "single hour" of the dark traveler's need and her trembling assistance. But we will see Rochester surprised and felled by life two more times in the novel, and we will see him in each painful case look to Jane for support.

Once at the house, Jane is told that the master of Thornfield has just ridden up—with a sprained ankle—and Jane marvels at the possible identity of the horseman, and thrills at the prospect of some change in her "passive," "monotonous" life. The next evening Mr. Rochester summons Jane and little Adèle to tea, and when Mrs. Fairfax ushers them into the drawing-room Jane immediately recognizes the rider's "broad and jetty eyebrows," his "decisive nose," his "grim mouth"—a middle-aged face, she sees now, and not handsome by any means, but a face full of character and intrinsic power.

Rochester, his leg propped on a pillow, barely acknowledges Jane's entrance, and then tells her to be seated, using an "impatient" tone, as if to say, "What the deuce is it to me whether Miss Eyre be there or not?" Under the circumstances, Rochester's "harsh" manner suits Jane far better than "a reception of finished politeness," for it eases her embarrassment, she tells us, and leaves her under no obligation to make conversation, a pressure to be amiable that Counselors often feel burdening them in even their most casual interactions. Jane merely sits quietly, waiting with great interest "to see how he would go on."

It is quite typical of Rationals to treat others coldly and stiffly; Keirsey says that they "tend to control and hide their emotions behind an immobile facial stance, with only their eyes transmitting depth of reaction."[50] And here Jane describes how Rochester "went on as a statue would, that is, he neither spoke nor moved," but only "searched my face with eyes that I saw were dark...and piercing." Moreover, Rationals are almost always strategical in their serious conversations, and Rochester is bent on investigating Jane's cast of mind in this interview—not in making her feel comfortable. Thus, when little Adèle asks innocently if he has brought a present for her governess, Rochester sees his opening and begins to question Jane: "did you expect a present, Miss Eyre?" and then, arching an eyebrow, "Are you fond of presents?"

Like all the Idealists, Jane is the soul of diplomacy[51] when unsure of her ground, and she answers tactfully, "I hardly

---

[50]David Keirsey, *Please Understand Me*, p. 86.

[51]The word "diplomatic" comes from the latin for "doubled" or "folded," in other words not straightforward or open. It is interesting to note that Jane's namesake god Janus (see footnote 46) traditionally has two faces, one young and one old, which made him known as the god of

know, sir...they are generally thought pleasant things."
FieldMarshal Rationals, on the other hand, are hardly ever
unsure of themselves, and they have little tolerance for
evasiveness. Rochester scoffs at Jane's fine phrase
"generally thought," and he demands, "but what do *you*
think?" Jane grows even more cautious under such scrutiny:
"a present has many faces to it," she offers, "and one should
consider all before announcing an opinion as to its nature."
Rochester again chides her for such equivocation—"Miss
Eyre...you beat about the bush"—and when Jane tries to
hide in humility, explaining shyly, "I have less confidence
in my deserts than Adèle," he blocks her once again: "Oh,
don't fall back on over-modesty!"

Rochester next examines Jane about her background and
qualifications (not her credentials—Rationals care nothing
for credentials): where was she educated? who
recommended her? and, most especially, how much has she
read? Mrs. Fairfax tries to speak up on Jane's behalf and
attest to her "kind and careful" character, but Rochester
silences her with a look, insisting "eulogisms will not bias
me; I shall judge for myself." Jane briefly describes her
lack of family, her strict life at school, and her meager
reading, and Rochester only shakes his head and comments,
"you have lived the life of a nun." Then, in a move
remarkably similar to Sergey's in *Family Happiness*, he
inquires if Jane can play the piano. When she tells him
politely, "a little," he frowns, "of course: that is the
established answer," and he orders her to "go into the
library" and "play a tune." Keirsey tells us that, of all the

---

"good beginnings" that would surely bring about "good endings." By
the way, these scenes of Jane and Rochester's getting to know each
other take place in January, the month of new beginnings, the month
named for Janus.

sixteen types, the role-directive FieldMarshal Rational is the most "deliberate and conscious" in taking charge of others and issuing orders,[52] and in this scene Rochester is quite aware of his own intransigent "tone of command": "I am used to say 'Do this,' and it is done," he explains to Jane, and "I cannot alter my customary habits for one new inmate."

Finally, having heard for himself that Jane can play "perhaps better than some, but not well," Rochester asks to see her portfolio of drawings, and his judgment of them expresses clearly the difference between the Rational and the Idealist view of art. Rochester dismisses most of the sketches out of hand, but three of the most original watercolors strike him as the product of "some time and thought," and he asks Jane if they are the creation of "that head I see now on your shoulders." "Yes, sir," she answers (gratified, but also somewhat embarrassed), and while Rochester pores over the paintings, Jane tries to explain that she goes about drawing in a more soulful way than he has suggested. She saw these subjects, she says, "with the spiritual eye"—they were inspired, mystical visions which she was unable to "embody" properly on paper. Most Rationals believe that drawing—all art, for that matter—is a matter of technical application, not inspiration, and Rochester re-phrases her explanation of the artistic process in words that suit his own theory: "Not quite," he corrects her: "you have secured the shadow of your thought; but...you had not enough of the artist's skill and science to give it full being." All the same, while the paintings lack something of the "artist's science" (only a Rational would use such a phrase), Rochester finds them strangely imaginative, full of rare effects of light and depth and air,

---

[52]David Keirsey, *Portraits of Temperament*, pp. 64, 75.

and he abruptly orders them put away, as if disturbed by what he calls their "elfish" power.

Rochester is even more disturbed over the next few days by Jane's own "elfish" presence in his household. Tiny and frail, plain and pale, she herself appears at times to be more "shadow" than "substance," and her spiritual, almost spectral manner (as she passes him quietly in the hallway or the gallery) gives her "rather the look of another world," and makes Rochester think "unaccountably of fairy tales."[53] And so, wanting to read further into the mysterious book of her, Rochester sends word one evening for Jane to join him after dinner in the dining-room. As before, Rochester directs her to be seated, though this time he pauses and adds "if you please" ("confound these civilities!" he mutters, "I continually forget them"). Jane's chair is near him by the fire, and when she tries to draw it off into the shadows, Rochester tells her to sit in the chair "exactly where I placed it"—stating bluntly, "I cannot see you without disturbing my position in this comfortable chair, which I have no mind to do." Again, Keirsey comments that role-directive FieldMarshals have such a "commanding" way about them that "most of us do not question or challenge such command."[54] And Jane reluctantly takes her seat, observing that "Mr. Rochester had such a direct way of giving orders, it seemed a matter of course to obey him promptly."

Rochester sits looking at the fire, and Jane—ever the student of faces—observes that his "granite-hewn features" and "great, dark eyes" seem somehow softer than before (she wonders if, perhaps, he has had too much wine).

---

[53]If Jane were not so plain, these first months with Rochester would indeed resemble the fairy tale *Beauty and the Beast*.

[54]David Keirsey, *Portraits of Temperament*, p. 74.

Rochester notices Jane's curiosity and tells her, simply, that he is "disposed to be gregarious and communicative to-night"—two words which describe the typical FieldMarshal quite accurately.[55] And yet, when he attempts to draw Jane out, his manner is so imperious and peremptory that he succeeds only in rousing her fierce sense of independence. "Speak," he orders her, "it would please me to learn more of you," but Jane (playing her own version of "mute withdrawal") sits smiling to herself "and said nothing."

Jane knows from long experience that a tactical "quiescence...gave [her] the advantage" with her superiors, letting her assert herself without appearing to assert herself, and in this case her "stubborn" silence pulls Rochester up short and makes him recognize that he has put what he calls his "request" in an "absurd, almost insolent form." Rochester sees something fine in this little governess—he admires independence—and he encourages her now to speak with him openly and plainly, as an equal, though he does *not* promise to change his manner. Rochester tells Jane she must be willing "to receive my orders now and then, without being piqued or hurt by the tone of command." And he also urges her to look ₊past the niceties of polite conversation with him—she must agree "to dispense with a great many conventional forms and phrases, without thinking that the omission arises from insolence."

Jane certainly senses something in Rochester more noble than insolence—an "unconscious pride," she terms it, that will not be bound by conventionality—and she responds boldly: "I should never mistake informality for insolence: one I rather like, the other nothing free-born would submit to, even for a salary." Rochester's eyes light up at such

---

[55]David Keirsey, *Portraits of Temperament*, p. 74.

spirit and intelligence in a woman, though his first thought is to rein in Jane's galloping idealism: "Humbug!" he snaps at her, "most things free born will submit to anything for a salary; therefore...don't venture on generalities of which you are intensely ignorant." But then he grows milder, and (for a Rational) very nearly complimentary:

> However, I mentally shake hands with you for your answer, despite its inaccuracy...the manner was frank and sincere; one does not often see such a manner: no, on the contrary, affectation, or...stupid, coarse-minded misapprehension of one's meaning are the usual rewards of candour.[56]

Rochester stops himself here—"I don't mean to flatter you," he clarifies—but he is indeed in an expansive mood and he soon finds himself opening up to this young girl about the most secret grief, and the most sudden hope, of his life. Staring into the flames, and casting his mind back over the last twenty years, Rochester tells Jane that, at eighteen, he was much like her, with a "clean conscience," an "unpolluted memory" and a kind of "rude tenderness of heart." But then Fate "wronged him" terribly, he says, and instead of proving himself superior to circumstances, he admits (with a good deal of disgust for his weakness), "I had not the wisdom to remain cool: I turned desperate; then I degenerated." Keirsey points out that Rationals typically seethe with "outrage when injustice is done" them, and are often disposed to revenge against their foes.[57] Unfortunately, Rochester, when he realized his fate was sealed, turned his rage against himself. Deprived of the prospects of anything like true happiness, he sought oblivion in mere "heartless, sensual pleasure—such as dulls intellect and blights feeling." Rochester succeeded in numbing his pain, but he became in the process, he tells

---

[56]Charlotte Brontë, *Jane Eyre*, pp. 137-138.
[57]David Keirsey, *Portraits of Temperament*, p. 70.

Jane, as cynical and "hard and tough as an India-rubber ball."

But now, as he sits with Jane and contemplates his wasted life, new possibilities for happiness begin to stir in Rochester's mind. He rouses himself and promises Jane that, though hard as rubber, he is "pervious" still, with "one sentient point in the middle of the lump"—and he wonders aloud, "Yes, does that leave hope for me?" Jane asks (somewhat uneasily), "Hope of what, sir?" And in answer Rochester introduces the theme that will virtually define his and Jane's relationship throughout the rest of the novel: "Of my re-transformation from India-rubber back to flesh."

Rochester could not have touched Jane closer to the heart. Personal transformation is what Keirsey calls the "primary and lifelong focus" of the Counselor Idealists,[58] and thus, though young and inexperienced, and feeling rather out of her depth, Jane is eager to offer Rochester her counsel. Jane's instinctive view of psychological change is of a slow, careful—and essentially moral—renovation from the inside out. "Repentance," she promises him, is the "cure" for a sinful life; and as for a "sullied memory,"

> It seems to me, that if you tried hard, you would in time find it possible to become what you yourself would approve; and that if from this day you began with resolution to correct your thoughts and actions, you would in a few years have laid up a new and stainless store of recollections, to which you might revert with pleasure.[59]

FieldMarshals, in contrast, believe in the quick, decisive stroke, and in their ability to transform anything in nature—including their own behavior—if they put their mind to it. Rochester smiles at Jane's cautious words about penitence

---

[58]David Keirsey, *Portraits of Temperament*, p. 87.
[59]Charlotte Brontë, *Jane Eyre*, p. 140. Jane's notion of therapy here sounds amazingly similar to L. Ron Hubbard's idea in Scientology of making "new tapes" in the brain in order to re-structure the mind.

and hard-won self-approval, for he has supreme confidence that he can re-direct the course of his life by an act of his own will: "I don't doubt myself," he assures her, "I know what my aim is, and what my motives are." And he announces grandly (though only half-seriously) that "at this moment I pass a law, unalterable," decreeing that his dissolute life is changed for the better—that his every thought and action now, as he puts it, "are right."

Counselor Idealists are drawn to such energy and self-confidence, and Jane feels a compelling "faith in" Rochester's inner power. But as a Counselor Jane also believes human beings are ruled by a higher power (by something like Levin's "God and goodness"), and she sees a dangerous arrogance in trying to take Fate in our own hands. Jane reminds Rochester that he is only "human and fallible," and warns him that "the human and fallible should not arrogate a power with which the divine and perfect alone can be safely trusted." But as a Rational, Rochester prides himself on living by his own rules (by what he calls his "household gods"), and he demands to know "What power?" is beyond him. Jane holds firm and answers with all her Counselor's conviction that our decisions must be based on a moral authority greater than our individual will: the power, she contends, to say "of any strange, unsanctioned line of action—'let it be right.'"

This idea of moral sanction[60] is crucial to our understanding of the difference between the Idealist's and the Rational's attitude toward human behavior. Most Idealists believe implicitly that our actions, to be considered "good" or "right," must be sanctioned by a code of ethics that respects some sort of transcendent authority and that insures social harmony—and such need for approval and cooperation

---

[60]See Ray Choiniere and David Keirsey, *Presidential Temperament* (Prometheus Nemesis Book Company, 1992), p. 8.

glows brightly in Jane's heart-of-hearts. Most Rationals, on the other hand, are pragmatic about their actions, believing "right and wrong" to be largely a matter of individual vision and operative usefulness—"efficiency is always the issue," as Keirsey puts it[61]—and such desire for utility and individual autonomy burns hot at Rochester's core. Without question, the seed of conflict we see in this scene between moral sanction and pragmatic self-determination is the basis for much of the tension in Idealist-Rational relationships; and in *Jane Eyre* it will grow into the controversy that strains Jane and Rochester's future happiness almost to breaking.

The argument is forgotten for now, however, and over the next few months the two take great pleasure in exploring the strengths and weaknesses of each other's personalities. Rochester is naturally "communicative," Jane discovers with delight, and he speaks to her with a "friendly frankness" that quickly "drew me to him." Rochester is equally delighted to have found what he calls a "unique mind" to place "in communication with my own," and he is amazed at how open this young woman is to "new ideas," how eager to follow him "in thought through new regions" of learning. Rochester also confides to Jane more about his old trouble (though giving her few details), and when he thanks her for being such a compassionate listener he astutely describes one of the Counselor's most characteristic skills. "You were made to be the recipient of secrets," he assures Jane, for

> it is not your forte to tell of yourself, but to listen while others talk of themselves...[to] listen with no malevolent scorn of their indiscretion, but with a kind of innate sympathy.[62]

[61]David Keirsey, *Portraits of Temperament*, p. 66.
[62]Charlotte Brontë, *Jane Eyre*, p. 139.

Nevertheless, for all her sympathy, Jane concedes that Rochester's many faults were "frequently before me." In spite of his kindness and intellectual generosity to her, and in spite of his sincere desire "to be a better man," he is "scornful" and "severe" with others, she is sad to say, "proud, sardonic, harsh to inferiority of every description," and he is also "hard and cynical, self-willed and resolute" in his hatred of his fate. Rochester is not a handsome man to begin with, but his face seems to Jane often twisted with "scowling abstraction," which makes him appear not only distant and aloof, but also surprisingly ugly.

And yet, as Jane spends more and more time with Rochester she finds herself readily "forgetting all his faults." Keirsey observes repeatedly in his writings that Idealists have a special affinity for the Rationals, a singular ability to appreciate their "iconoclasm,"[63] their "strong will,"[64] their "ingenuity,"[65] and their "resoluteness "[66] And, indeed, Jane begins to acquire a taste for what she thinks of as Rochester's "faults": his arrogance and willfulness give relish to her life "like keen condiments in a choice dish"; his harsh brilliance becomes precious to her, like "pure gold"; his blunt directiveness ceases to intimidate her and becomes "more cheering than the brightest fire"; and even his glowering expression helps her feel more closely "akin to him," as if able to understand intuitively "the language of his countenance and movements."

Jane knows she is seeing Rochester now through the eyes of love—"I had rejected the real," she confesses, "and rabidly devoured the ideal." But I must say that Jane's feelings for

---

[63]David Keirsey, *Please Understand Me*, p. 75.

[64]David Keirsey, *Portraits of Temperament*, p. 71.

[65]David Keirsey, *Portraits of Temperament*, p. 94.

[66]David Keirsey, *Portraits of Temperament*, p. 106.

Rochester also seem rooted in their earlier conversation about his "re-transformation," and they seem, sadly, to include plans for an Idealist Pygmalion project. Jane mentions, with fully the best of intentions, that

> I believed he was naturally a man of better tendencies, higher principles, and purer tastes than such as circumstances had developed, education instilled, or destiny encouraged. I thought there were excellent materials in him.[67]

In the same way, while Rochester praises Jane's "gravity, considerateness, and caution," and while he deeply envies her the integrity of a conscience "without blot or contamination," he wonders if Jane is not at times too serious and pure for her own good. "Do you never laugh, Miss Eyre?" he asks her, and have "you never felt jealousy?" Also, it irks him that a young girl "not passed the porch of life" should take it upon herself to advise him on his moral improvement—once he even growls at her, "you are not my conscience-keeper!" And though he too is coming to feel an extraordinary "natural sympathy" with Jane, he bedevils her with a Gypsy-like reading of what he thinks is her one real barrier to happiness, an over-scrupulous attitude which says to the world,

> "I have an inward treasure, born with me, which can keep me alive....The passions may rage furiously, like true heathens, as they are...but judgment shall still have the last word in every argument, and the casting vote in every decision. Strong wind, earth-quake-shock, and fire may pass by: but I shall follow the guiding of that still small voice of conscience."[68]

Although, under normal circumstances, Rationals are remarkably objective and non-manipulative with their loved ones, Rochester's questions and criticisms of Jane during these months are far from disinterested. Much as Jane

[67]Charlotte Brontë, *Jane Eyre*, p. 150.
[68]Charlotte Brontë, *Jane Eyre*, p. 203.

cherishes her dreams of restoring Rochester to his "higher principles" and "purer tastes," so Rochester secretly hopes he can somehow relax Jane's conscience and open her mind to a desperate proposal—indeed, a proposal of marriage. Thus, early one spring morning, Rochester tells Jane that, after growing so close in their friendship, he is certain she would follow him in doing "all that is right"—but then he poses a suspicious question to her: what would happen, he wonders, "if I bid you do what you thought wrong?" Rochester is certain he knows Jane's answer: "my little friend," he predicts, "would then turn to me, quiet and pale, and would say, 'No, sir; that is impossible: I cannot do it, because it is wrong.'"

Jane nods solemnly in agreement, and Rochester retraces his steps and tries a more hypothetical approach. Bidding Jane to "call to aid your fancy," he describes the case of how a "heart-weary" man meets by chance a "good and bright" young girl who miraculously revives in him those "higher wishes" he thought were lost to him forever. Then he presents Jane with a dilemma:

> Is the wandering and sinful, but now rest-seeking and repentant, man justified in daring the world's opinion...in over-leaping an obstacle of custom...in order to attach to him for ever this gentle, gracious, genial stranger; thereby securing his own peace of mind and regeneration of life?[69]

Put this way, the problem is deeply perplexing to Jane. Does the goal she treasures most in life (personal regeneration) justify a type of behavior (unsanctioned action) she finds profoundly wrong? Do moral ends, in short, justify immoral means? Jane doesn't know what to say, and is calling upon some "good spirit" to help her find a "judicious response," when Rochester sees her conscience arching its back and tries to change the intense mood of the

---

[69]Charlotte Brontë, *Jane Eyre*, p. 220.

conversation. He laughs bitterly and pretends he has been talking about another girl he escorts in society, and he jokes that "if I married her she would regenerate me with a vengeance."

This mystifying and aborted exchange is as near as Rochester ever comes (before their wedding day, at least) to telling Jane the horrible truth he is hiding from the world: that he is already married, duped as a very young man by a rich Creole girl, a deceiving Artisan beauty who dragged him through four years of "hideous and degrading agonies," who fell eventually into a violent, murderous insanity—and who has lived ever since locked in a cell on the third floor of Thornfield, fed and tended by Grace Poole. Rochester knows he should tell Jane the tale of his tortured life plainly, "and make my proposals openly" (he will admit to Jane later, "I was wrong to attempt to deceive you....This was cowardly"). But Jane's love and trust mean so much to him, and he is so wary of what he calls the moral "stubbornness...in [her] character," that he decides to withhold the truth from Jane until he has safely married her.

There is, however, a more fundamental reason for Rochester's decision than the power of his love or his fear of Jane's conscience. Again, Keirsey argues that Rationals are pragmatic in their behavior, which is to say that they are more interested in judging by their own lights and "achieving their aims" than in "observing the rules"[70] of law or morality that govern most human interactions. In essence, Rochester sees himself as married to the monstrous woman on the third floor only in a legal sense, or perhaps a religious sense, and he regards any arbitrary law as "a mere conventional impediment" to him marrying someone else

---

[70]Ray Choiniere and David Keirsey, *Presidential Temperament*, p. 9.

he truly holds dear. Though he knows that "in the eyes of the world" such disregard for legality would surely cover him in "grimy dishonour," Rochester insists he cares only "to be clean in my own sight," and he sees it as "absolutely rational that I should be considered free to love and be loved." His marriage contract might be legally binding, the wedding ceremony might have been witnessed by God, but Rochester, Brontë tells us, "reasoned thus: 'That woman, who has so...sullied your name; so outraged your honour; so blighted your youth—is not your wife: nor are you her husband.'" Life bound to her "is hell!" he cries, and he concludes (like Prometheus chained to the rock), "'I have the right to deliver myself from it if I can.'"

Acting out of the great passions of love and fear, then, but also out of his Rational's passionate pragmatism, Rochester disdains moral sanction and reaches out of his personal hell for the hand of Jane Eyre, his "angel of light," as he calls her, and the consequences unfold inexorably. Rochester proposes to Jane in the garden at Thornfield, vowing almost savagely, "For the world's judgment, I wash my hands thereof. For man's opinion—I defy it." And Jane, believing he means only society's opinion of her as a poor governess, quickly overcomes her shyness, and her doubts about Rochester's sincerity, and lets the love she has kept for months under a "wholesome discipline" finally bloom in her heart.

The ominous storm blows up without warning and, as I have said, lightning splits the chestnut tree, but Jane loves Rochester too devotedly—with all her "heart, soul, and strength"—to heed nature's warning. Jane does sense some unspoken anguish near Rochester's heart, and she does read a "sign" in the gaping trunk of the chestnut; but she is sure the message is one of enduring love, telling her to cleave to

Rochester and support him in his pain, just as the two charred halves of the tree even now intertwined their branches and held "fast to each other...at the faithful, honest roots."

The wedding day soon arrives, and with it Rochester's brother-in-law from the West Indies, whose lawyer stands up in the village church and stops the ceremony at the altar. And indeed, the truth he delivers—"Mr. Rochester has a wife now living"—seems more shattering than any lightning bolt in the orchard. The Guardian clergyman (named Mr. "Wood") is stunned and thrown back onto canon law, insisting that the proceedings must be halted. Rochester is shaken to his roots by a "spasm...of fury [and] despair," his black eyes glowing with a "bloody light...as from spreading heartfire." And Jane remembers her own nerves vibrating violently, "as they had never vibrated to thunder."

Rochester's every instinct tells him to disregard the "priest of the gospel and man of the law," and hold onto Jane by the strength of his will—and turning from the minister to face the lawyer, he "twined my waist with his arm," Jane recalls, "and riveted me to his side." Jane, on the other hand, confesses to feeling almost immediately torn and deadened by Rochester's falseness—"struck with a subtle doom," she calls it—and she can think only of freeing herself from Rochester's grasp. Keirsey points out that Counselors (like all the other Idealists) often idealize their loved ones beyond "the realities of human nature," and have grave difficulty accepting the fact that "though some of us have hearts of gold we also have feet of clay."[71] And such fatal disillusionment certainly seems to be Jane's

---

[71]David Keirsey, *Portraits of Temperament*, p. 89.

reaction to the disclosure: as soon as she is alone she rushes to her room, shuts herself in, and stares vacantly at her lost image of Rochester, knowing in her heart that

> never more could [she] turn to him; for faith was blighted—
> confidence destroyed! Mr. Rochester was not to me what he
> had been; for he was not what I thought him...the attribute of
> stainless truth was gone from his idea; and from his presence I
> must go.[72]

After hours of silent grief, her "head swimming" in confusion, her "heart...weeping blood," Jane steals downstairs to make her escape, only to stumble into Rochester's waiting arms. Rochester recognizes her desperate intention and he vows to stop Jane from leaving Thornfield, first (in his exasperation) by threat of force: "Jane, I am not a gentle-tempered man—you forget that." But Rochester knows that physical violence can never capture what he loves most in Jane, her Counselor's "spirit...and energy," and so, regaining his composure, he marshals a series of rational arguments, designed to prove that he "had a right to break the [marriage] compact." Demanding, "Jane, you must be reasonable," "Jane, will you hear reason?" Rochester first tries to make the case that his marriage was a swindle, explaining how his father secretly arranged the marriage for money, and how the girl's family concealed her madness from him. Next he tries to discredit his wife, telling Jane the long story of her loathsome depravities and her growing viciousness (citing her "coarse, perverse" nature and her "pygmy intellect"). Then he tries to appeal to Jane's sense of justice, describing the "horrible...wretched" life she condemns him to if she

---

[72]Charlotte Brontë, *Jane Eyre*, p. 298. I will discuss this issue of over-idealizing at great length in Chapter Five in my portrait of Angel Clare—who, I might add, uses many of these same words about his stained bride, Tess Durbeyfield.

leaves Thornfield, and reminding her (this is very important to Rationals) that staying with him as his wife involves "no man being injured."

Jane's heart fills with pity and forgiveness as she listens to Rochester; she knows that she loves him "more than ever," and that "no human being...could wish to be loved better than I was loved." And yet, almost immediately (and as Rochester had always feared), Jane's "conscience, turned tyrant, held passion by the throat," and she clings fiercely to her belief in the need for moral sanction. "I will keep the law given by God [and] sanctioned by man," she resolves, answering Rochester with an argument persuasive to Idealists (and absolutely binding to Guardians), that our commitment to moral law is the only thing standing between us and social or personal chaos:

> Laws and principles are not for the times when there is no temptation: they are for such moments as this, when body and soul rise up in mutiny against their rigour....If at my individual convenience I might break them, what would be their worth? They have a worth—so I have always believed; and if I cannot believe it now, it is because I am insane—quite insane.[73]

Rationals also believe rigorously in laws and principles—the laws of science and the principles of personal fidelity—and Rochester declares his "resistless *bent* to love" Jane "faithfully and well," and he commands her to step above "mere human law" and give him her pledge of love: "Jane—give it to me now." But, again, Jane's conscience grips her heart in this dreadful moment like "a hand of fiery iron," and she can think only of what she calls her "intolerable duty." Despite confessing that she "worshipped" Rochester and "longed to be his," she is determined to "renounce" his love and leave him "decidedly, instantly, entirely." Rochester, withering Jane

---

[73]Charlotte Brontë, *Jane Eyre*, p. 319.

with "his flaming glance," argues on against such self-sacrifice—"what a distortion in your judgment, what a perversity in your ideas, is proved by your conduct!" But Jane, her heart "beating faster than [she] can count its throbs," stands firm on what she calls the "preconceived" principles she has always held dear: they "are all I have at this hour," she feels, and "there I plant my foot."

Although Jane seems steadfast in her decision to tear herself from Rochester (and indeed she slips away early the next morning with little more than the clothes on her back), she is still badly caught on the horns of her Pygmalion dilemma. She knows that if she consents to stay with Rochester, she might well pull him back from the abyss and regenerate him spiritually: she might "soothe him, save him, love him...be his comforter—his pride; his redeemer from misery; perhaps from ruin." But to live with Rochester on his shameless Rational terms—essentially as his mistress—would mean to abandon her own vital Idealist values, and thus cost her the very essence of her self-esteem, her integrity.[74] To save Rochester, in short, would mean to lose herself.

And so she is left (like so many Idealists) struggling with a deeply divided moral commitment, longing fervently "to do what was right, and only that," and yet punishing herself for having chosen the rigors of moral sanction over the tenderness of human love and sympathy. "In the midst of my pain of heart, and frantic effort of principle," Jane realizes, "I abhorred myself. I had no solace from self-approbation: none even from self-respect." Instead of holding fast like the scorched fragment of the chestnut tree, Jane turns away when she is most needed, and she condemns herself for having "injured—wounded—left my master." Jane tells herself that she has kept "inviolate" the

---

[74]David Keirsey, *Portraits of Temperament*, pp. 91, 102-103.

laws of morality, and that in spite of temptation she "still possessed [her] soul," but as she presses blindly to reach the road leading away from Thornfield Hall, such thoughts of virtue and purity are cold comfort.

And yet, on some level, the spirit of the chestnut tree endures in Jane. She had marvelled after the storm that "the cloven halves were not broken from each other, for the firm base and strong roots kept them unsundered below." And now, though separated from Rochester by more than distance, Jane feels this unconscious connection at her deep heart's core. As I have said, Brontë strains Jane and Rochester's underlying sense of unity almost to breaking in *Jane Eyre*, but at the last moment their love prevails in the most fantastic way.

After fleeing Thornfield and very nearly dying as a beggar on the road, Jane is taken in and nursed back to health at the house of a handsome young clergyman named St. John Rivers. As his name suggests, St. John (a Monastic) is a figure of saintly virtue and purity in the novel, and he eventually asks Jane to turn her talents to God by marrying him and sharing his life as a missionary in India. Clearly, St. John is the moral alternative to Rochester in *Jane Eyre*—the contrast could not be more pointed—and in this way Brontë severely tests Jane's decision to live by the dictates of her Idealist's conscience. Jane does not love St. John, and she understands that marrying him now would be "an error of judgment," quite as much as marrying Rochester before "would have been an error of principle." But she admires St. John's brooding godliness and his earnest morality, and one moonlit night she is about to give in to his entreaties—when a sudden, mysterious thrill passes through her heart and limbs, not "like an electric shock," she says, but "quite as sharp, as strange, as startling" as a lightning storm. Jane looks quickly around her and listens "expectant," and she hears a faint voice—Rochester's—somewhere crying, "Jane! Jane! Jane!" in tones of "pain and woe, wildly, eerily, urgently." Jane does not know what this unearthly summons means, but she realizes she cannot marry St. John without seeing her beloved master again, and she leaves for Thornfield the next morning.

Although this moment of telepathic communication is the climax of *Jane Eyre*, and surely one of the most memorable scenes in nineteenth century fiction, it has been dismissed by a good many critics as merely one of a number of trappings which Brontë borrowed from the Gothic novel to add a touch of mystery or ghostliness to Jane's narrative. But while the scene does strain credulity, it should not be dismissed too easily as melodramatic supernaturalism. Keirsey suggests that "what is known as ESP" may well be a kind of extraordinarily dynamic intuition—in both its forms, projection and introjection—and he observes that this ability to transmit and receive information empathically is found in Counselor Idealists "more than in any other types":

> this capability extends to people, things, and often events, taking the form of visions, episodes of foreknowledge, premonitions, auditory and visual images of things to come. [Counselors] can have uncanny communications with certain individuals at a distance.[75]

Charlotte Brontë (herself a Counselor) certainly believed in the possibility of extrasensory perception, "at least for finely tuned individuals," and she defended the authenticity of the phenomenon in *Jane Eyre*: "But it is a true thing,"

---

[75]David Keirsey, *Please Understand Me*, p. 171.

she insisted to her biographer, "it really happened!"[76] And Jane, in turn, tells us several times in the novel of the "strange presentiments" she has felt throughout her life, and of her belief that "signs, for aught we know, may be but the sympathies of Nature with man."[77]

At all events, whether Jane's empathic ability is "natural" or not, her reconciliation with Rochester is truly miraculous. Returning to Thornfield, Jane finds the manor burned to ruin, the lunatic wife dead—consumed in the fire she set herself—and Rochester alive, but gruesomely scarred, lame in one hand, and virtually blind. Rochester's devastation, however, is just as horrible on the inside, and Jane's eyes fill with tears when she sees how much of his personal fire has been burned out of him, leaving him sullen and defeated: "it was mournful, indeed," she remembers, "to witness the subjugation of that vigorous spirit."

In truth, we see the FieldMarshal at his most weakened in these last pages of *Jane Eyre*. Rationals pride themselves on their power to be independent and their ability to achieve,[78] and having to live with what Rochester calls such insufferable "infirmities" and "deficiencies" is the cruellest fate imaginable. When Jane arrives, Rochester seems all but crushed under that fate: he is self-conscious about his "hideous" disfigurement; he is ashamed of his "crippled strength"; and he feels nullified and impotent, left useless by his "seared vision." But most surprising of all, Rochester seems morally chastened by the fire. He has been "an irreligious dog," he confesses to Jane, but now he says he

---

[76]Quoted in Arthur Zeiger's "Afterword" to *Jane Eyre* (Signet Classic, 1960), p. 459.

[77]Behavioral scientists—Keirsey included—have been and still are divided in opinion on how to regard research reports on so-called "psychic phenomena" and "parapsychology."

[78]David Keirsey, *Portraits of Temperament*, pp. 67, 71.

regrets his "stiff-necked rebellion" against God's law, and he understands that in asking Jane to live with him in sin, "I did wrong: I would have sullied my innocent flower—breathed guilt on its purity.[79]

In one way, Jane is grateful that Rochester has learned to curb his arrogance and show the first signs of a Christian conscience; the fire seems to have done much of her Pygmalion work for her, and she assures him he is a better man now than "in your state of proud independence." The point must not be lost, however, that Idealists are also drawn to Rationals in great part *because of* their their proud independence, and while Jane is pleased that Rochester seems tamed and contrite, she can hardly bear to see him so deeply mired in his weakness and frustration. Once her "fierce falcon" and "royal eagle," he now looks to Jane like a "caged eagle...chained to a perch." His once fiery countenance (with flashing "falcon eye") now reminds her of a "lamp quenched, waiting to be relit." And though Jane has never thought of Rochester as a handsome man (no "graceful Apollo" like St. John), it breaks her heart to hear him refer to himself now as "Vulcan," the only god the Greeks pictured as lame and ugly.

Ironically, while the fire has shackled and humbled Rochester, it has granted Jane her most fervent wish, freeing her from her soul's dilemma. With the lawful wife now dead, Jane no longer need defy moral sanction in order to love Rochester and regenerate him, and almost immediately she takes up the task of bringing his spirit alive: "it is time," she says, "some one undertook to rehumanise you." The light in Rochester's eyes might be nearly out, but Jane has all her Counselor's confidence that

---

[79]Charlotte Brontë, *Jane Eyre*, pp. 449-450.

she can "waken the glow" of life in him again, and "kindle the lustre" of joy in his soul.

Jane was reluctant to join St. John Rivers on his mission in India, but to this mission of revitalizing Rochester she gladly devotes her Counselor's two great interpersonal talents: her enthusiasm and her love. "I accosted him with...vivacity," she recalls—and almost at once Rochester responds: "Blind as he was," she remembers, "smiles played over his face, joy dawned on his forehead: his lineaments softened and warmed." And when Jane finally tells Rochester that to love him and help him is her most "sincere...prayer," the delight is so great in him, "his features beamed" so brightly, that she is able to bask in the radiance: "it brought to life and light my whole nature: in his presence I thoroughly lived; and he lived in mine."

Rationals are skeptical to the end, however, and Rochester must question Jane one last time how she can possibly love "a crippled man, twenty years older than you, whom you will have to wait on." Rationals disparage themselves almost unrelentingly for their flaws and frailties, and Rochester fumes to Jane, "I am no better than the old lightning-struck chestnut-tree in Thornfield orchard." But Jane is the master of this metaphor, and she welcomes the chance to come full circle and let the image of a gnarled but newly-branching tree express her message of personal rebirth through love:

> You are no ruin, sir—no lightning-struck tree: you are green and vigorous. Plants will grow about your roots, whether you ask them or not, because they take delight in your bountiful shadow; and as they grow they will lean towards you, and wind round you, because [of] your strength.[80]

---

[80]Charlotte Brontë, *Jane Eyre*, pp. 447-448.

Although Jane is delighted with her metaphor, such a prospect of clinging friendship is not at all what Rochester had in mind. "Ah! Jane," he stops her, "but I want a wife," and it is on this point that Jane knows she must encourage Rochester most sensitively. Rochester is too humiliated by his deformities to ask openly for Jane's hand; in fact, he puts himself into her hands to decide the matter, telling Jane that she must choose *for* him the woman he will marry, and promising her that "I will abide by your decision."

While such new-found power and independence in the relationship thrill Jane, and while her heart's desire has always been to become Rochester's wife, she knows that she must not play the dominant role he has assigned her. Jane realizes that Rochester, as a Rational, and especially as a FieldMarshal, must take command of his own life, and she understands that reviving his autonomy and strength of will is more important than exercising her own. And so she gently counsels Rochester to search his heart and make up his own mind: "Choose then, sir—*her who loves you best.*" And Rochester, urged thus to assert his old self-confidence and decisiveness, steps forward to settle the issue: "I will at least choose—*her I love best.* Jane, will you marry me?"

Jane and Rochester quickly wed—within three days, Rochester insists—and the "natural sympathy" they have felt for each other, almost from their first meeting, does indeed grow bountifully. Although Jane recognized immediately that some differences would "sever us widely," she also knew instinctively that "I have something in my brain and heart, in my blood and nerves, that assimilates me mentally to him." And even after ten years of marriage (when she sits down to write her life's story), she can take sublime pleasure in the compatibility—especially in the rare ability to communicate about their interior worlds—that many Idealists develop with their Rational mates:

> To be together is for us to be as once as free as in solitude, as gay as in company. We talk, I believe, all day long: to talk to each other is but a more animated and an audible thinking. All my confidence is bestowed on him, all his confidence is devoted to me; we are precisely suited in character.[81]

* * * * *

To arrive at this sort of consummate interpersonal unity is the dream of all the Counselors (all the Idealists, for that matter), and Konstantin Levin and Jane Eyre illustrate two different but rather typical paths to happiness for Counselors and their loved ones. In relationships with relatively little "natural sympathy" (as is frequently the case with Guardians), Counselors can come to appreciate the domestic responsibility and social skill of their mates, and often, as Levin shows us, the soul-searching they go through in such relationships brings them to a deeper understanding of themselves and their expectations. In relationships with Rationals, on the other hand, Counselors often feel an immediately satisfying "meeting of minds," and their future happiness, like Jane's, depends on finding some kind of workable reconciliation between their own ethical, respectful nature and the Rational's deeply grained pragmatism and iconoclasm.

No matter what the mix in their relationships, however, Counselors must guard against instigating Pygmalion projects that try to coerce such ideal unity with their loved ones. Keirsey reminds us that Counselors, armed with their enthusiasm for personal development, and proceeding with surely the best of intentions, believe that they are simply

---

[81]Charlotte Brontë, *Jane Eyre*, p. 454.

helping their Artisan or Guardian loved ones "find soul and significance" in their lives, and that they are merely rescuing their Rational mates "from [the] seeming folly"[82] of their promethean defiance.

---

[82]David Keirsey, *Please Understand Me*, p. 75.

Chapter 5

The
Teacher

> She became inspired....A great eagerness to open the door of life...for the understanding of life, had possession of her.
>
> ———Sherwood Anderson[1]

Although Miriam Leivers (a Monastic) ushers herself through a "gate of suffering" in her sexual awakening, although Newland Archer (an Advocate) hopes to "open doors" for his wife's imagination, and although Jane Eyre (a Counselor) can trace her very name to the Roman god of gates and doorways, the Idealist most committed to guiding others through the doors of life, or along the pathways of learning and understanding, is the type that Keirsey has named the Teacher (Myers's "ENFJ").

Teachers are natural facilitators in all their relationships, encouraging those around them, urging their personal growth, and taking charge of others (particularly of groups)

---

[1] Sherwood Anderson, *Winesburg, Ohio* (Viking Compass edition, 1971), p. 164.

with an extraordinary enthusiasm and confidence. Indeed, Teachers are so expressive and charismatic in their leadership—in a word, so *inspiring*—that they seem in some ways less coercive than the other Idealists. Keirsey says that, though Teachers are both expressive and role-directive, they manage to "command without seeming to do so,"[2] not by means of explicit orders, nor through saintly patience, romantic longing, or mute withdrawal, but by kindling in their students and colleagues their own passion for self-exploration and development. Teachers are masters of the art of positive expectation (or "front-loading"), and they communicate their belief in the evolution of the "self" with such a glow of promise that quite often, as Keirsey tells us, their optimism "induces action" in others, and the "desire to live up to [their] expectations."[3]

Teachers bring all this infectious energy to their intimate relationships as well, and they make passionate and delightfully creative companions. However, at such close range the intensity of their wishes for their loved ones can create interpersonal conflict. Teachers can overwhelm their loved ones with their exuberance, and with their Pygmalion presumption that *everyone* wants to be helped along the path of self-discovery. Then, when their loved ones either resist their pressure or fail to meet their idealistic expectations, Teachers can feel frustrated, disillusioned, or even betrayed by the persons they care most about.

Angel Clare

This Pygmalion scenario of attribution-and-disappointment is acted out to some extent by all the Idealists, and I have

---

[2]David Keirsey, *Portraits of Temperament*, p. 97.
[3]David Keirsey, *Portraits of Temperament*, p. 97.

touched on it in nearly all of my portraits in this book. But Keirsey emphasizes that Teachers, with their vibrant imaginations and their radiantly hopeful outlook, are "especially vulnerable to idealizing interpersonal relationships, raising these relationships to a plane which seldom can sustain the realities of human nature."[4] To a novelist interested in the complexities of human interaction, such an idealizing imagination—and such a denial of reality—holds the seeds of tragic disaffection. And I know of no work of English or American literature that presents this tragedy more poignantly than Thomas Hardy's *Tess of the d'Urbervilles* (1891)

As I detailed in *Volume Two: The Guardian*, Hardy's novel tells the sorrowful story of Tess Durbeyfield, a beautiful Wessex village girl (and Protector Guardian ["ISFJ"]), who comes to ruin at the hands of her false cousin, Alec d'Urberville, a wealthy and unscrupulous Promoter Artisan ("ESTP"). While the events in the first two sections of the novel, which culminate in Tess's seduction, her pregnancy, and the death of her baby, are certainly painful to read, Hardy's attitude in *Tess* is that the workings of fate are not merely unhappy, but profoundly malicious, a view perhaps best expressed (as Hardy himself points out) by Gloucester in Shakespeare's *King Lear*:

> As flies to wanton boys are we to the gods;
> They kill us for their sport.[5]

Very likely reflecting the terrible estrangement in his own marriage, Hardy came to regard the human aspiration to find fulfillment in love as an "irksome, outworn game,"

---

[4]David Keirsey, *Please Understand Me*, p. 167.
[5]Hardy cites these lines in his "Preface to the Fifth and Later Editions" of *Tess of the d'Urbervilles*.

with the hope for happiness first held out and then cruelly
dashed by the gods, apparently for no larger purpose than
their own sadistic amusement. Rephrasing Robert
Browning's well-known lines (which became almost the
motto of the Victorian age), Hardy admonishes his readers
that "God's *not* in His Heaven; all's *wrong* with the world."
And, accordingly, he portrays Tess's search for love not as
a triumph over adversity, not even as a noble descent into
catastrophe, but as an "impish—demoniacally funny"
entanglement of "anxieties, disappointments, [and] shocks,"
until the "President of the Immortals," as Hardy puts it,
"ended his sport with Tess" and destroys her utterly.

Hardy ponders these mocking twists of fate when Tess first
meets Alec d'Urberville in the novel, wondering why she
"was doomed to be seen and coveted that day by the wrong
man and not by some other man, the right and desired one."
Tess had, in fact, encountered this "right" young man only a
month earlier, during a May-day festival on the village
green, when a stranger (a student on a walking tour of the
countryside) paused to dance with some of the farm girls.
After a round or two with the bolder girls, the young
gentleman caught Tess's bashful eye, lingered a moment as
if to say something, then turned with a sigh and resumed his
journey. Tess watched him longingly until he disappeared
in the distance, and then turned back to her modest,
innocent life, a life which was soon to be torn from her
forever by Alec's deceitfulness. Tess is destined to meet
this young man, Angel Clare, again in the novel, but only
when her fate has been decided, and when his Teacher's
idealizing imagination can only further her destruction.

In pointed contrast with the black-haired and full-blooded
Alec d'Urberville, Angel Clare takes his place in the novel
as a slight and "sensitive" young man, with "fixed,

abstracted eyes," a thin, straw-colored beard, and a mouth perhaps "too small and delicately lined for a man's," though Hardy adds that Angel now and again shows "an unexpectedly firm close of the lower lip...enough to do away with any inference of indecision." As I explained in the last chapter, Mentor Idealists display a curious combination of diffuseness and decisiveness in their character, and Hardy observes quite accurately that, while Angel is impossibly "nebulous" and "vague" about the details of his "material future," and while he is forever "neglecting the particulars of an outward scene for the general impression,"[6] the young man nevertheless has clearly-defined personal goals. Indeed, about the time of his excursion past Tess's village, Angel is deciding how to tell his father that he intends to go to Cambridge, earn a university degree, and become "a teacher of men."

Angel's father, unfortunately, has other plans for his somewhat headstrong son. The Reverend James Clare (an Inspector Guardian ["ISTJ"]) is a village parson of the old Evangelical school—a man "not merely religious," Hardy calls him, "but devout; a firm believer." Mr. Clare is also a Guardian parent, with firmly established expectations for his sons, one of which is that Angel, like his two older brothers before him, will go to Cambridge to prepare himself to enter the Anglican Church. Hardy tells us that this view of Cambridge as a stepping-stone to holy orders is a "family tradition" with Angel's father, a custom so deeply "rooted" in the "straightforward and simple-minded" vicar that, when Angel begins secretly to order books on Greek

---

[6]David Shapiro describes the cognitive style of the Hysterical personality as "lacking in sharpness, particularly in sharp detail. In a word it is *impressionistic*" (*Neurotic Styles*, p. 111).

mythology, and then to voice his own ideas about his education, Mr. Clare is "shocked" and "stultified."

Angel's view of religion, like many Idealists', is humanistic and reforming, not "literal and grammatical" like his father's, and though Angel promises sincerely that he will always have "the warmest affection" for Church history, he also confesses to his father that he is far more interested in studying Platonic moral philosophy than Anglican "theolatry," and he insists that he cannot in good conscience allow himself to be ordained a minister in such a rigid institution. Again, Mr. Clare is appalled at these blasphemies, and tries a familiar Guardian tactic to shame Angel into obedience: he grieves so piteously for his son's waywardness that, Hardy says, "it made Angel quite ill to see him." But if an Idealist holds contempt for anything, as Keirsey points out, it is for "the bigot with his blind prejudices."[7] And thus, when Angel's father finally comes out and implores him, "what is the good of...a university education if it is not to be used for the honour and glory of God?" Angel answers without hesitation, "why, that it may be used for the honour and glory of man."

Despite his confident reply, Angel feels the pangs of having failed his father, and instead of arguing further he surprises everyone by renouncing any claim he might have to follow his brothers to the university. This rash sacrifice of his rightful education has unforeseen consequences, both for Angel himself and ultimately for Tess. First, without the discipline of an organized course of study Idealists tend to let themselves wander and browse intellectually, and Hardy tells us that Angel gives himself over for several years to "desultory studies, undertakings, and meditations." Instead

---

[7]David Keirsey, *Portraits of Temperament*, p. 92.

of pursuing his passionate interest in teaching, Angel finds he prefers "reading as his musings inclined him, without cramming for a profession." Angel is not proud of his mental aimlessness, but he justifies it by telling himself he is exercising his "intellectual liberty"—a stubborn independence of mind which typifies the Mentor Idealists, and which Hardy says Angel "valued even more than a competency."

At the same time, giving up Cambridge makes Angel feel deep in his heart that he has "been made to miss his true destiny through the prejudices of his family," and so with a good deal of underlying bitterness he turns his back on almost all the Guardian "social forms and observances" his parents and his brothers hold dear. He comes to resent the "material distinctions of rank and wealth" which his father and mother religiously observe. He develops an "almost unreasonable aversion to modern town life," which sorely tries the patience of his brothers, two more Inspector Guardians whom Hardy caricatures as "correct to their remotest fibre" and snobbishly devoted to "civilized society." And flying in the face of his father's idea of a "truly Christian" woman (and his mother's notion of "a lady"), Angel has a brief and sordid affair with an "older woman" in London. Eventually, Angel abandons Victorian religion and society altogether, deciding that he will seek his destiny in rural farming life, which he has romanticized as being like the "pastoral life [of] ancient Greece."

In several ways, Angel's experience at this time parallels Tess's. Both "had been made to break an accepted social law" (Tess in society at large, Angel in his family). Both feel cheated of their dreams and see themselves as outcasts from their homes. And both (as the gods look on and laugh) are drawn to the same southern corner of Wessex county to begin their lives over again.

Thus, the next spring, as Angel settles in as an apprentice at Talbothay's dairy in the Froom valley, Tess arrives at the same destination to take up work as a milkmaid. Tess has lived through her shame, buried her baby, and believes she is finished forever with the treacherous attentions of men. But as fate would have it the valley is sprawling and lush, the season is irresistibly fertile—the whole of nature seems "surging up anew," Hardy tells us, "with an "invincible instinct towards self-delight"—and inevitably Tess and Angel begin falling under each other's spell.

Angel rooms upstairs in an attic over the dairy-house, and as his name "Angel" suggests he spends much of his free time "up above" the rest of the farm hands, pensively "strumming upon an old harp," or reading "abstractedly from some book." Keirsey points out, that while all the Idealists are "interested in people-watching."[8] Teachers are especially prone to "read other people,"[9] for their personalities. And Hardy, in turn, describes Angel as so intent "to read human nature" that he insists on taking his meals downstairs with the assembled dairyfolk, a practice which soon leads him to regard the workers not as the "Hodge" (i.e., "hayseed") characters made fun of in the popular press, but as distinct and varied individuals, and to take a "real delight in their companionship."

This bright young gentleman, so "educated, reserved, subtle," and yet so kindly and so eager to be friendly, becomes the hopeless dream of all the milkmaids, and Tess is drawn reluctantly into the romance of his odd situation at

---

[8]David Keirsey, *Please Understand Me*, p. 65.
[9]David Keirsey, *Please Understand Me*, p. 168.

the dairy, daydreaming about him as an "admirable and poetic man" laboring secretly at Talbothay's, like Peter the Great in the shipyards. Tess also clearly remembers Angel as the sensitive young student from the May-day dance (from a time before her trouble), and "like a fascinated bird" she watches him now with his books and music, believing him to be far above her morally and intellectually, very much "an intelligence rather than a man," and surely out of place in what she thinks of as her own "Valley of Humiliation." This is not to say that Tess entirely loses her head over Angel. Tess is a cautious young Guardian who is well aware of social and intellectual barriers, and who has learned the harsh consequences of loving above her station in life. And for a time she manages to keep her feelings under control and to continue in what Hardy calls her "repressed life."

Angel, on the other hand, is enchanted by Tess's extraordinary beauty, and by the deep tinge of sadness in her character, and he quickly begins to idealize her out of all recognition. Angel first notices Tess when she is shyly explaining to the dairyman (in "her own native phrases") the unfairness of life and her feeling of being a lost soul in the world. Tess has certainly had more than her share of sorrow, but Angel (who knows nothing of her past) immediately projects his own Idealist beliefs about "the ache" of nineteenth century industrial civilization into her simple Guardian expressions of grief. Angel is astonished—and delighted—to find in a provincial dairy farm what he believes to be "a milkmaid [with] just that touch of rarity about her," and he offers to become her teacher and develop her rude understanding: "I should be only too glad," he promises her, "to help you to anything in the way of history or any line of reading you would like to take up." Tess declines moodily, but when Angel presses her (with "some enthusiasm")—"What, really, then, you don't want to learn anything?"—she finally confesses, "I shouldn't mind learning why...the sun do shine on the just and the unjust alike."

The conflict of personality type in this interchange—the Teacher's natural enthusiasm for self-development, against the Protector's weary concern with portion and punishment—is unmistakable, but Angel's imagination here is waxing more and more poetical, and he proceeds to exalt Tess in her despair, to project his own Idealist spirituality into her Guardian dispiritedness. In the spectral early morning light, for example, before the rest of the workers are up, Tess the humble milkmaid seems to Angel to take on "a dignified largeness both of disposition and physique, an almost regnant power." Then, walking in the mist to the meadow, Tess appears to transcend the gloom and float over the earth in what Angel sees as "a sort of phosphorescence...as if she were merely a soul at large."

At these times (Hardy calls them the "non-human hours"), Tess is no longer a slim, somber young girl to Angel, but "a visionary essence of woman," and even when he recognizes Tess as a down-to-earth personality he invests her with mythical proportions. Hardy observes that Angel likes to call Tess "Artemis, Demeter, and other fanciful names,"[10] transforming her from a vulnerable young farm girl into a powerful "divinity who could confer bliss" onto mere mortals. Needless to say, Angel's spiritualized, goddess-like vision of Tess is in some ways the harmless fantasy of

---

[10]As goddess of the hunt and wild things, Artemis is clearly associated with the Artisan ("SP") temperament, and as goddess of the corn and the harvest, Demeter is indeed the totem deity of the Guardians ("SJs"). See *The Pygmalion Project, Volumes One* and *Two*.

a young man in love, but Tess clearly feels the burden of his romanticizing. Against the pressure of being named "Artemis" and "Demeter," Tess pleads with Angel simply to "call me Tess."

Though as a Teacher he likes to believe his interest in Tess is purely intellectual, perhaps even platonic—"no more than a philosopher's regard"—Angel is poised on the edge of a more physical passion, and as the spring ripens into summer his feelings grow more heated. Angel might have been initially charmed by Tess's "strange and ethereal beauty," but amid what Hardy calls the "warm ferments of the Froom Vale" he soon finds himself responding more and more to her "pink-gowned form" and the "infatuating, maddening" curve of her upper lip. Idealists are often torn between the attractions of spiritual and physical beauty, and indeed, Angel concedes now that "there was nothing ethereal" about Tess's appeal, "all was real vitality, real warmth, real incarnation." Angel's natural inclination, Hardy reminds us, is to idealize Tess's charms—"perfect, he, as a lover, might have called them"—but in this more sensual mood he stops himself:

> no—they were not perfect. And it was the touch of the imperfect upon the would-be perfect that gave the sweetness, because it was that which gave the humanity.[11]

Even in this statement, however, Angel's restless (and contradictory) imagination is at work, striving to make Tess all the more sweetly perfect for her touch of imperfection. More than any other temperament, Idealists (particularly male Idealists) are thrown into spiritual distress by physical beauty—trembling as if in the presence of something

---

[11]Thomas Hardy, *Tess of the d'Urbervilles* (Signet Classic edition, 1964), p. 166. All quotations from *Tess of the d'Urbervilles* are from this edition.

divine—and Hardy concludes his analysis of Angel's growing passion with an observation that shows us this confusion quite well. Angel dreams of Tess's voluptuous red lips, and "could reproduce them mentally with ease"; but when he sees them in reality, "clothed with colour and life," they send "an *aura* over his flesh, a breeze through his nerves," like "nothing...on the face of the earth."

In any event, Tess's beauty—human or divine— overwhelms Angel, and "all resolutions, reticences, prudences, fears, fell back like a defeated battalion." He kneels at Tess's milking stool one fateful morning, takes her in his arms, and declares his love. Tess, taking alarm from her only other experience of men, breaks into tears (whether of joy or of sorrow it is impossible to tell), but Angel knows at once that "his heart had outrun his judgement." Though he is driven towards Tess "with every heave of his pulse," he quickly checks himself "for tender conscience's sake," begging her to forgive his passionate outburst. As an Idealist (and unlike Alec d'Urberville), Angel is very much "a man with a conscience," who feels that Tess is "no insignificant creature to toy with and dismiss," and Hardy's explanation of the source of Angel's moral sensitivity offers us an important insight into the Idealist character.

Hardy's argument, in essence, is that Angel's conscientious attitude toward Tess derives from his instinctively subjective view of existence. That is to say, Angel (like most Idealists) believes intuitively that one's life—indeed, reality itself—is the unique and personal creation of each individual's imagination, an internal dream of life which is then projected onto the outside world. Angel is a "contemplative being," Hardy points out, and as he struggles to come to grips with his feelings for Tess, he realizes that her "whole world depended" not on some external objective reality, but on her own internal vision and the richness of her "subjective experience." Angel sees that "the universe itself only came into being for Tess on the particular day in the particular year in which she was born," and that her personal envelope of "consciousness...was [her] single opportunity of existence." And because Tess's life is, to her, so unspeakably valuable,

> how, then, should he look upon her as of less consequence than himself; as a pretty trifle to caress and grow weary of; and not deal in the greatest seriousness with the affection which he knew that he had awakened in her?[12]

The contrast with Alec d'Urberville's concrete and utilitarian Artisan view of life—that people simply exist in the world to be used and enjoyed—couldn't be clearer. But let me add that, while the Idealists' subjective view of reality can lead to this kind of fundamental respect for other people, it also explains why Idealists so unconsciously project their own "reality" into those around them. And the tragic irony of Angel and Tess's relationship is that, while Angel shows careful consideration for Tess physically and emotionally, vowing not to approach her again unless she wishes it, he continues to violate her psychologically, forcing his ideal image onto her as surely as Alec d'Urberville did his sexual desire, and with similarly ruinous consequences.

From the first, Angel romanticized Tess as "a fresh and virginal daughter of Nature," thinking of her not as part of "real" nature at the dairy, but as a figure in some abstract Nature—Nature with a capital "N"—the innocent, idyllic Nature of poets and myth. And as his feelings for Tess bloom all that summer, so too does his poetical image of

---

[12]Thomas Hardy, *Tess of the d'Urbervilles*, p. 171.

her. He sees the morning mist, for instance, clinging to Tess's hair and eyelashes "like seed pearls." He compares her beautiful mouth (using his favorite "Elizabethan simile") to a garland of "roses filled with snow." He likens Tess in her purity to "the wild convolvulus out there in the garden hedge that opened itself this morning for the first time." Indeed, when he goes home to tell his parents of his intentions to marry a farm girl, he insists that

> she's brim full of poetry—actualized poetry, if I may use the expression. She *lives* what paper-poets only write.[13]

And when Tess reluctantly reveals to him that she is descended from the ancient d'Urberville line, Angel (despite his contempt for "rank and wealth") seems strangely pleased at the sound of calling his little Tess Durbeyfield "Mistress Teresa d'Urberville"—for Angel, Hardy tells us, "it was a pretty lover's dream."

Again, however, the Pygmalion pressure of Angel's idealizing is a terrible burden on Tess, and she resists it as best she can. When Angel, with his Teacher's role-directiveness, playfully instructs Tess, "you must spell your name correctly—d'Urberville—from this very day," she objects to such pretentiousness, replying timidly, "I like the other way rather best." But Tess can tell she has little chance of holding out against Angel's romantic image of her. Keirsey explains that Teachers often "unwittingly overpower" their loved ones with their ideals, even when their loved ones believe, like Tess, "that they cannot possible live up to [the Teacher's] perception of them."[14] And Hardy, turning around Angel's own metaphors of nature, describes Tess as very nearly wilting under the

---

[13]Thomas Hardy, *Tess of the d'Urbervilles*, p. 180.
[14]David Keirsey, *Please Understand Me*, p. 168.

intensity of his apollonian imagination: "she seemed to flinch under it," he says, "like a plant in too burning a sun."

The metaphor is fitting, for as summer burns toward fall Tess begins to give way under "the ardour of [Angel's] affection." Despite the secret shame she carries next to her heart, and despite her guilt-ridden refusal of Angel's first offer of marriage ("Oh, Mr. Clare—I cannot be your wife— I cannot be!"), Tess is inevitably "drifting into acquiescence," her "every pulse in revolt against her scrupulousness." And so, when Angel pleads with her again to marry him, Tess finally relents in what is clearly a terrifying moment of emotional abandon for a Guardian—it is a "reckless, inconsiderate acceptance of him," Tess confesses, a frantic decision to follow her heart and "close with him at the altar, revealing nothing and chancing discovery." Thus, for all her Guardian strictures, her "months of self-chastisement" and her "schemes to lead a future of austere isolation," Tess knows she must in the end listen to "love's counsel." Sobbing, she promises Angel "Yes, yes, yes!" and then turning and embracing him almost desperately,

> for the first time Clare learnt what an impassioned woman's kisses were like upon the lips of one whom she loved with all her heart and soul.[15]

Angel and Tess now seek each other's company openly, and begin making their plans to marry in accordance with what Hardy believes is an "'appetite for joy' which pervades all creation." Sadly, however—and ominously— neither Angel nor Tess is able to get free from the lies and illusions upon which their relationship is founded. On her side, Tess shows the Protector Guardian's fundamental

---

[15]Thomas Hardy, *Tess of the d'Urbervilles*, p. 207.

need to find security in life, hoping she can rest in what Hardy calls the safe "nest" of Angel's "protection and sympathy." Tess's need is so great, in fact, that she cannot quite bring herself to tell him the truth of her time with Alec d'Urberville, though she tries sincerely to confess her shame, right up to the eve of the wedding. But even more troubling—Hardy makes this very clear—is the illusory nature of Angel's Idealist love.

At first, in contrast with "the impassioned thoroughness of her feeling for him" (what Guardian "long-suffering it guaranteed, what honesty, what endurance, what good faith"), Hardy admits that Angel loves Tess "rather ideally and fancifully." Hardy steps carefully in his remarks about Angel in this part of the novel, not wanting to criticize his hero, but insisting all the same that Angel will not allow himself to love Tess as a flesh-and-blood human being, envisioning her instead as a Greek goddess, perhaps even as Pygmalion saw Galatea—Angel once actually remarks to Tess that her arms look to him like "wet marble." Hardy next concedes that Angel "was, in truth, more spiritual than animal," although again he characterizes Angel's apollonian way of love with a good deal of compassion:

> though not cold-natured, he was rather bright than hot—less Byronic than Shelleyan; could love desperately, but with a love more especially inclined to the imaginative and ethereal.[16]

The worst Hardy will say of Angel is that "Clare's love was doubtless ethereal to a fault, imaginative to impracticability," and he poses the "odd paradox" that, perhaps, "with more animalism he would have been the nobler man." But while Hardy is more or less sympathetic

---

[16]Thomas Hardy, *Tess of the d'Urbervilles*, p. 210.

in judging Angel's character, he is merciless in portraying his behavior, and its inescapable consequences.

As I have suggested, Teachers glow brightly with their dream of love, often kindling the imaginations of their loved ones, inspiring them with their own ardent illusions. And as the wedding approaches week by week the "radiance" of Angel's affection (his last name "Clare" means "light" in French) becomes, as Hardy puts it, "the breath and life of Tess's being; it enveloped her as a photosphere, irradiated her into forgetfulness of her past sorrows." Tess's love for Angel lifts her into "spiritual altitudes...approaching ecstasy," and she seems to become "a sort of celestial person, who owed her being to poetry—one of those classical divinities Clare was accustomed to talk to her about when they took their walks together." But, again, such luminous expectations have no basis in reality, and Hardy warns us that the "gloomy spectre" of truth prowls around Tess and Angel's love, "like wolves just outside the circumscribing light." Then, on their wedding night, truth springs its attack.

Angel has engaged rooms in a nearby farmhouse for their honeymoon, but both he and Tess arrive with heavy hearts concerning their secretly compromised virginities. Angel knows Tess has placed sublime trust in him as "a guide, philosopher, and friend," believing he has "the soul of a saint," and "the intellect...of a seer"—once she even called him "her Apollo." And because of her innocent faith in him, Angel feels obliged to bare his soul and tell her of his "forty-eight hours' dissipation" years ago with the woman in London. Tess forgives Angel without a second thought, indeed gratefully, for now she feels able to reveal the story of her own fall with Alec d'Urberville—"'tis just the same!" she cries, "I will tell you now."

However, as his beautiful young bride humbly opens her heart to him, Angel's face turns ashen with pain and disbelief. "Treading fitfully on the floor" (and as the "fire in the grate" grins impishly), Angel hears Tess out, and though every material thing in the room remains strangely, hideously, the same, he knows that, in this most important relationship of his life, "the essence of things had changed." Tess watches him silently "smothering his affection for her," and she begs Angel to forgive her—as she has forgiven him—but Angel can only whisper hoarsely, "Oh, Tess, forgiveness does not apply to the case! You were one person; now you are another." Tess is stunned and terrified—"I thought, Angel, that you loved me...my very self!" But Angel now sees Tess for the first time "without irradiation—in all her bareness," and feeling the depths of his soul becoming "paralysed," he answers her coldly, almost numbly,

> "I repeat, the woman I have been loving is not you."
> "But who?"
> "Another woman in your shape."[17]

Angel's reaction is instructive, suggesting as it does the "paralytic"[18] nature of the Teacher's response to severe stress, and also how easily personal identity can shift and transform itself in the Idealist's metaphorical imagination.[19] And yet, in explaining what can only be described as Angel Clare's hysterical[20] rejection of Tess, or of his image of

---

[17]Thomas Hardy, *Tess of the d'Urbervilles*, p. 246.

[18]David Keirsey, *Portraits of Temperament*, p. 9

[19]In his theory of madness, Keirsey argues that the Idealists are particularly prone to defend themselves by masquerading behind a split or multiple personality.

[20]Shapiro observes that, since the Hysterical person "does not seem rooted in a sense of his factual being and history, in firm convictions, and a sense of the factual, objective world," he is easily "captured by

Tess, I am not proposing that this is the normal Teacher's response to such shattered illusions. In most cases, as Keirsey tells us, Teachers "are extraordinarily tolerant of others, seldom critical, and always trustworthy,"[21] and Hardy himself defends Angel's character, even at this distraught time, observing how "gentle and affectionate he was in general."

But few Idealists are ever fully prepared for the chilling moment of recognition, when they suddenly see the imperfect reality of their loved ones—all too many of their relationships fail to survive this disillusionment. And Hardy also points out another undeniable facet of Angel's personality, and one that has come to dominate him for the moment: the immediate and stubborn decisiveness of the Mentor Idealists, which can make them judge others harshly, particularly for the kind of calculated deception that Angel believes Tess guilty of. "Within the remote depths of his constitution," Hardy tells us,

> there lay a hard, logical deposit, like a vein of metal in a soft loam, which turned the edge of everything that attempted to traverse it. It had blocked his acceptance of the Church; it blocked his acceptance of Tess....When he ceased to believe he ceased to follow.[22]

Mentors, I should say, are not "logical" in the Rational's sense of "systematic" or "deductive." Hardy's point is simply that, to some extent at least, Angel's heart follows his head when making important decisions, and certainly this is more true for Mentors than for Disciples (contrast Angel's obduracy, for instance, with Alyosha Karamazov's

vivid impressions, romantic provocations, transient moods of his own, or the fantasy characters that, for whatever reason, appeal to him" (*Neurotic Styles*, pp. 120-121).

[21]David Keirsey, *Please Understand Me*, p. 168.

[22]Thomas Hardy, *Tess of the d'Urbervilles*, p. 258.

patience and pliancy in Chapter Two). Put another way, the struggle between the head and the heart is somewhat more evenly-matched in Mentors than in Disciples, and Hardy describes how, over the next few days, in trying to decide what to do about Tess, Angel is "ill with thinking; eaten out with thinking; withered with thinking," and also wracked with the "incoherent multitude of his emotions."

Anticipating by several years Freud's interest in dreams and unconscious mental processes,[23] Hardy shows dramatically in the novel that Angel, in his heart-of-hearts, forgives Tess and loves her deeply. The second night, in a harrowing sleep-walking scene (that is, while his "reason slept"), Angel lifts his bride in his arms and murmurs his soul's affection: "my dearest, darling Tess! So sweet, so good, so true." Angel carries Tess outside, across a meandering stream, to the ruins of a church, retracing symbolically the innocent path of their courtship and wedding. But Angel's tenderness fades with the light of morning, and returning to consciousness he feels no less betrayed and cheated of his ideal: "here," he laughs bitterly, "I was thinking you a new-sprung child of nature," and that "I should secure rustic innocence as surely as I should secure pink cheeks."

Much like the "frequently divided" stream he carries Tess over in his sleep, with its rivulets "distorting, and splitting" the moonlight, Angel is torn and confused in his feelings for Tess, and as I have argued, Mentor Idealists cannot live for long with such unresolved relationships. And so, revealing his Teacher's iron determination "in the depths of this gentle being," Angel hastily makes up his mind that he and Tess must live apart until he "can bring [himself] to

[23]*Tess* was published in 1891, while Freud and Breuer published *Studies in Hysteria* in 1895, and Freud began writing *The Interpretation of Dreams* in 1896 (published in 1900).

endure" the "terrible and total change that her confession had wrought in his life, in his universe."

Although, to his credit, Angel is appalled at his hypocrisy, his self-awareness is helpless to lift what Hardy calls "the shade of his own limitations," and as he parts from Tess the earth seems stripped forever of all its former beauty: "the gold of the summer picture was now grey, the colours mean, the rich soil mud, and the river cold." At bottom, Angel's "heart was troubled," and Hardy diagnoses the problem with both precision and a severe beauty. Hardy observes that "humanity stood before [Angel] no longer in the pensive sweetness of...art," and he understands that Angel's heart is blocked, at least for now, by the very intensity of his idealism, by his unyielding "will to subdue...the substance to the conception, the flesh to the spirit." Very simply, Hardy knows that Angel cannot love Tess because she has failed his illusion of her perfection. And he suggests that, until Angel is able to learn the harder lessons of human forgiveness and compassion—which he does at the very end of the novel—all of his Idealist's gifts of affection, enthusiasm, and benevolence are no more than "dead leaves upon the tyrannous wind of his imaginative ascendancy."

Margaret Schlegel

With the critical success in the mid-1980s of two motion pictures, a wide new audience was introduced to the fiction of E.M. Forster, and in particular to two of his finest novels, *A Room With a View* (1908), his sparkling comedy of manners, and *A Passage To India* (1927), the more "public and political" book (in Lionel Trilling's phrase) which many regard as his late masterpiece.[24] Though enormously different in style and setting, these two stories frame in their characters' relationships the dialectic that seemed to fascinate Forster in all of his fiction, the awkward intercourse between Dionysus' Artisan world of flesh and blood on the one hand, and Demeter's Guardian world of social authority on the other—with Apollo's lofty Idealists often caught ironically in the middle. Throughout his novels, Forster's Idealists are both intrigued and betrayed by Artisan sensuality, while they both respect and feel thwarted by stiff-necked Guardian traditionalism. Indeed, the Idealist's confused attempts to resolve these conflicts is Forster's great theme, and his most masterful statement of the ironies of reconciliation, at least between an Idealist and a Guardian, takes place in what is to my mind his very best novel, *Howards End* (1910),[25] in the courtship and marriage between a spirited Teacher, Margaret Schlegel, and a stolid Inspector ("ISTJ") businessman named Henry Wilcox.

Margaret Schlegel is certainly not looking for a man in her life. Though twenty-nine at the beginning of *Howards End*, Margaret only rarely thinks about passing quietly into middle-aged spinsterhood. She has had an occasional suitor, and has felt from time to time a "yearning for the masculine," but none of her young men have inspired in

---

[24]Both David Lean's film *A Passage to India* (1984) and James Ivory's *A Room With a View* (1986) won many international awards, including Academy Awards in the United States. In addition, Ivory directed a less acclaimed film, *Maurice* (1987), based on Forster's long-unpublished novel (written in 1913-14) of homosexual love. And in 1991 Charles Sturridge directed an exquisite but little known film of Forster's first novel, *Where Angels Fear to Tread* (1905).

[25]At this writing, Ivory's 1992 film version of *Howards End* had become by far the most popular of all of the five recent films based on Forster novels.

Margaret the kind of love that, she says, she "would shout from the rooftops." Bright and strong-minded, Margaret is known in her modest London circle as quite an "independent young woman," both in her comfortable income, which she inherited from her English mother, and in her idealistic views of the world, which she inherited from her German father. Margaret's dead father Ernst was a philosophy professor in Germany, a fervent Teacher himself whom Forster classifies "as the countryman of Hegel and Kant, as the idealist, inclined to be dreamy, whose Imperialism was the Imperialism of the air." To the horror of the Schlegel family, Ernst abandoned Germany as a young man because of the pervasive materialism and will-to-power he saw strangling the aesthetic and intellectual life there. He left the German universities to their "empires of facts" and emigrated to England hoping to "rekindle the light within."

Though her father died when Margaret was only a teenager, she is very much Ernst Schlegel's daughter. Listening at his knee, Margaret drank in his fervent views on Art and Literature, Socialism, Temperance, and Women's Suffrage—all the "Schlegel fetiches," as Forster calls them—and she (and her younger sister Helen) soon became known as "tremendous talkers" in the intellectual discussions that filled the Schlegel household. Margaret was not as pretty as Helen, and so relied less on charming people to her views; she preferred to go "straight ahead" at philosophical issues, and even at thirteen she could seem "offensive" in her hunger to exchange ideas. Her older cousins tried shielding her from controversial adult issues (such as, is God on Germany's side or England's?), but Margaret was an "odd girl...in many ways far older than [her] years," and she could not understand their reticence:

"Papa," she would ask pointedly, in front of all her relatives, "why will they not discuss this most clear question?"

All her life Margaret is driven to ask such "impetuous questions," just as she can barely wait to expound her views on complex social problems and moral dilemmas. Teachers, Keirsey tells us, have "a remarkable fluency with language, especially in speech,"[26] and Margaret grows up to have a rare talent for expressing herself—or, as one friend admits, "Miss Schlegel puts everything splendidly." Keirsey also mentions that (unlike Counselors) Teachers "have no hesitation about speaking out, no matter how large or small the group may be,"[27] and as an adult Margaret belongs to a number of art societies and informal discussion clubs, where she often leads the conversation with what Forster teasingly calls her "clever nonsense." And Forster explains her delight in speaking her mind (what she confesses to be her "demon of vociferation") by giving us a wonderful insight into the Teacher's nature: Margaret is

> not beautiful, not supremely brilliant, but filled with something that took the place of both qualities—something best described as a profound vivacity, a continual and sincere response to all that she encountered in her path through life.[28]

This is not the objective, analytical curiosity that characterizes the Rational approach to life; Margaret is not "brilliant" in that way, and Forster reminds us twice in the novel that she "is not a barren theorist." As a Teacher, Margaret is intrigued with people, their problems, and with developing the personal or human side of social institutions.

---

[26]David Keirsey, *Please Understand Me*, p. 168.

[27]David Keirsey, *Please Understand Me*, p. 168.

[28]E.M. Forster, *Howards End* (Vintage Books edition, 1921), p. 10. All quotations from *Howards End* are from this edition.

Forster says that "on the whole...everyone interested" Margaret—as does every aspect of public life. She cares a great deal about politics, for example; "not as politicians would have us care," Forster adds, but as one who desires that "public life should mirror whatever is good in the life within." She is also deeply "interested in ideas" about Art and Society, though she insists that one's intellectual life must always be open to the spiritual mysteries, responding to what she calls "the kink of the unseen." In her religious beliefs as well, Margaret is unconventional and profoundly personal. Though she has sympathy with the place of the Christian Church in western culture, her own religion is private and very nearly pantheistic, finding divinity in places and things—in houses and trees, for example—and in blessed individuals. She believes that "any human being lies nearer to the unseen than any organization," and she speaks for many Idealists when she questions the lack of privacy in traditional Church services: "in public," she wonders, "who shall express the unseen adequately?" and then she concludes,

> it is private life that holds out the mirror to infinity; personal intercourse, and that alone, that ever hints at a personality beyond our daily vision.[29]

Thus, for all of Margaret's fascination with the outer world, she remains strongly devoted to the inner spiritual life, and often tries to keep her mind "focussed on the invisible." And yet, a mind "focussed" on something as formless as "the invisible" can hardly be said to be focused at all, and Forster describes with great skill in Margaret what I have cited several times in this book as the "global and diffuse" workings of the Idealist imagination. Forster tells us that her mind "darted from impulse to impulse," and that her

---

[29]E.M. Forster, *Howards End*, p. 81.

brain "darted up and down" as she considers an issue. He pictures her "zig-zagging with her friends over Thought and Art" and swinging "rapidly from one decision to another." He says that she hates fixed "plans" and clear "lines of action," and that she wishes she could "do all...things at once," even though "so contradictory." Keirsey observes in *Portraits of Temperament* that Idealists "fuse and blend otherwise distinct ideas almost effortlessly"[30] in their thought process, giving them a panoramic understanding of the world. And with a remarkable grasp of the Idealist mind Forster explains that Margaret naturally confuses the categories and blurs the particulars of whatever she is thinking about, preferring to let all her thoughts impinge on each other freely and form an undifferentiated "global" view. When she is thinking of house-hunting, for example,

> She could not concentrate on details. Parliament, the Thames, the irresponsive chauffeur, [all] would flash into the field of house-hunting, and all demand some comment or response. It is impossible to see life steadily and see it whole, and she had chosen to see it whole.[31]

Keirsey also speaks of the Idealist's consciousness as innately metaphorical, creating its own "romantic or mysterious"[32] reality by fluidly transforming one idea into another. And again, with extraordinary awareness, Forster characterizes Margaret as a person who meditates "half-sensibly and half-poetically" on the world around her, who believes life is "sometimes only a drama," who insists "Houses are alive," and to whom something as mundane as a railway station "had always suggested Infinity."

---

[30]David Keirsey, *Portraits of Temperament*, p. 104.
[31]E.M. Forster, *Howards End*, p. 161.
[32]David Keirsey, *Portraits of Temperament*, p. 104.

Forster apologizes for exposing Margaret's fanciful, symbolical imagination to criticism from what he calls his more "practical" (i.e. Guardian) English readers: "If you think this ridiculous, remember," he cautions, "this is the way her mind worked." And Forster also assures the sensible reader that Margaret is not the extreme of her temperament in the novel. Although her Guardian Aunt Juley[33] thinks of Margaret as "a little hysterical," Forster explains with good humor that "she was not mad really," and insists more seriously that "Margaret was no morbid idealist." The morbid Idealist in *Howards End* is unquestionably Margaret's younger sister Helen, an over-zealous Advocate who clings more and more desperately to the "halo of Romance" that crowned her once in a doomed love affair—a magical twenty-four hours that dissolved into the harsh reality of family telegrams and clumsy denials.

Far more than the quixotic Advocates, Teachers appreciate the indispensable strengths of the Guardian way of life, and indeed Margaret has what Forster calls a "deeper sympathy, a sounder judgment" than her sister concerning the role of economic "types" among us. Thus, after Helen's humiliation in love, Margaret lectures her that the practical life, hateful and insensitive though it is, has its virtues. "It's one of the most interesting things," Margaret begins in her intense way,

> the truth is that there is a great outer life that you and I have never touched—a life in which telegrams and anger count. Personal relations, that we think supreme, are not supreme there. There love means marriage settlements, death, death duties. So far I'm clear. But here my difficulty. This outer life,

---

[33]Aunt Juley is a sweetly meddlesome Provider Guardian ("ESFJ"), and Forster describes her intellectually cautious Conservator nature with a brilliant image, commenting that the dear old woman "collected new ideas as a squirrel collects nuts."

though obviously horrid, often seems the real one—there's grit
in it. It does breed character.[34]

Helen, however, will have none of Margaret's sense of
perspective, and her growing fanaticism gives her sister a
good deal of concern. When Helen announces fervently, for
example, that the "real [world] is purely spiritual,"
Margaret agrees that "all vistas close on the unseen—no
one doubts it—" but she confesses in a private moment that
"Helen closed them rather too quickly for her taste." Helen
also begins to denounce all forms of commerce, insisting
with many socialist-minded Advocates that "poverty is
somehow" more "'real'" than wealth; but while Margaret
does not think money-making should be the first goal of
life, she also understands that money "pads the edges of
things," and she reminds her sister that their own mother's
estate rests "firm beneath our feet." And finally, when
Helen becomes infatuated with the Freudian cult-idea of the
"subconscious self" (which Forster chides as "the Punch
and Judy aspect of life"), Margaret happily acknowledges
the "superiority of the unseen to the seen"; but she also
insists that "at every turn...one was confronted with reality,"
and she worries that "there was something a little
unbalanced in the mind that so readily shreds the visible."

The idea of "balance" that Margaret mentions here emerges
in the course of the novel as her—and very much
Forster's—personal creed. Since Idealists are so susceptible
to black-and-white extremes in their feeling and thinking,
they almost invariably come to the idea of balance
(harmony, wholeness) as their spiritual goal in life, and in
this case Margaret the Teacher shares her wisdom often and
energetically with many of the other characters. She writes
her sister, for example, not to "brood" on the difference

----

[34]E.M. Forster, *Howards End*, p. 27.

between "the seen and the unseen": "to brood on it is mediæval," she warns her; "our business is not to contrast the two but to reconcile them." She instructs her new friend Ruth Wilcox how to resolve the contradiction between the surface part of living and "the submerged": "It's then that proportion comes in—to live by proportion." And she has held forth over the years to her Aunt Juley that "proportion is the final secret" for balancing life:

> The business man who assumes that this life is everything and the mystic who asserts that it is nothing, fail, on this side and on that, to hit the truth....No; truth, being alive...was only to be found by continuous excursions into either realm.[35]

Teachers, even well-balanced ones, love to share with others the profound lessons of enlightened living, and Margaret is all too ready to proclaim her insights to her loved ones: "Gracious me," she catches herself, "I've started preaching!" In *Howards End*, however, Margaret does more than instruct those around her; she also acts on her words, entering the realm of the outer world herself, when she develops a curious affection for a good English couple, Ruth and Henry Wilcox.

Margaret and Helen meet the Wilcoxes on tour in Germany before the novel opens, and though the romantic Schlegel girls have little in common with this salt-of-the-earth middle-aged Guardian couple, the four strike up a pleasant travelers' friendship. Back in England, the Wilcoxes send the Schlegel sisters a gracious invitation to visit them at Howards End, their "old and little" house in the country, and to meet their children. Helen ends up going by herself (Margaret has a cold), and it is there, at Howards End, impressed by the honest simplicity of the family, and enchanted by the overwhelming beauty of the gardens, that

---

[35]E.M. Forster, *Howards End*, p. 195.

Helen falls in love with the handsome son Paul, who kisses her under a vast, ancient-rooted wych-elm. And it is there, the next morning, that she watches her dream of love fade into strained apologies.

Sorely disillusioned, Helen comes home and turns against the Wilcoxes with growing animosity, eventually developing what Forster calls an "idée fixe"[36] against them. However, Margaret's relationship with Ruth Wilcox, resumed amid the awkwardness, grows steadily into dear friendship over the next few months. And even after this serene and gracious lady unexpectedly dies, leaving her husband and three grown children virtually shipwrecked without her,[37] Margaret maintains her heartfelt "interest in the survivors."

I have said that Margaret's friendship with the Wilcoxes is curious, but it is certainly not contrary to type. Keirsey argues in *Please Understand Me* that, with their extraordinary powers of sympathy, Teachers often become "deeply involved" in the lives of their friends, even their casual friends,[38] and Margaret immediately takes a concerned, almost nurturing attitude toward the Wilcoxes,

---

[36]Pierre Janet coined the phrase "idée fixe" in the 1890s to describe certain traumatic subconscious memories in the hysterical personality (Keirsey's Idealists), and his warning that fixed ideas "are apt to be very dangerous" throws a good deal of light onto Helen's strangely hostile behavior: "such fixed ideas are dangerous because they are no longer under the control of the personality, because they belong to a group of phenomena which have passed beyond the dominion of the conscious will" (*Psychological Healing*, Vol I, p. 596).

[37]Though she dies quite early in *Howards End*, Ruth Wilcox's memory, and her legacy, haunt much of the rest of the novel. In this and many other ways, Ruth compares closely with another earth-mother Protector Guardian ("ISFJ"), Mrs. Ramsay in Virginia Woolf's novel *To the Lighthouse*, (see *The Pygmalion Project: Volume Two*).

[38]David Keirsey, *Please Understand Me*, p. 168.

as if wanting to put them in touch with higher things—with "beauty and all the other intangible gifts that are floating about the world." At the same time, Keirsey tells us that Teachers need their lives to be "settled and organized,"[39] and Margaret admires Ruth Wilcox's deep roots in traditional English life, as well as Henry's ability to live so capably in the real world. At times, Margaret finds the Wilcoxes rather thick and over-conventional, but she also feels that "they led a life that she could not attain to—the outer life of 'telegrams and anger,'" and she senses that in this outer world

> they could protect her, excelling where she was deficient. Once past the rocks of emotion, they knew so well what to do, whom to send for; their hands were on all the ropes, they had grit as well as grittiness, and she valued grit enormously.[40]

In short, while Helen cannot bear them, Margaret finds something solid, and also oddly endearing, about the Wilcoxes—they are "the right sort," she says—and even after Ruth's death she keeps up a friendly acquaintance with the widowed Henry, one of the most splendid examples of an Inspector Guardian I have found in literature.

Forster sums up Henry Wilcox as a "steady man"—to be sure, a man for whom the word steadiness "included all praise." Though his eyes are capable of "kindness and good fellowship," there is no "hint of weakness" in his expression, and no note of vacillation or abstraction in his features, particularly in his forehead, which Forster describes as "high and straight, brown and polished," having

---

[39]David Keirsey, *Please Understand Me*, p. 169.
[40]E.M. Forster, *Howards End,* p. 103.

the effect of a bastion that protected his head from the world.
At times it had the effect of a blank wall. He had dwelt behind
it, intact and happy, for fifty years.[41]

Henry is also a highly successful business man, "an important figure," Forster tells us, in the Imperial and West African Rubber Company, and in true Guardian fashion "a reassuring name on company prospectuses." Not an impulsive Artisan entrepreneur, nor a far-seeing Rational strategist in business, Henry is a reliable company man, one who knows "the ropes" of company regulations and procedures, who has worked "regularly and honestly" up the ladder, and who is at his best, Forster notes, "when serving on committees."

In his family life, too, Henry is the essential Inspector Guardian, a dependable father-figure and a good provider, though Forster admits that he treats his wife and children sternly, formally, and largely "without sentiment." Forster explains that Henry is not unfeeling with his loved ones, but simply that he "dodged emotion successfully"—and then he generalizes the point: "All Wilcoxes," he says, "avoided the personal in life. It did not seem to them of supreme importance." As Keirsey points out, social *ceremonies* are the important thing to Guardians,[42] and when Henry puts on his daughter Evie's wedding Forster observes that "the management was excellent, as was to be expected with anything that Henry undertook." Henry, with his "sensible and generous brain," sees to every comfort of his guests. He is "inherently hospitable," Forster tells us, but in a darker image he comments that "Henry treated a marriage like a funeral, item by item," so that "the emotional content was minimized, and all went forward smoothly."

---

[41]E.M. Forster, *Howards End*, p. 91.
[42]David Keirsey, *Portraits of Temperament*, p. 50.

Make no mistake, Inspector Guardians have strong feelings, and Henry "suffered acutely" after Ruth's death, closing himself upstairs, away from his children, where he honors his wife's "gentle conservatism," and where he weeps and remembers her

> goodness....Not anything in detail—not courtship or early raptures—but just the unvarying virtue, that seemed to him a woman's noblest quality. So many women are capricious, breaking into odd flaws of passion or frivolity. Not so his wife. Year after year, summer and winter, as bride and mother, she had been the same, he had always trusted her.[43]

But giving in to grief seems self-indulgent to an Inspector when there are public duties to perform, and so, at his wife's funeral, and when presiding over the reading of her will, Henry gladly retreats behind "his fortress" of procedural details and resumes his best committee-room manner. He disposes of his troublesome personal affairs "sharply"—even tearing up and burning a codicil in his wife's will leaving Howards End to Margaret Schlegel—and then he passes "on to the next point."

Forster does not try to explain why, after some two years as a widower, Henry begins to take a romantic interest in Margaret. The usual reasons do not seem to apply. Though some twenty years younger than he, Margaret is not a particularly attractive woman, her figure "meagre," her face "all teeth and eyes." Henry certainly does not covet her modest income, and her outspoken liberal views and passionate intellectualism make her disturbingly different from his constant Ruth. But something in Margaret's mental and emotional vivacity intrigues him—differences do seem to attract—and perhaps in his own way he begins to admire Margaret for the same reason that she keeps up

---

[43]E.M. Forster, *Howards End,* p. 89.

with him: "collision with [the Wilcoxes]," she once admitted, "stimulated her." In any event, having bumped into Margaret socially one or two times, Henry discretely asks his daughter Evie to invite her for luncheon at the venerable Simpson's on the Strand, where he "happens" to join them.

After securing a table for the party, ordering the traditional saddle of mutton, and making "some preliminary inquiries about cheese," Henry tries to settle into serious conversation with Margaret, and Forster's dialogue captures much of the good-humored incongruity of Idealist-Guardian relations. Margaret feels out of place in such a "thoroughly Old English" restaurant, and (smiling at the slices of mutton he piles on her plate) she threatens to invite Henry to lunch with her progressive, health-conscious circle of friends: "It's all proteids and body-buildings," she tells him, "and people come up to you and beg your pardon, but you have such a beautiful aura." Henry inquires suspiciously, "A what?" and Margaret teases him: "Never heard of an aura...nor of an astral plane?" Henry had indeed "heard of astral planes," Forster comments bluntly, "and [he] censured them."

Margaret agrees that such spiritualism goes too far, but she cannot help poking fun at Henry's intolerance: "You're bound to have [an aura]," she teases him, "but it may be of such a terrible colour that no one dares mention it." Henry knows he's being joshed, but forges ahead in his earnest manner: "Tell me, though, Miss Schlegel, do you really believe in the supernatural and all that?" Then, as Margaret gathers her thoughts to respond, Henry interrupts to settle another weighty issue—selecting the cheese: "Gruyère or Stilton?" "Gruyère, please." "Better have Stilton."

Margaret puts herself in Henry's capable hands concerning the cheese, but she gently reserves her options regarding the supernatural, despite his obvious disapproval. "Though I don't believe in auras," she begins, "and think Theosophy's only a halfway-house—"

> "—Yet there may be something in it all the same," he concluded with a frown.
>
> "Not even that. It may be halfway in the wrong direction. I can't explain. I don't believe in all these fads, and yet I don't like saying that I don't believe in them."
>
> He seemed unsatisfied, and said: "So you wouldn't give me your word that you *don't* hold with astral bodies and all the rest of it?"
>
> "I could," said Margaret, surprised that the point was of any importance to him. "Indeed, I will....But why do you want this settled?"[44]

Though I have argued that Mentor Idealists are quite decisive in "settling" the significant issues in their lives, they pale in comparison with Monitor Guardians— "practical persons," as Forster calls them, "who know what they want at once, and generally know nothing else." Inspectors like Henry want everything in their lives settled and decided almost as soon as possible; they cannot rest until they have tied up all the loose ends that fray their nerves. And so, within a few muddled, miserable days, Henry arranges to meet with Margaret at his large vacant house on Ducie Street in London, ostensibly to show her the place and offer her the lease, but actually with a much more private intention. Indeed, as he shows her officiously through the immense rooms, quoting their exact dimensions ("Thirty by fifteen. No, wait a minute. Fifteen and a half"), and pointing out the heavy, comfortable furnishings, Henry works himself up to ask Margaret to marry him.

---

[44]E.M. Forster, *Howards End,* p. 154.

Inspectors are not usually at their best in romantic moments, and Forster confesses that "the proposal was not to rank among the world's great love scenes." Henry has been awkwardly personal throughout the tour of the house, and just as they enter the Chelsea drawing-room he clears his throat and launches formally: "Miss Schlegel...could you be induced to share my—is it probable—" Margaret has sensed this moment was coming, and stops him gently: "I see, I see" she interjects, averting her eyes, "I will write to you afterwards if I may." Henry falters, straining to make himself clearly understood: "Miss Schlegel—Margaret—you don't understand...I am asking you to be my wife." Margaret assures him she understands perfectly, but she continues to look away—"she had too much intuition," Forster explains, "to look at him as he struggled for possessions that money cannot buy."

Though filled with sympathy, and though she knows her hesitation must bring him pain, here again Margaret has no desire to settle the matter too hastily, and she relies on the prudish phrase, "Oh, sir, this is so sudden," to escape without a definite reply. Embarrassed and uncertain, Henry inspects for damage—"You aren't offended, Miss Schlegel?"—and Margaret can tell that, exhausted with the effort of so much emotion, "he was anxious to get rid of her." Margaret promises him warmly that she is not offended, and takes her leave before Henry can apologize any further.

Margaret certainly does understand the meaning of Henry's proposal—with a good deal more insight than he understands it himself—and she is far from being offended. Indeed, Forster tells us that "an immense joy" wells up in Margaret almost the moment Henry asks for her hand. And over the next few days, as she sounds the depths of her feelings and discusses with her sister the strengths and weaknesses of Henry's personality, Margaret's "pale cast of thought" (Forster quotes Hamlet) gives way to her Teacher's "native hue of resolution," and she comes quickly to a decision.

As I have said, Margaret has always somewhat theoretically admired the competent, honest-English character of the Wilcox men. Their way of life, she has argued with Helen, demonstrates "such values as neatness, decision, and obedience, virtues of second rank, no doubt, but they have formed our civilization." And she has insisted that for all their "defects of temper" (i.e., their lack of imagination), "such men give me more pleasure than many who are better equipped." Now, as she contemplates joining her life with one of what Forster himself calls this practical "type," Margaret's feelings are generally consistent with her abstract position. Forster tells us that as she listens to Henry in his drawing-room "she thrilled with happiness" to have the competent and distinguished head of the Wilcox family—such a "man of standing"—want to marry her. The next day she assures Helen, "it is wonderful knowing that a real man cares for you," and she praises "all those public qualities" in Henry that "enable...you and I to sit here without having our throats cut."

Undoubtedly, Margaret is romanticizing Henry to some extent—Idealists always do. Helen has cautioned her before about glorifying the "Wilcox ideal," and Forster describes Margaret in the masculine rooms of Ducie Street as paying "homage" to Henry's authority and self-confidence, and as "keen to derive the modern capitalist from the warriors of the past." But Keirsey points out that Teachers "know what they prefer, and can read other people with outstanding accuracy,"[45] and during Henry's proposal Margaret keeps her head amazingly well, deliberately resisting her inclination to "clothe the struggle with beauty." Besides, Margaret believes herself too old and too wise to fall head over heels, and she can honestly tell her sister the next day that, while she does not love Henry yet, in due time she will, "of that I'm pretty sure."

Though the prospect of marrying Henry the competent "man of business" charms Margaret in one way, Forster clearly suggests that a vital element is missing for her as she mulls over the "strange love-scene" of his proposal. No matter how mature and level-headed a Teacher might be about a "practical" marriage, the Idealist's need for a mating of souls is always just beneath the surface. And thus, though Henry's words make Margaret "happy, and longing to give happiness," she remembers her joy as essentially impersonal and soulless: "it had nothing to do with humanity," she confesses, and she recalls feeling no "central radiance" in her heart, no glowing apollonian spirituality that she knows would have "been love." In Henry's place, she feels, she would have spoken of love and promised "*Ich liebe dich*," but she also understands that "it was not his habit to open the heart":

> he might have done it if she had pressed him—as a matter of duty, perhaps; England expects every man to open his heart once; but the effort would have jarred him.[46]

Margaret seems bravely aware of this lack of radiance in Henry's character. She understands that Henry views their marriage in "tints of the quietest grey," and not in her own sunlit, "shining" hues of love. She knows that he expects only steady "comradeship and affection" from their

---

[45]David Keirsey, *Please Understand Me*, p. 168.
[46]E.M. Forster, *Howards End*, p. 166.

marriage, not the "waves of emotion" that she feels washing over her. And she admits to her sister that the book of her marriage will be written in "a very good kind of prose," but not in the inspiring poetry of romantic love.

Forster describes the almost comical tension between Henry's prose and Margaret's poetry in another wonderfully ironic scene, the evening after Margaret has written Henry accepting him. Henry arrives with the engagement ring, and after a hearty dinner they take a turn on the Parade—"it would be her first love scene," Margaret trembles to think. Henry speaks of the ring (its value? its size?), while Margaret is more intimate and tries to discover the beginnings of Henry's love for her, asking him when he first thought of her "this way"—"How extraordinarily interesting, Henry! Tell me." But Henry meets her Teacher's romantic inquisitiveness with his own Inspector's stubborn concreteness:

> Henry had no intention of telling. Perhaps he could not have told, for his mental states became obscure as soon as he had passed through them. He misliked the very word "interesting," connoting it with wasted energy and even with morbidity. Hard facts were enough for him.[47]

If Henry will not reveal the origins of his feelings, Margaret is excited to tell him of hers. The moment of Henry's proposal brought to light "unexpected mysteries" in Margaret's life, intimations about the real meaning of love and marriage that literature had never provided her. And in a striking Idealist metaphor she strives to express the infinite promise she found symbolized in Henry's proposal. In novels and plays, she explains, a proposal of marriage is "a kind of bouquet"—a formal prize presented to the heroine at the end of the story. But in real life a proposal is

---

[47]E.M. Forster, *Howards End*, p. 178.

literally "a proposal...a suggestion, a seed," as she calls it, holding all the possibilities for the relationship in its few fateful words.

Unfortunately, Henry holds very little stock in ideas of mystical potential, and before Margaret finishes her sentence he interrupts to bring the conversation down to earth:

> By the way...I was thinking, if you don't mind, that we ought to spend this evening in a business talk; there will be so much to settle.[48]

Margaret watches her beautiful thought fly "away into darkness" and then she turns with a sigh to Henry's business.

Margaret assumes that Henry wants to compare notes on how the two families can be reconciled to their marriage. Helen is aghast at the prospect, while Henry's children are sour and suspicious, and Margaret chatters happily about trying to warm family relations, especially hoping Henry will make a diplomatic effort with her sister: "I am so anxious you two should be friends." Henry *does* want to discuss settlements, but not the emotional kind, and not with Margaret's relatives. And so, after putting up patiently with a good deal of "drifting from our business," Henry voices his inevitable Guardian concern:

> I am anxious, in my own happiness, not to be unjust to others....I am determined that my children shall have no case against me.[49]

Margaret finally catches on—"You mean money. How stupid I am!"—and her immediate, heartfelt advice to Henry points up quite clearly the difference between the

---

[48]E.M. Forster, *Howards End,* p. 178.
[49]E.M. Forster, *Howards End,* p. 179.

Teacher's and the Inspector's regard for money: "Be generous with them," she urges him; "Bother justice!" Though she does not resent money as her sister does (along with many other Advocate Idealists), Margaret has no use for being more than comfortably well-off, and she encourages Henry to divide his wealth liberally among his children. Henry shudders at the thought of such careless generosity, and cautions Margaret about his financial position: "We've none too much, I assure you; you're marrying a poor man." No matter how wealthy Guardians are (and Henry is very nearly a millionaire), they are so innately frugal and distrustful that, whenever money is mentioned, their instinct is to hide their fortune and "talk poor," as if nearly destitute. And, thus, in this scene Henry nervously avoids divulging specific amounts—"I hadn't any intention of bothering you with details"—and he changes the conversation abruptly.

Henry insists on walking Margaret safely home, and as they make their way he brings up other concrete matters of time and property—the date of the wedding ("We can scarcely think of anything before...September"), and where they will live ("Ducie Street has huge drawbacks"). But then, in Aunt Juley's garden, away from the lights of the road, he suddenly takes Margaret in his arms and kisses her. Margaret is startled by the embrace and "nearly screamed" with fright, though she catches her breath and returns the kiss lovingly. Henry sees her to the door, rings for the maid, and without another word he disappears into the night. Margaret has had her "love scene," but once again she finds it brusque and impersonal, sadly lacking in intimacy. "On looking back," Forster tells us,

> the incident displeased her. It was so isolated. Nothing in their previous conversation had heralded it, and, worse still, no tenderness had ensued. If a man cannot lead up to passion, he can at all events lead down from it, and she had hoped, after

her complaisance, for some exchange of gentle words. But he
had hurried away as if ashamed.[50]

Guardians raised in the Victorian era, I might point out,
were so bound in their lives by propriety and self-denial
that they were often timid about shows of physical
affection, and could easily feel guilty about their sexual
desires—a facet of their character that Forster sums up in a
single sentence about Henry: "Whether as boy, husband, or
widower, he had always the sneaking belief that bodily
passion is bad, a belief [in which] Religion had confirmed
him."

However, despite her misgivings about his proposal, despite
her sister's frantic disapproval, and despite her profound
disappointment with their first kiss, Margaret is unshaken in
her determination to marry Henry, and Forster's
explanation again emphasizes the role of temperament in
her decision: "Others had loved her in the past," Forster
says, but "never before had her personality been touched."
More than physical affection, more than romance, more
even than spiritual communion, Margaret's love for Henry
is based on her Teacher's express need to be "settled and
organized," and on her admiration for the kind of man
whose capable hands steer the course of civilization and
guarantee the stability of society. Margaret firmly believes
that "Henry would save" the Advocate Idealists and all their
noble causes. "Without fine feelings or deep insight," and
while "Helen and her friends were discussing the ethics of
salvation," Henry would save their English homes and their
English way of life. And glowing with pride and
compassion "she loved him for" such Rock of Gibraltar
reliability.

---

[50]E.M. Forster, *Howards End,* p. 184.

But Margaret has one other belief about Henry, or rather about what she can make of Henry, that quietly informs her decision, and Forster describes Margaret's hidden agenda with some of his most powerful writing in *Howards End.* Initially (and wisely), Margaret vows never to expect of Henry more sensitivity than he can give. She seems to accept his Inspector's emotional limitations: that "he's afraid of emotion," that his "sympathy lacks poetry," and that "he's not as spiritually honest as I am." And she resolves never to inflict on Henry her own Idealist's needs for "emotional talk, or...display of sympathy."

But soon after the engagement, when Margaret has begun to take more personal responsibility for Henry's happiness, she conceives a new role for herself in the relationship. Margaret has always believed implicitly that her Teacher's "birthright...was to nourish the imagination," and it now occurs to her that, in the name of love, she might be able to help Henry learn about the exquisite balance between the inner life and the outer life (the "Invisible" and the "Visible") which she has always sought in her own personality. "Mature as he was," she believes

> she might yet be able to help him to the building of the rainbow bridge that should connect the prose in us with the passion. Without it we are meaningless fragments, half monks, half beasts, unconnected arches that have never joined into a man. With it love is born, and alights on the highest curve, glowing against the grey, sober against the fire.[51]

As is typical of the Idealists, Margaret assumes in this line of thinking that all people suffer from a sense of internal fragmentation in their lives, and specifically from the peculiar Idealist division into "monk" and "beast." Her soaring imagination has blinded her to the possibility that

---

[51]E.M. Forster, *Howards End*, p. 185.

Henry is not fragmented, or not in those terms, and that perhaps he experiences life and love in his own Guardian ways. In Margaret's view, Henry is not simply unemotional and unspiritual, he is "afraid of emotion," and "not spiritually honest," as if to say that he is hiding from his true (i.e. Idealist) feelings. And thus she regards her desire to knit up the fragments of Henry's soul not as an invasion of his privacy, nor even as interference with his legitimate Inspector personality, but as a loving attempt to put Henry in touch with a higher ideal—to help him to a rebirth of spirituality, and to a new, more poetical understanding of the physical world:

> Only connect! That was the whole of her sermon. Only connect the prose and the passion, and both will be exalted, and human love will be seen at its height. Live in fragments no longer. Only connect, and the beast and the monk, robbed of the isolation that is life to either, will die.[52]

Although as a Teacher Margaret is a role-directive type, she intends no bold assault on the fortress of Henry's Guardian sensibility, urging him outright to heal the breach in his inner self. Again, Keirsey argues that Teachers "command without seeming to do so," not so much telling their loved ones what to do, as telling them what they *need* to do for their own happiness, and taking for granted that their loved ones will rise to meet their exalted expectations. Indeed, Margaret feels that her message of spiritual-physical wholeness is so irrefutable, so rightly the aim of all healthy-minded persons, that she need only acquaint Henry with his need to "connect" and he will inevitably embrace her ideal:

> She would only point out the salvation that was latent in his own soul, and in the soul of every man....Nor was the message difficult to give. It need not take the form of a good "talking."

---

[52]E.M. Forster, *Howards End,* pp. 185-186.

> By quiet indications the bridge would be built and span their lives with beauty.[53]

Differences of temperament are too intrinsically a part of us, however, for this kind of manipulation to succeed, even if subtle and well-intentioned, and Forster is quick to suggest the difficulties in store for Margaret's Pygmalion project, commenting with his gentle irony that it "was hard going in the roads of Mr. Wilcox's soul." In the first place, Henry is not at all curious to discover "the mysterious or the private" aspects of his internal life, and he stiffens against Margaret's first subtle Pygmalion probings by warning her, "I am not a fellow who bothers about my own inside." And even more of a problem, Henry simply misses most of Margaret's "quiet indications" for changing him. After failing again and again during the first few weeks of their engagement to awaken Henry's "latent" spirituality, Margaret finally admits her frustration:

> there was one quality in Henry for which she was never prepared, however much she reminded herself of it: his obtuseness. He simply did not notice things, and there was no more to be said.[54]

Of all the temperaments, Idealists are the most interpersonally sensitive,[55] responding intuitively to all of what Forster calls the "lights and shades that exist in the greyest conversation," and clearly Margaret believes that such "people" awareness is another quality latent in Henry's soul. But when she gently scolds him about his thick-skinned "obtuseness to personal influence" he replies

---

[53]E.M. Forster, *Howards End,* pp. 185-186.   In *Portraits of Temperament* Keirsey describes the "integrative" imagination of the Idealists, which lets them "fuse and blend otherwise distinct and separate ideas almost effortlessly" (p. 104).

[54]E.M. Forster, *Howards End,* p. 187.

[55]See *Portraits of Temperament,* pp. 104-105.

with a laugh: "My motto is Concentrate. I've no intention of frittering away my strength on that sort of thing." Margaret protests, using the familiar Teacher's rhetoric of personal development: "It isn't frittering away the strength," she assures him; "it's enlarging the space in which you may be strong." But Henry really isn't concerned about enlarging his space, and answers, "You're a clever little woman, but my motto's Concentrate."

Disillusioned month after month by Henry's immovable concreteness, Margaret instinctively falls back on the part of life she shares with him—the outer life: "Her surface," she finds, "could always respond to his without contempt, though all her deeper being might be yearning to help him." And she largely abandons what she calls her "plan of action" to inspire the spiritual passion in Henry's soul. Simply loving him is best, Margaret decides, "and the more she let herself love him, the more chance was there that he would set his soul in order." Clearly, in the hands of a determined Idealist love itself can have a coercive, purposeful agenda, and, indeed, "disappointed a hundred times" in Henry's lack of tenderness and sentiment, Forster tells us that Margaret "still hoped" to make a difference in his life, certain that "some day she would use her love to make him a better man."

Margaret's hope as well as her love for Henry are severely tested in the second half of *Howards End*, as Forster interweaves their essentially serio-comical relationship with sorrowful, ill-fated events in both their families, what he calls a "jangle of causes and effects." For a while, however, Margaret is convinced that their marriage is proceeding amicably along the same lines as their courtship, she working quietly to create "new sanctities" in Henry's inner life, and he "blustering and muddling into a ripe old age."

Margaret believes she has seen the best and the worst in Henry, and she takes comfort in a thorough knowledge of her husband's heart: "To have no illusions and yet to love—what stronger surety can a woman find?"

The truth, however, is that Margaret has kept her one illusion about Henry—that she can make him more of an Idealist—and when she is forced to abandon this vision she comes perilously near to giving up on her marriage. In the crisis of the novel, when Henry, the traditional Guardian moralist, sets his face sternly against her sister Helen's illegitimate pregnancy, Margaret must finally acknowledge that her Pygmalion project has failed. Henry will not open his doors to Helen in her trouble; his "position in society," he says, prevents him. Nor does Henry recognize his hypocrisy: embarrassing facts about an affair of his own during his first marriage have emerged, but he cannot understand why his case and Helen's are the same, and he cannot bring himself to forgive Helen as he has "actually been forgiven" by Margaret.[56] Margaret sees on these clear issues that Henry will never be the "better man" of affection and sensitivity she had dreamed of making him, and she resigns herself to leaving him: "he had refused to connect," she says, setting her jaw, "and their love must take the consequences." But at the last moment, when Henry's son Charles is sentenced for manslaughter against Helen's lover—"her seducer," as Henry archly refers to him—and when Henry, broken with despair, turns to Margaret for salvation, her anger mysteriously gives way to tenderness, and she comes to a profound new understanding of her marriage, and of the nature of love.

---

[56] See Chapter Three, footnote 19.

Margaret has always felt caught between Helen and her husband, hovering in "the gulf between Henry as he was and Henry as Helen thought he ought to be." Margaret has tried to reconcile these opposites, "now accepting men as they are, now yearning with her sister for Truth." But at the end (indeed, at Howards End), as she nurses Henry and helps to care for Helen's baby, she seems to have found the insight needed for creating what she calls "truer relationships, beyond the limits that fetter us now." Margaret has learned what Helen calls a "heroic" lesson in interpersonal relations through the turbulent last events of the novel. She has learned that personal differences are to be respected and appreciated, not seen as shortcomings to be coerced into some ideal "sameness." We waste our lives, Margaret explains now to her sister, trying to develop our loved ones as we think "they are supposed to develop." "Develop what you have" in your own life and in yourself, she advises Helen, and let others "catch the glow" of healthy living in their own unique ways. Margaret knows now that "people are far more different than is pretended," and she understands finally that, no matter how difficult living with these differences might be, the "diviner" beauty of family love, like the glorious garden at Howards End, grows from the sacred "seed-bed" of diversity:

> Differences—eternal differences, planted by God in a single family, so that there may always be colour; sorrow perhaps, but colour in the daily grey.[57]

David Keirsey counsels each of us in *Please Understand Me* to

> Abandon the Pygmalion Project, that endless and fruitless attempt to change the Other into a carbon copy of Oneself....Put down your chisel. Let be. Appreciate.

---

[57]E.M. Forster, *Howards End,* p. 338.

And Margaret, having come so painfully to the same attitude of appreciation, looks forward to the remaining years of her marriage with serene patience, "loving Henry, and understanding him better daily."

This is not to say that all of Margaret's frustrations with Henry magically melt away at the end of the novel. Forster's sense of irony is too pervasive to let him close on a purely optimistic note. Margaret's deepest belief about human relations—virtually her Idealist's philosophy of life—is that "it all turns on affection," and on this point Henry remains a disappointment to her. Though Henry's anguish in the last pages exhausts him, so that he seems (like so many depressive Guardians) "eternally tired" of the burden of living, he is little more sympathetic than before, and continues to behave toward his loved ones in much the same business-like manner, essentially "without sentiment" or "real affection." Thus, our final glimpse of Henry shows him still the meticulous Inspector managing his financial affairs, dividing his property once and for all between Margaret and his children—"is all that clear?" he demands, "does everyone understand?" And even though Henry finally makes Margaret the legal owner of Howards End, he has little idea that she is also the spiritual keeper of the cottage.

As an Idealist, Margaret had hoped for a deeper understanding and a more personal expression of affection in her marriage, but, again, she seems to have found the wisdom she needs to let Henry be himself. Margaret knows she will never receive from Henry the heart's intimacy she longs for. But no matter: Margaret has come to know "her own heart," Forster tells us, and apparently that is enough for her. Forster promises us early in *Howards End* that there are times "when the inner life actually 'pays,' when years of self-scrutiny...are suddenly of practical use," and now, indeed, Margaret is able to find within herself the satisfaction Henry cannot give her. To insure the "healthy life" and "harmony" of her marriage, Margaret lets her "soul retire within, to float upon the bosom of a deeper stream," while she turns outward to her husband, loving him in what she calls "the noblest way," not as the tender soul-partner she would have him be, but as the decent Guardian man he is.

*   *   *   *   *

As a record of the growth of interpersonal maturity, then, *Howards End* leads us out of the darkness of *Tess of the d'Urbervilles*, for by staying with Henry and loving him in his time of trouble, Margaret proves that she has learned the lessons of compassion and forgiveness that Angel could not understand when he turned away from Tess. Angel, I might add, eventually gains a similar wisdom, and by the end of *Tess of the d'Urbervilles* Hardy can tell us that "tenderness was absolutely dominant in Clare at last." But Teachers need to remember that, while they might take pride in Margaret's hard-won commitment to Henry, they are also capable of Angel's cruel abandonment of Tess. Indeed, while Keirsey describes Teachers as remaining remarkably true to their mates, preferring to live with a feeling of "vague dissatisfaction" than to begin searching for a more ideal partner, he also cautions us that their loyalty often exists "side by side with a dream of the perfect relationship—a characteristic of all Idealists, but one which is particularly strong in a Teacher."[58]

---

[58]David Keirsey, *Please Understand Me*, p. 169.

Afterword

Just such a retrospect
Hath the perfected Life
——Emily Dickinson[1]

Naming the apollonian temperament the "Idealists" is misleading in one sense, because surely all types of human beings have "ideals" in their lives, all have goals they strive to accomplish and dreams they want to realize. Artisans, for instance, chase after "peak" sensory experiences; Guardians hope to establish unwavering stability in an unruly world; and Rationals aspire in their more abstract way to design the most elegant theoretical models. Idealists also have ambitions of this outward kind—to found utopias, for example—but as the evidence of literature suggests, they are not content merely to dream of *doing* something perfect. The Idealists' "inside dream" is to *be* perfect, to unfold their wings and ascend into what Emily Dickinson called "the perfected life." In other words, their ideal is to become

---

[1] Emily Dickinson, "The Props assist the House," ll. 8-9.

their own ideal, and thus they, more than any other temperament, are the Idealists.

The authors I have discussed in this volume certainly portray the Idealist's search for the perfected life with extraordinary insight and sympathy; these characters are their authors' heroes, and are presented with deep-seated affection. We might well expect this to be the case, since all these authors are Idealists (except for Thomas Hardy, a Guardian), and each temperament intrinsically admires its own way-of-being. At the same time, I must say that these authors present their Idealists with remarkable honesty, showing us many of the conflicts and shortcomings in the pursuit of the perfect self—and of the perfect mate. It is a curious quirk of personality that Idealists are more harshly critical of their own temperament than they are of Artisans or Guardians or Rationals. Jung himself was harder on his own "introverted intuitive" type than any other,[2] and several of these authors (Tolstoy is a good example) seem more comfortable finding fault with their Idealist characters than with the other types, as if needing to protect everyone else's self-image but their own.

Such surprisingly cruel self-criticism is most apparent in portraits of the Disciples, and particularly of the Monastics, who in some cases are characterized as overwrought personalities, and as excessively manipulative with their loved ones. Although Alyosha is Dostoevsky's admitted "hero" in *The Brothers Karamazov*, he seems almost neurotically intent on serving God (or Father Zosima) and bringing a spiritual dimension to the other characters, as does Miriam with Paul in *Sons and Lovers*, St. John Rivers with Jane Eyre, and Forster's "morbid idealist" Helen

---

[2]See Jung's *Psychological Types* (1920).

Schlegel with the Wilcoxes in *Howards End.* Indeed, the
most graphic description I have found of an Idealist's
Pygmalion project is in Jane Eyre's criticism of St. John:

> He wanted to train me to an elevation I could never reach; it
> racked me hourly to aspire to the standard he uplifted. The
> thing was as impossible as to mould my irregular features to
> his correct and classic pattern, to give to my changeable green
> eyes the sea-blue tint and solemn lustre of his own.[3]

Why Disciples seem to bear the brunt of this criticism
puzzles me a good deal, but I suspect it has something to do
with many Idealist authors' rather ambivalent attitude
toward their own religious enthusiasm. While all Idealists
(even D.H. Lawrence) are profoundly religious in their
approach to life—Eduard Spranger defines them as having
the "Religious attitude"[4]—they do not like to think of
themselves as over-zealous or proselytizing in relation to
others. And since the Disciples are more willing than
Mentors to display their religious devotion, and perhaps
more prone to cross the line from what Jung called being
"the mystical dreamer" to "the crank,"[5] they are the ones
literature most often characterizes as fanatical.

In truth, literature shows all the Idealists—Disciples and
Mentors—as having a full complement of fears and
weaknesses, of moral dilemmas and self-deceptions, of
vanities and Pygmalion agendas. But what is to my mind
the most significant pattern in the lives of most of these
characters is their ability to grow in wisdom and arrive at
some sort of saving insight by the end of their stories.
Newland Archer and Masha, Levin and Jane Eyre, Angel

---

[3]Charlotte Brontë, *Jane Eyre* (Signet Classic edition), p. 401.

[4]See Eduard Spranger's *Types of Men* (1928).

[5]Carl Jung, *Psychological Types* (Bollingen Series, Princeton), p. 401.

Clare and Margaret Schlegel—all these Idealists develop as persons ("self-actualize") in their stories and achieve a level of self-awareness by the end that brings them a profound personal peace, and also quite often a serene reconciliation with their loved ones.

Not that these Idealists become their ideal selves, or create their ideal relationships, in the course of their stories. (Remember, Idealists are often happier searching for themselves than finding themselves.) But they do follow a path of enlightenment—again, Plato's "upward journey of the soul"—that is perhaps the distinguishing feature of Idealist literature, and that brings them to understand how their grand efforts at Pygmalion projects result in little more than resentment, frustration, and disillusionment. E.M. Forster counsels Margaret in *Howards End* that "visions do not come when we try," and Idealists, it appears, are able to learn that the same is true of "perfected lives."

The Keirsey Temperament Sorter

Please use the answer sheet at the end.

1. At a party do you

    (a) interact with many, including strangers

    (b) interact with a few, known to you

2. Are you more

    (a) realistic that speculative

    (b) speculative than realistic

3. Is it worse to

    (a) have your "head in the clouds"

    (b) be "in a rut"

4. Are you more impressed by

    (a) principles   (b) emotions

5. Are you more drawn toward the

    (a) convincing   (b) touching

6. Do you prefer to work

(a) to deadlines   (b) just "whenever"

7. Do you tend to choose

(a) rather carefully   (b) somewhat impulsively

8. At parties do you

(a) stay late, with increasing energy

(b) leave early, with decreased energy

9. Are you more attracted to

(a) what is actual   (b) what is possible

10. Are you more interested in

(a) sensible people   (b) imaginative people

11. In judging others are you more swayed by

(a) laws than circumstances

(b) circumstances than laws

12. In approaching others is your inclination to be somewhat

(a) objective   (b) personal

13. Are you more

(a) punctual   (b) leisurely

14. Does it bother you more having things

(a) incomplete   (b) completed

15. In your social groups do you

(a) keep abreast of others' happenings

(b) get behind on the news

16. In doing ordinary things are you more likely to

(a) do it the usual way   (b) do it your own way

17. Writers should

(a) "say what they mean and mean what they say"

(b) express things more by use of analogy

18. Which appeals to you more:

(a) consistency of thought

(b) harmonious human relations

19. Are you more comfortable in making

(a) logical judgments   (b) value judgments

20. Do you want things

(a) settled and decided   (b) unsettled and undecided

21. Would you say you are more

(a) serious and determined   (b) easy-going

22. In phoning do you

(a) rarely question that it will all be said

(b) rehearse what you'll say

23. Facts

(a) "speak for themselves"   (b) illustrate principles

24. Are visionaries

(a) somewhat annoying   (b) rather fascinating

25. Are you more often

(a) a cool-headed person   (b) a warm-hearted person

26. Is it worse to be

(a) unjust   (b) merciless

27. Should one usually let events occur

(a) by careful selection and choice

(b) randomly and by chance

28. Do you feel better about

(a) having purchased   (b) having the option to buy

29. In company do you

(a) initiate conversation   (b) wait to be approached

30. Common sense is

(a) rarely questionable   (b) frequently questionable

31. Children often do not

(a) make themselves useful enough

(b) exercise their fantasy enough

32. In making decisions do you feel more comfortable with

(a) standards   (b) feelings

33. Are you more

(a) firm than gentle   (b) gentle than firm

34. Which is more admirable:

(a) the ability to organize and be methodical

(b) the ability to adapt and make do

35. Do you put more value on the

(a) definite   (b) open-ended

36. Does new and non-routine interaction with others

(a) stimulate and energize you

(b) tax your reserves

37. Are you more frequently

(a) a practical sort of person

(b) a fanciful sort of person

38. Are you more likely to

(a) see how others are useful

(b) see how others see

39. Which is more satisfying:

  (a) to discuss an issue thoroughly

  (b) to arrive at agreement on an issue

40. Which rules you more:

  (a) your head   (b) your heart

41. Are you more comfortable with work that is

  (a) contracted   (b) done on a casual basis

42. Do you tend to look for

  (a) the orderly   (b) whatever turns up

43. Do you prefer

  (a) many friends with brief contact

  (b) a few friends with more lengthy contact

44. Do you go more by

  (a) facts   (b) principles

45. Are you more interested in

  (a) production and distribution

  (b) design and research

46. Which is more of a compliment:

  (a) "There is a very logical person"

  (b) "There is a very sentimental person"

47. Do you value in yourself more that you are

  (a) unwavering   (b) devoted

48. Do you more often prefer the

  (a) final and unalterable statement

  (b) tentative and preliminary statement

49. Are you more comfortable

  (a) after a decision   (b) before a decision

50. Do you

    (a) speak easily and at length with strangers

    (b) find little to say to strangers

51. Are you more likely to trust your

    (a) experience   (b) hunch

52. Do you feel

    (a) more practical than ingenious

    (b) more ingenious than practical

53. Which person is more to be complimented: one of

    (a) clear reason   (b) strong feeling

54. Are you inclined more to be

    (a) fair-minded   (b) sympathetic

55. Is it preferable mostly to

    (a) make sure things are arranged

    (b) just let things happen

56. In relationships should most things be

    (a) renegotiable

    (b) random and circumstantial

57. When the phone rings do you

    (a) hasten to get to it first

    (b) hope someone else will answer

58. Do you prize more in yourself

    (a) a strong sense of reality (b) a vivid imagination

59. Are you drawn more to

    (a) fundamentals   (b) overtones

60. Which seems the greater error:

    (a) to be too passionate   (b) to be too objective

61. Do you see yourself as basically

   (a) hard-headed   (b) soft-hearted

62. Which situation appeals to you more:

   (a) the structured and scheduled

   (b) the unstructured and unscheduled

63. Are you a person who is more

   (a) routinized than whimsical

   (b) whimsical than routinized

64. Are you more inclined to be

   (a) easy to approach   (b) somewhat reserved

65. In writings do you prefer

   (a) the more literal   (b) the more figurative

66. Is it harder for you to

   (a) identify with others   (b) utilize others

67. Which do you wish more for yourself:

   (a) clarity of reason   (b) strength of compassion

68. Which is the greater fault:

   (a) being indiscriminate   (b) being critical

69. Do you prefer the

   (a) planned event   (b) unplanned event

70. Do you tend to be more

   (a) deliberate than spontaneous

   (b) spontanteous than deliberate

Answer Sheet

Enter a check for each answer in the column for **a** or **b**.

	A	B		A	B		A	B		A	B		A	B		A	B		A	B
1		✗	2		✗	3		✗	4		✗	5		✗	6		✗	7			✗
8		✗	9		✗	10		✗	11		✗	12		✗	13		✗	14	✗	
15	✗		16		✗	17		✗	18		✗	19		✗	20		✗	21		✗
22		✗	23		✗	24		✗	25		✗	26		✗	27		✗	28	✗	
29	✗		30		✗	31		✗	32		✗	33		✗	34		✗	35		✗
36	✗		37		✗	38		✗	39	✗		40		✗	41		✗	42		✗
43		✗	44		✗	45		✗	46	✗		47		✗	48		✗	49	✗	
50		✗	51		✗	52		✗	53		✗	54		✗	55		✗	56		✗
57	✗		58		✗	59		✗	60		✗	61		✗	62		✗	63		✗
64	✗		65		✗	66		✗	67		✗	68	✗		69		✗	70		✗

1 6 | 4 2   3 0 | 6 4   3 0 | 6 4   5 2 | 8 6   5 1 | 9 6   7 0 | 0 8   7 3 | 7 8

→ 6 | 10   → 2 | 0   → 0 | 1

1 | 6 | 4 | 2   3 | 0 | 4 | 4   5 | 6 | 7 | 6   7 | 3 | 7 | 8

E   I   **S   N**   **T   F**   **J   P**

Directions for Scoring

1. **Add down** so that the total number of "a" answers is written in the box at the bottom of each column (see next page for illustration). Do the same for the "b" answers you have checked. Each of the 14 boxes should have a number in it.

2. **Transfer the number** in box no. 1 of the answer sheet to box no. 1 below the answer sheet. Do this for box no. 2 as well. Note, however, that you have two numbers for boxes 3 through 8. Bring down the first number for each box beneath the second, as indicated by the arrows. Now add all the pairs of numbers and enter the total in the boxes below the answer sheet, so that each box has only one number (see illustration on next page).

3. **Now you have** four pairs of numbers. Circle the letter below the larger number of each pair (again, see illustration). If the two numbers of any pair are equal, then circle neither, but put a large X below them and circle it.

You have now identified your "type." It should be one of the following:

INFP	**ISFP**	**INTP**	**ISTP**
ENFP	**ESFP**	**ENTP**	**ESTP**
INFJ	**ISFJ**	**INTJ**	**ISTJ**
ENFJ	**ESFJ**	**ENTJ**	**ESTJ**

Sample Answer Sheet

See "Directions for Scoring" on the facing page.

	A	B		A	B		A	B		A	B		A	B		A	B		A	B
1	X		2	X		3	X		4		X	5		X	6	X		7		X
8	X		9	X		10	X		11		X	12		X	13	X		14	X	
15	X		16	X		17	X		18		X	19		X	20	X		21	X	
22		X	23	X		24	X		25		X	26		X	27	X		28	X	
29	X		30	X		31		X	32		X	33		X	34	X		35	X	
36	X		37	X		38	X		39		X	40		X	41	X		42	X	
43		X	44		X	45	X		46		X	47		X	48	X		49		X
50	X		51	X		52	X		53		X	54	X		55	X		56	X	
57	X		58	X		59	X		60		X	61		X	62	X		63		X
64	X		65	X		66		X	67		X	68		X	69	X		70	X	

1 | 8 | 2 | 2   3 | 9 | 1 | 4   3 | 8 | 2 | 4   5 | 0 | 10 | 6   5 | 1 | 9 | 6   7 | 10 | 0 | 8   7 | 7 | 3 | 8

9 | 1   0 | 10   10 | 0

1 | 8 | 2 | 2   3 | 17 | 3 | 4   5 | 1 | 19 | 6   7 | 17 | 3 | 8

(E) I   (S) N   T (F)   (J) P

If you have an X in your type, yours is a mixed type. An X can show up in any of the four pairs: E or I, S or N, T or F, and J or P. Hence there are 32 mixed types besides the 16 listed above:

XNTP	**EXTP**	**ENXP**	**ENTX**
XNTJ	**EXTJ**	**INXP**	**INTX**
XNFP	**EXFP**	**ENXJ**	**ENFX**
XNFJ	**EXFJ**	**INXJ**	**INFX**
XSTP	**IXTP**	**ESXP**	**ESTX**
XSTJ	**IXTJ**	**ISXP**	**ISTX**
XSFP	**IXFP**	**ESXJ**	**ESFX**
XSFJ	**IXFJ**	**ISXJ**	**ISFX**

Having identified your type, the task is now to read the type description and to decide how well or how poorly the description fits. You will find a description or portrait of your type on the page indicated in the table of contents of *Please Understand Me*. If you have an X in your type, yours is a combination of two types. If, for example, the E and I scores are equal and the type is, say XSFJ, then you would read both ESFJ and ISFJ portraits and decide for yourself which parts of each description are applicable.

Bibliography

Angyal, Andras. *Neurosis and Treatment: A Holistic Theory.* New York: John Wiley & Sons, 1965.

Bateson, Gregory. *Steps to an Ecology of Mind.* New York: Ballantine Books, 1972.

Choiniere, Ray, and David Keirsey. *Presidential Temperament.* Prometheus-Nemesis Book Company, 1992.

Cohen, B. Bernard. *Writing About Literature.* Glenview, Illinois: Scott, Foresman and Company, 1973.

Forster, E.M. *Aspects of the Novel.* New York: Harcourt, Brace & World, 1954.

Hamilton, Edith. *Mythology.* New York and Toronto: New American Library.

Henry James, "The Art of Fiction" in *Partial Portraits.* Ann Arbor: The University of Michigan Press, 1970.

Howe, Irving. *Thomas Hardy.* New York: Macmillan, 1967.

Janet, Pierre. *Psychological Healing.* London: George Allen & Unwin, Ltd., 1925.

Jung, Carl. *Psychological Types.* Princeton: Princeton University Press, 1971.

Keirsey, David. *Portraits of Temperament.* U.S.A.: Gnosology Books, Ltd., 1987.

Keirsey, David, and Marilyn Bates. *Please Understand Me: Character and Temperament Types.* U.S.A.: Gnosology Books, Ltd., 1984.

Kjetsaa, Geir. *Fyodor Dostoevsky: A Writer's Life.* New York: Viking Press, 1987.

Laing, R.D. *The Divided Self.* London: Penguin Books, 1965.

Lewis, R.W.B. *Edith Wharton: A Biography.* New York: Harper & Row, 1975.

Lilly, John C. *The Deep Self.* New York: Warner Books, 1977.

Maslow, Abraham. *Motivation and Personality.* New York: Harper, 1954.

MacLeod, Sheila. *The Art of Starvation.* New York: Viking Press, 1970.

Rogers, Carl. *On Becoming a Person.* Boston: Houghton Mifflin, 1961.

Rosenthal, Robert, and Lenore Jacobson. *Pygmalion in the Classroom; teacher expectation and pupils' intellectual development.* New York: Holt, Rinehart and Winston, 1968.

Sagar, Keith. *D.H. Lawrence: Life into Art.* Athens: The University of Georgia Press, 1985.

Scholes, Robert, Carl H. Klaus, and Michael Silverman. *Elements of Literature.* New York: Oxford University Press, 1978.

Shapiro, David. *Neurotic Styles.* New York and London: Basic Books, 1965.

Spranger, Eduard. *Types of Men.* Halle: Max Niemeyer Verlag, 1928.

Trilling, Lionel. *E.M. Forster.* New York: New Directions, 1943.

Watzlawick, Paul, Janet Beavin, and Don D. Jackson. *Pragmatics of Human Communication.* New York: W. W. Norton & Company, 1967.

Watzlawick, Paul, John Weakland, and Richard Fisch. *Change: Principles of Problem Formation and Problem Resolution.* New York: W. W. Norton & Company, 1974.

Wilson, A.N. *Tolstoy.* New York: W. W. Norton & Company, 1988.

Advocate Idealists ("ENFPs"), 35, 93f., 166, 233, 259f., 273f.

Apollo, 11, 12, 13, 51, 88, 96, 153, 197, 228, 247f., 254, 283

Artisans ("SPs"), 6, 7, 12, 14, 22, 25, 38, 39, 44, 47, 54f., 68, 74, 94, 96, 103f., 113, 153, 173, 174, 219, 231, 235, 245, 254, 264, 283

Bateson, Gregory, 26

Brontë, Charlotte, 201f., *204*, 226

Brontë, Emily, *38*

Camus, Albert, 28, 29

Chaucer, Geoffrey, 6, 21

Conrad, Joseph, 28, 30

Counselor Idealists ("INFJs"), 36, 50, 163f.,233, 256

Dickens, Charles, 4, 6, 30

Dickinson, Emily, 283

Disciple Idealists ("NFPs"), 35, 42, 67, 73, 163, 164, 169, 170, 251f., 284f.

Don Quixote, 14, 16, 30, 31

Dostoevsky, Fyodor, 23, 28, 31, 43f., 284

Eliot, George, 28, 41

Fitzgerald, F. Scott, 29, 30

Forster, E.M., 7, 16, 21, 29, 30, 253f., 284, 286

Freud, Sigmund, 31, 43, 252, 2ʋu

Goethe, 13, 109

Guardians ("SJs"), 6, 12, 15, 16, 22, 25, 44, 54, 59f., 71, 74, 95, 96, 98f., 113, 173f., *196*, 205, 221, 230f., 235f., 254, 259, 261f., 283

Hamlet, 4, 19, 22, 24, 30, 31, 269

Hardy, Thomas, 29, 235f., 284

Hawthorne, Nathaniel, 28, 29

Hemingway, Ernest, 6, *112*

Hesse, Hermann, 1, 24, 25, 34

Husserl, Edmund, 18, 20

James, Henry, 4, 6, 18, 30, 42

Janet, Pierre, *262*

Jung, Carl, 31, 284f.

Kant, Immanuel, 18, 19, *166*, 255

Keirsey, David, 3, 5, 8, 12, 17, 21, 25, *28*, 41, 48, *49*, 53, *59*, *61*, 72, 84, 93, 96, 100, 106, 114, 115, 122, 125f., 129, 131f., 139, *141*, 143f., 148f., 156f., 159, *162*, 164, *167*, *168*, *170*, 175, 179, 187f., 191, *193*, 203, 207f., 210f., 219, 221, 224, 226, *227*, 231, 233f., 238, 240, 246, *250*, 251, 258, 262f., 269, *277*, 280, 282

Laing, R.D., 23, *31*, 64, *65*, *77*
Lawrence, D.H., 6, 17, 66f., 154, 285

MacLeod, Sheila, *77*
Maslow, Abraham, *22*
Melville, Herman, 28, 31, 93
Mentor Idealists ("NFJs"), 36, 163, 164, 169, 170, 171, 237, 239, 251f., 285
Monastic Idealists ("INFPs"), 35, 41f., 93, 94, 166, 178, 225, 233, 284

Nietzsche, Friedrich, *12*, 43

Percy, Walker, 32f.
Plato, 18, 27, *166*, 170, 183, 243, 286
Please Understand Me, 3, 5, 8, 12, 41, 72, 84, 96, 100, 262
Portraits of Temperament, 6, 41
Proust, Marcel, 19, 30
Pygmalion project, 1, 2, 3, 7, 8, 32, 35, 36, 38, 39, 51, 54, 56, 59, 61f., 70, 80f., 106, 109, 116, 124, 135, 146, 150, 152, 155, 160f., 163, 187, 217, 224, 228, 234, 246f., 276f., 285f.

Rationals ("NTs"), 6, 12, 15, 18, 22, 25, 27, 39, 54, 57f., 73, 75, 111, 113, 124f., 170f., 182, 188, 201f., 251, 256, 264, 283
Rogers, Carl, *22*
Rosenthal, Robert, *56*

Shakespeare, William, *4*, 6, 17, 19, 28, 235
Shapiro, David, *21*, *96*, *190*, *195*, *237*, *250*
Shaw, Bernard, 16, 28
Siddhartha, 25, 26, 32
Spranger, Eduard, 285
Stevens, Wallace, 20

Teacher Idealists ("ENFJs"), 36, 61f., 71f., 167, 202, 233f., 236f.
Tolstoy, Leo, 29, 124f., 165f., 284

Watzlavick, Paul, *27*, *60*
Wharton, Edith, 95f., 162
Williams, Tennessee, 30, 31
Woolf, Virginia, 20, 29, 31, *262*
Wordsworth, William, 19

LOVE, COERCION, AND THE ARTISAN

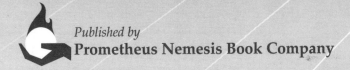

The Pygmalion Project: Volume I, The Artisan, by Dr. Stephen Montgomery (the editor of *Please Understand Me*) investigates the styles of love and coercion among the Keirseyan temperaments, taking famous characters from literature and film as provocative case studies. *Volume I, The Artisan* approaches the art of loving from the artisans' point-of-view, by examining their playful and charming way in relationships with Guardian ("SJ"), Rational ("NT"), and Idealist ("NF") partners. Begin by completing Keirsey's new personality test, and then read about the Artisan mating game, how they delight and dismay their loved ones, as presented in the pages of D. H. Lawrence, Ernest Hemingway, F. Scott Fitzgerald, and eight other authors. More importantly learn more about Keirsey's concept of the Pygmalion Project—how we try to sculpt our loved ones into copies of ourselves, and how we are manipulated by them in return. If you've ever been in love with an Artisan (or ever been fooled by one), *The Pygmalion Project* will prove fascinating reading.

Published by
Prometheus Nemesis Book Company

THE GUARDIAN'S
PYGMALION PROJECT

T he second part of Dr. Stephen Montgomery's quartet on love and coercion among the types focuses on the Guardians' ("SJ") uniquely responsible style of caring for others. Montgomery (the editor of *Please Understand Me*) has selected characters from works of Jane Austen, Sinclair Lewis, Virginia Woolf, and half a dozen other authors, to bring to life the Guardian's parental way in love and marriage, and to illustrate their earnest style of interpersonal manipulation—what Keirsey calls the Pygmalion Project. The book examines the Guardians both as instigators and as victims of marital games with the Rationals ("NTs"), the Idealists ("NFs"), and particularly with the childlike Artisans ("SPs"). If you have a Guardian spouse (or even a Guardian parent), *The Pygmalion Project Volume 2, The Guardian* will help you understand and appreciate them.

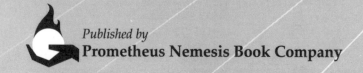

Published by
Prometheus Nemesis Book Company

PORTRAITS OF TEMPERAMENT

Portraits
of
Temperament

DAVID

KEIRSEY

Portraits of Temperament is David Keirsey's most recent thinking on the ingrained attitudes and habitual actions of the four basic personality types, which he now renames the Artisans, Guardians, Rationals, and Idealists. Keirsey summarizes the four temperaments, showing how the behavior of each is either concrete or abstract, cooperative or pragmatic, directive or informative, and finally, assertive or responsive. The book includes two brief self-scoring personality tests to assist in observing the differences and similarities among us.

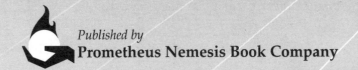

Published by
Prometheus Nemesis Book Company

	Qty	$

Please Understand Me Keirsey & Bates   208 pages—$11.95   **Qty**   **$**
> *National Best Seller.* Over one million copies sold. A 25 year clinical study of differences in temperament in mating, parenting, teaching, and leading. Defines four types: Dionysians (SP), Epimethians (SJ), Prometheans (NT), and Apollonians (NF). *Keirsey Sorter* included.

Comprendeme Por Favor   *Please Understand Me* in Spanish   238 pages—$11.95   **Qty**   **$**
Versteh Mich Bitte   *Please Understand Me* in German   276 pages—$11.95   **Qty**   **$**
Presidential Temperament Keirsey, Choiniere   **Introducry Offer** 610 pages—$9.95   **Qty**   **$**
> Depicts temperament-determined lives of forty U.S. presidents, from youth to old age. Authors found 20 Guardians [SJ], 12 Artisans [SP], 8 Rationals [NT], and *no* Idealists [NF]. Shows how character always dominates circumstance in determining presidential behavior.

Portraits of Temperament Keirsey   124 pages—$9.95   **Qty**   **$**
> The four Keirseyan temperaments are named Artisan, Guardian, Rational, and Idealist, each with two variant patterns of behavior based on differing kinds of competence and interest.

The Pygmalion Project: 1 The Artisan Montgomery   180 pages—$9.95   **Qty**   **$**
> The Artisan [SP] style of relating to Guardian [SJ], Rational [NT], and Idealist [NF] mates, shown by characters in novels, plays, and films, such as D. H. Lawrence's *Lady Chatterly's Lover*, Ernest Hemingway's *The Sun Also Rises*, and Sinclair Lewis's *The Great Gatsby*.

The Pygmalion Project: 2 The Guardian Montgomery   258 pages—$9.95   **Qty**   **$**
> The Guardian [SJ] style of relating to Artisan [SP], Rational [NT], and Idealist [NF] mates, as shown by characters in novels, plays, and films, such as C.S. Forester's *African Queen*, Jane Austen's *Pride and Prejudice*, Henrik Ibsen's *A Doll House,* and others.

The Pygmalion Project: 3 The Idealist Montgomery   325 pages—$9.95   **Qty**   **$**
> A careful and imaginative study of how Idealists [NF] relate to their Artisan (SP), Guardian (SJ), and Rational (NT) mates, as illustrated by characters in novels and films such as Forster's *Howards End*, Tolstoy's *Anna Karenina*, Brontë's *Jane Eyre*, and others.

Children The Challenge Dreikurs, Soltz   335 pages—$8.95   **Qty**   **$**
> There is no substitute for this manual for those parents, teachers, and counselors who wish to establish and maintain cooperative and productive relations with children.

Talk So Kids Will Listen & Listen So Kids Will Talk Mazlish, Faber   242 pages—$8.95   **Qty**   **$**
> For parents, teachers, and counselors who wish to learn the gentle art of talking with children about important matters.

Abuse it—Lose it Keirsey   20 pages—$2.00   **Qty**   **$**
> Applies the principle of logical consequences and the abuse it—lose it method for developing self-control in mischievous school boys who are all too often stigmatized as cases of "attention deficit disorder" and then drugged into obedience.

Drugged Obedience in the School Keirsey   8 pages—$.25   **Qty**   **$**
> A comparison between drugging mischievous school boys with cocaine-like narcotics, and the abuse it—lose it method of teaching self-control to kids in school.

Temperament in Leading (includes The Temperament Sorter)   48 pages—$ 3.00   **Qty**   **$**
> Styles of management and teaching, from *Please Understand Me*.

The Sixteen Types (includes The Temperament Sorter)   48 pages—$3.00   **Qty**   **$**
> From *Please Understand Me* , featuring portraits of the 16 types.

The Keirsey Temperament Sorter $.25   **Qty**   **$**
> A self-scoring test to identify 16 types, from *Please Understand Me*.

The Keirsey Temperament Sorter on Disc—Specify Macintosh (Hypercard) or IBM $7.00   **Qty**   **$**
A Brief Test of Character Traits $.25   **Qty**   **$**
> A self-scoring test to identify 4 types of temperament: Artisans, Rationals, Guardians, and Idealists, reprinted from *Presidential Temperament*.

ORDER FORM

Name_____

Address _____

City _____

State _____ Zip _____

Order Subtotal	USA	Abroad
$ 00.00 - $ 49.99 —	$2.00	$ 3.50
50.00 - 99.99 —	3.50	6.00
100.00 - 149.99 —	4.50	9.00
150.00 - 199.99 —	5.00	10.50

Subtotal _____

7% Sales Tax _____
(CA Only)

Shipping _____

Total Enclosed

Mail order and check (U.S. Dollars only) to Prometheus Nemesis Books
Box 2748, Del Mar, CA 92014. CALL 619-632-1575; FAX 619-481-0535